And Also With You

Books by Will D. Campbell

Race and Renewal of the Church

Up to Our Steeples in Politics (with James Holloway)

Brother to a Dragonfly

The Glad River

Cecelia's Sin

Forty Acres and a Goat

God on Earth (with Bonnie Campbell)

The Convention

Chester and Chung Ling

Covenant: Faces, Places, Lives

Providence

The Stem of Jesse

The Pear Tree that Bloomed in the Fall

And Also With You

DUNCAN GRAY

AND THE

AMERICAN DILEMMA

Will D. Campbell

PROVIDENCE HOUSE PUBLISHERS

Franklin, Tennessee

TENNESSEE HERITAGE LIBRARY
Bicentennial Collection

01   00   99   98   97   5   4   3   2

Library of Congress Catalog Card Number: 97-73595

ISBN: 1-57736-036-2

Dust jacket by Bozeman Design. Cover illustrations: Front—Color transparency of Confederate monument by Robert Jordan, University of Mississippi; Inset—"Rev. Duncan M. Gray Jr., St. Peter's Episcopal Church, Oxford, 1962." Photograph by Martin J. Dain, © Center for the Study of Southern Culture. Back—Oil painting of campus riot at University of Mississippi, September 30, 1962, by Elizabeth Willis, courtesy Ruth Miller Spivey Gray.

Author photo—L. Webb Campbell II

Endsheet—Photograph of Greek lettering on Confederate monument courtesy Archives Department, J. D. Williams Library, University of Mississippi.

PROVIDENCE HOUSE PUBLISHERS
238 Seaboard Lane • Franklin, Tennessee 37067
800-321-5692

For Ruthie

Contents

Preface

The story I begin here is both biography and history. Or maybe neither in the ivy-tinged scholastic sense. What I want it to be is a meditation and a brief inquiry. A meditation on the life of Duncan Montgomery Gray Jr., a man who has been a significant player in the drama of twentieth-century history (generally with little note from those who record the affairs of a people). Gray—spelled with an "a."

The brief inquiry is to be of a company of young men known as the University Greys (Company A, Eleventh Mississippi Infantry Regiment, Confederate States of America) who in 1861 stacked their books and went away to fight a war that would haunt and sap their people long beyond the rotting of their bones; the Greys—spelled with an "e."

Where Mr. Gray with an "a" is concerned, it is without apology a tribute. There are few heroes left in America. Duncan Montgomery Gray Jr. is one of mine. Since heroes are in such short supply, I want to share him with those who have that primal yearning for someone to look up to, admire, applaud, and perhaps even emulate. From America's dismal ghettoes to Aspen's most extravagant slopes, we hear the plaintive cries for heroes. Yet we live in a time of exuberant cheers of scripted evil, a time when our celebrities are often those who have fallen far short of moral compass. As this millennium winds down and we take into the new century a climate of perplexity bordering on despair, cynicism approaching unfaith, a politic more nihilistic than truths that are self-evident, we *do* need heroes. Someone who won't let us down. Some idea or ideal to hold onto; someone to trust, believe in. A village Nestor, pointing higher still. So I am not searching for Duncan Gray's warts and foibles. Nor am I attempting a scholarly dissertation.

In writing of heroes one does well to remember some words of the apostle Paul:

> Finally, brethren, whatsoever things are true, whatsoever things are honest, whatsoever things are just, whatsoever things are pure, whatsoever things are lovely, whatsoever things are of good report; if there be any virtue, and if there be any praise, think on these things.

Can I follow the same subjective guideline with the Greys with an "e"? At this point I don't know. I know too little of them now to say they are also my heroes. They left the Mississippi Central depot in Oxford, Mississippi, on May 1, 1861, a happy lot, undaunted by an early morning rain, with only the brief admonition of L. Q. C. Lamar that they would soon see hard service as mild bridling of their exuberance. They never came back. I know Duncan Gray. I know the Greys hardly at all. I shall strive to know them better and, perhaps later, be able to strike the ambiguity from my present estimate of them. For now I know only that their cause was the far opposite of the cause of Duncan Montgomery Gray Jr. He has been a champion of equality, freedom, fairness, and decency in general. The Greys were involved in a chattel dispute. Yes, there was the matter of which region of the young country would emerge as dominant. Yes, there were constitutional questions, states' rights, and other matters debated. But those things might have been settled short of sword and canister. The bottom line had to do with the buying and selling, the owning, of human beings. It was for that the Southern elders met in legislative halls and shouted the citizenry to rebellion. Then the drums, bugles, and banners lured the youthful and prankish Greys from their studies and onto fields of carnage.

I am of the yeomanry, one whose progenitors neither bought nor sold other human beings but who worked their own little patches of cotton, cane, and corn when their indenture expired and they could call themselves free. I must confess that I might have difficulty listing as heroes those who fought for the merchandising of fellow creatures and propagation of the manor. Why, then, should the Greys be part of the story at hand? What place do they have alongside a man named Gray? The answer, I believe as I begin, is more than the similarity of the spelling—Greys and Gray. Is it because the Greys with an "e" were victims of the seeds of time, seeds they did not plant but whose harvest was imposed upon them? Maybe. But most of those of Company A, I am told, who left hearth and household to fight the Civil War had a personal stake in the battle. They were, for the most part, of the landed gentry. They came from slave-owning families, while most Confederates in the ranks owned no slaves and had little investment in the things that brought about that tragic war. Perhaps I can come to terms more quickly with the rank-and-file yeoman butternut falling at the charge of a bluecoat than with the Greys who had plantation acres to safeguard. Maybe it is because my *po-white* genes continue at war with the patricians. Maybe I feel more pity for them than admiration; for what, really, is there to admire? We hear of honor. That elusive, and, sometimes illusive, soul-spice generally more stoic than Christian. A notion used often for manipulation and deception, but nevertheless a virtue unto itself. After the battles were over, won or lost, when the Blue and the Grey lay together, when Gettysburg was again quiet for they had all gone away, honor, we have been taught, remained. Remained, though perhaps badly violated. Still and yet: honor.

I don't know about all that. I do know that the very concept of race over which the war was fought is a principality with which we should wrestle and not serve, but a principality that yet prevails over righteousness in America. My own history in the matter is mixed. My great-granddaddy fought in the Battle of Shiloh, was injured, decided he was fighting a bad war, deserted, and came home to Amite County, Mississippi, and died. His body lay in a pine box at the northern entrance to the dogtrot to keep it cool until the circuit-riding preacher came by to bury him. He owned no slaves. How did he know it was a bad war? I don't know that either. But he did know it and passed it along to his son, my Grandpa Bunt, who passed it along to me. "There ain't no 'niggers' in this world," Grandpa told me more than once. And perhaps that is why I can exult in Duncan Gray's own wrestling with that principality we have named *race*; that sickness that yet today wins national elections, perpetuates an economy in which rich people get richer and poor people keep getting poorer. For despite the sophistication of contemporary futuristic rhetoric, when the veneer is scraped away, for too many white folk welfare is the myth of black people driving a Cadillac to the grocery store and buying beer and sirloins with food stamps. Crime in the streets means black criminals. Teenage pregnancy means black teenagers who have babies to get more welfare. And everyone knows it. No longer do we have, or need, a Bilbo, or Pitchfork Ben Tillman to scream "nigger!" from courthouse steps on the eve of elections. Principalities are smarter than that. Still I know my whiteness has served as an advantage all the days of my life, so I claim no immunity.

For whatever reason, my muddled feelings regarding the University Greys tarry. Might the romance of their epic be a reason for my mild flirtation with them as potential heroes? But where was the romance of Seminary Ridge as screaming missiles sent birds falling from the sky, men and horses falling in loaf-size pieces, their blood marking a nation's history? Where exactly is the glory of handsome young Captain William Benjamin Lowry living out his life with half a face, or Jeremiah Sanders Gage signing his Gettysburg death letter to his mother with his own blood? Where is the valor of the vaunting, irascible adolescent Thomas Fondren McKie, who would harangue his mother into signing his enlistment, but five months later as a sniffling, whining sixteen year old plead that she write President Davis to grant his release as a minor? "You recollect, Mother, on the very evening that I mustered into service, that we walked out into the garden and you cryed and asked me to go up to the depot and get off," he wrote. Was theirs a tragedy in the classical understanding of tragedy? Or was it a matter of geographic legacy, something dinned into the psyche of all afflicted with this incurable skin disease called *whiteness*, born below that line bequeathed us by Charles Mason and Jeremiah Dixon, two Englishmen who in 1763 meant us no harm but who with their chains and transits left another principality to be wrestled with in lore and literature all these years? But not yet conquered. That wretched, glorious, evil, righteous, often sadly wrong but ever-present principality we still call *The South*. After all these years, somehow we can't let it go. Duncan Gray, even in the throes of persecution, reveled in it. "I am a Southern Churchman," he insisted. And I, with Duncan Gray as subject and hero, cannot let it go. The years, times, and a creed we can neither articulate nor understand have driven a wedge between two causes and at the same time welded and melded them together. From Mark Twain to William Faulkner to Flannery O'Connor, the subject of race has dominated the landscape of our literature. The delicate fabric of civility, essential to any respectable society, has been torn asunder by it. And it has been the subject of race that has claimed ascendancy over other powers and principalities against which Gray's Bible told him he should wrestle.

Searching for a man so readily at hand as Duncan Montgomery Gray Jr. would not appear much of an undertaking. It seems simple enough. Ask and he will explain himself. I have known him for many years, but that has not been the case. He doesn't talk much about himself. So I shall pry.

Yet, am I sure my search is precisely about him? Finally about him alone? Mr. Gray is a Mississippi man. As am I. So perhaps I am beginning now another search for Mississippi, that place that to many has been a land to curse and a land to hallow. A plague and an anointing.

Mississippi: Land of the haughty, workers of iniquity. Those who trust in chariots and all manner of perdition.

Mississippi: A glorious blessing. Kith and kin. Shepherds. Green pastures to lie down in. Founded upon the seas; established upon the floods. Land of the meek who will inherit the earth; those who trust in the Lord.

Mississippi: That place I had run from in the fall of 1941 when I was just turned seventeen. To go away to a little college in Louisiana where for three weeks I prayed fervently, without ceasing and out loud when I was alone in my room, that the school would burn to the ground—the whole of it. So that I might go home to Mississippi. None of that is germane to my subject except as it relates to my first meeting Duncan Montgomery Gray Jr. fourteen years later. Forty years ago. In Mississippi. His land and mine. The place he has given a lifetime to make better. Even to relate the details of that meeting is not appropriate at this juncture of the story, and might never be for I intend this as his story; not my own.

All these years he has seemed at once close at hand and far away. Somehow he was ever on the sidelines of my life. I saw him seldom, though we seemed continuously to be moving down the same trails, fighting similar battles, espousing related causes. I kept hearing of him.

Now I want to learn more about him, learn what has shaped him to the thing he is and share what I find. I am, however, fearful of so bold an undertaking. Such is my regard for him.

My interest in learning of him also seems to parallel that adventuresome and tragic company of young men who departed from the very ground on which Duncan Gray, a hundred years later, fought one of his most courageous and life-threatening battles. The University Greys. More than their having the same name with different spelling, however, interests me. Greys and Gray. It is more that the two major battles they fought, one on the third day of the battle of Gettysburg, the other when the first Negro student was enrolled at the university the Greys left, were both high-water marks, each a turning point—or *could* have been a turning point—in America's chronic preoccupation with the race question. For a long time, in my mind, the story of Duncan Montgomery Gray Jr. and the University Greys (Company A, Eleventh Mississippi Infantry Regiment, CSA) have somehow been related stories.

As we enter the new millennium, we still have not settled America's dilemma: the thing that has claimed so very much of the life and energy of Duncan Gray and the cause for which the Greys went away—race.

Or, maybe my effort here will be just a recital of madness. The South. The land of one man named Duncan Montgomery Gray Jr. and fourscore or so young men who called themselves the University Greys. They as much of the South as he, each like a minstrel trying to learn the lyrics of a tune that is so easy to sing off meter. Race, of course, is not just the preoccupation of the South. It is as the Swedish scholar Gunnar Myrdal called it, "An American Dilemma." From the 1600s when the first slaves were delivered to this day, the Africans who became Americans have been the obsession of Americans of European lineage. Politics, religion, social movements, ideologies; what are we going to do about the colored people? What are we going to do about the Negroes? What are we going to do about the blacks? What are we going to do about the African Americans? (That is not to mention the vulgar who asked, and still ask, "What are we going to do about the niggers?") Whatever the appellative in vogue, the question has been the same. In a sense it has prescribed our history. One is hard pressed to recall an era of our story when it was not a commanding question. What of them? Wars. National elections. Social ordering. What of them?

It is to America's shame that we have not listened to our black prophets. From Frederick Douglass to Sojourner Truth to Martin Luther King Jr. We should have listened. Out of our own self-interest and well-being, we should have heard and heeded. But we haven't. It is what the University Greys were about. More than any other one thing, it is what Duncan Montgomery Gray Jr. has been about. Unfreedom versus freedom. How long? How long? White America cries "What do they want now?" Always they. They want what Langston Hughes wanted:

The land that never has been yet And yet must be.

It was what Duncan Montgomery Gray Jr. has wanted also.

The events that follow really happened. The manner in which they are presented may not in some instances be precisely as they occurred. Since I was not present as the stories were lived, most obviously in the case of the University Greys, I have sometimes manufactured dialogue to carry a specific happening. Some scenes may be composites; none a fabrication. In painting a forest, a tree might be pruned, moved aside, or even lost. But an oak never becomes a pine. The portrait remains honest. Truth and fact are not always the same. This is a narrative in the spirit of Duncan Gray and his times, and in the spirit of the University Greys, that tragic company of Confederates that left to fight elsewhere. Not one of the Greys ever came back. And yet, in the final analysis, they never left at all and are very much with us. Duncan Gray never went away. Perhaps that is why the Greys and Gray belong in the same story; both are yet with us. Fidelity to their stories is my sole objective.

And also with you.

And Also With You

Go forth
into the world in peace:
Be of good courage,
Hold fast that which is good,
Render to no one evil for evil.
Strengthen the fainthearted,
Support the weak,
Help the afflicted,
Honor all persons.
Love and serve the Lord,
Rejoicing in the power
of the Spirit.
And the blessing of God,
the Father, the Son,
and the Holy Spirit
be upon you and remain
with you always.

Amen

Chapter One

GO FORTH INTO THE
WORLD IN PEACE

The signature benedictory blessing of the Right Reverend Duncan Montgomery Gray Jr. for most of his adult life begins with the words, "Go forth into the world in peace." On September 30, 1962, every line, every word of the prayer carried a special meaning for him. James Howard Meredith, the first Negro ever admitted to the University of Mississippi had just been brought to the campus, accompanied by high-ranking federal officials and U.S. Marshals. The university campus and the town of Oxford would soon be a battlefield. The sermons Gray had preached earlier, capped by the one preached that Sunday morning, were already sending shock waves throughout the congregation, community, and state. A white Mississippi preacher was openly and aggressively advocating integration of the races, an intolerable aberration for most white Mississippians in 1962.

"Kill him! Kill him! Kill him!" Those were the only words the thirty-six-year-old Episcopal priest could hear from a clamoring throng beneath him. He was clinging precariously to the side of the Confederate monument at the entrance to the University of Mississippi campus, trying to address a mob gathered beneath where he struggled to steady himself. It had been eight hours since he had said his benediction on that destined Sunday.

Others remember hearing, "I'll bet he belongs to the National Council of Churches!" And, "Kill him! Kill him!" Over and over.

"Traitor! Traitor! Let me at the goddammed scalawag!"

Gray had been called a scalawag before, that insult hurled at Southern white Republicans who cooperated with the victorious federals during

Reconstruction. He had heard it said of him back in the Delta, his first parish, by some of the more vehement segregationists. However, his accusers had not stood in such menacing immediacy before.

At a few minutes past six o'clock that evening, Meredith had been brought to the university, drawing a line in the sand at the heretofore impregnable symbol of that indefinable something called "the Southern way of life," affectionately known by white fans as Ole Miss—this after nearly two years of court actions and obstreperous behavior by citizens' groups and every level of state government.

Soon the marshals—actually deputy marshals, border patrolmen, and guards from federal prisons—would be joined by federalized members of the Mississippi National Guard and twenty thousand U.S. Army troops to protect the lone black student. For the five thousand then enrolled on the generally serene Oxford campus, there would be no thoughts of diphthongs, metaphors, and logarithms for now. There was a new problem to solve. The problem was a twenty-nine-year-old black man; a veteran, a citizen of the state. And he wanted to go to school with them.

The anger of this crowd, however, was not directed at Meredith. Rather, they were about silencing the rector of St. Peter's Church of Oxford who was trying to quell a riot.

The scabrous tongues drowned the rector's pleading for attention. "Let the general speak," a slightly calmer voice said. "We have a leader now!"

The leader the crowd clamored to hear was retired Major General Edwin A. Walker. Clinging to the side of the aging obelisk, a few feet from where the five-foot-eight-inch rector stood, the general was also trying to address the raging assemblage that had chosen to follow him instead of the man of peace.

General Walker was born in 1909 in the Texas Hill Country. He was a graduate of West Point. In recent years, perhaps to make up for a rather lackluster military career, the retired general had excelled both on polo ponies in a sporting flirtation with the patricians, a rank to which he aspired, and in ultra-conservative politics. Five years earlier, in 1957, he had commanded the 101st Airborne when President Eisenhower had sent the unit to Arkansas to protect the nine Negro students at Little Rock's Central High School. (Governor Orville Faubus had defied a court order and refused to admit the Negro students.) In 1961, after a political dispute with the army, Walker resigned and devoted his energy as a private citizen and member of the John Birch Society to doing battle with various alleged communist factions. When it became certain that Meredith would be brought to the university with federal force of arms, Walker used radio, television, and newspaper interviews to appeal for massive and direct intervention. From his home in Dallas, Texas, he had stated on radio that in Little Rock he had been on the wrong side but now that he was out of uniform and on the right side, he would be in Mississippi. "Ten thousand strong from every state in the union," he had urged. "Bring your flags, your tents, and your skillets. It is time. Now or never." Thousands vowed to join him in Oxford.

True to Walker's promise he had come to Oxford, flying first to Jackson, Mississippi, in a private plane for more press appearances and more appeals for warriors. And true to their word, many had heeded his beckoning. Standing over six feet tall, his big Stetson bespeaking the Texas Hill Country of his youth, he appeared the epitome of Southern machismo. The Reverend Duncan Gray knew that General Walker had come to town on a hostile mission.

Duncan M. Gray Jr. was not the first rector of St. Peter's Church to be caught in the vise of racial conflict. Over the years, race played an important role in the life of St. Peter's. Some stayed on and fought. Some departed. In 1861, Frederick Augustus Porter Barnard was both chancellor of the University of Mississippi and rector of St. Peter's Church. He was a graduate of Yale, friend of the poet and abolitionist John Greenleaf Whittier and a vehement opponent of secession and war. Despite his opposition, Barnard was a delegate to the convention in Montgomery, Alabama, in July of 1861 that formed the Episcopal Church of the Confederacy. Soon thereafter, he went from Mississippi to New York where he became president of King's College, later Columbia University.

Albert Taylor Bledsoe was also an important leader in the early days of St. Peter's. A polemicist on both religious and political matters, he had been ordained an Episcopal priest in Ohio, though he left the ministry in a dispute over infant baptism before coming to the University of Mississippi faculty. He had been a friend of Abraham Lincoln, but he was also a staunch defender of slavery and secession. During the war he was in Jefferson Davis's cabinet.

Not long after the war a Confederate general, Francis A. Shoup, was rector. Shoup then became a professor at the University of the South at Sewanee.

On the other hand, there were those who would have applauded Gray's progressive stand. In 1884, Bishop Hugh Miller Thompson made St. Peter's the cathedral church for three years and sounded a warning that, if heeded, might have prevented the troubles Mississippi and Duncan Gray experienced eight decades later. "A day of reckoning will come if we neglect our duty to our black neighbors." A day of reckoning did indeed come, and it was in full tenor as the twenty-sixth rector of St. Peter's Church risked his life on that night of turbulence.

Duncan Gray was a priest in Cleveland and Rosedale, Mississippi, on May 17, 1954, when the U.S. Supreme Court ruled that segregated public education was unconstitutional. Since then he had been a leader among the few whites advocating compliance. It was a lonely voice, but he expressed it with dignity and theological certainty. Now his pulpit was the slippery bevel of the Confederate monument on the University of Mississippi campus.

It was a test his familiar benediction had not known before. Every line of it would be tried before this crucible of insurrection was over. Peace was an elusive dream; courage anachronistic, and yet at that moment in unfettered flower. For certainly there was no deficiency of courage in the young rector. And no dearth of courage in the black man whose entrance the screaming throng was trying to undo. As the priest tried to balance himself against the riotous tugging of the crowd, few knew or cared that inside the clerical attire was a fourth generation Mississippian. Nor did they note the Greek lettering directly beneath Mr. Gray's lifted right hand, lifted for silence but in seeming papal fashion as if to bless the multitude.

Ω ξειυ, αγγελλειυ Λακεδαιμουιοις, οτι τηδε
κειμεθα, τοις κειυωυ ρημαοι πειθομευοι.

Stranger, go tell the Lakedaimonians that we are
lying here in obedience to their command.

The command to the Spartans to which Simonides referred had been: "Come back with your shield, or on it." So they are still lying there; still obeying the command. Not with their shield. Obeying. As soldiers have done in all wars. Such is the message of the monuments of Gettysburg, Antietam, Manassas, Argonne, Normandy, Guadalcanal, and the marble of Vietnam. Lying in obedience. The prevailing present. With anyone who stands before the monument as the stranger. In the presence of those still, in death, obeying *their* command.

A friendly face beneath the priest was Professor William Willis, a communicant of St. Peter's at the time and from whose house Mr. Gray had just come. Willis, the noted classical scholar (later of Duke University), stood regarding the indignity of the scene and the threat upon his rector's life with reverence and moral shock, yet as helpless as

6

the overpowered Spartans at Thermopylae. At that moment, his rector and friend reminded him of the crucifix on the altar of St. Peter's. A few in the crowd had been his students. They would have recognized, though perhaps not heeded, the lesson of Thermopylae. Ironically, the general whom the crowd cried out to hear and the priest they were trying to silence would have known well the words of Simonides, as did, of course, Professor Willis. All three would also have known also whether their sentiments were with the Spartans or the Persians.

In addition to the students, others in the crowd were unlettered denizens from machine shops, farms, and factories of Alabama, Louisiana, West Tennessee, and throughout Mississippi. They neither knew nor cared the rendering of the ghostly epigram. But the degree of anger coming from the crowd was not in proportion to intellect, academic achievement, place of residence, nor social ranking. Nor, as events would soon show, were they all seeking the blood of the young priest.

Gray's detractors were counterfeiting the battlefield tenor of the Lost Cause, bravado grafted into their being by the songs and stories and banners and emotional intensity of a real and supposed past; anger unleashed now by incautious words of unworthy heroes and ambitious poltroons of the day, singing off-key the songs and orations of their ancient ancestry; things that make for war.

"Kill him! Kill him!" they roared anew as Mr. Gray continued to beseech the mob to stop their madness. "Let the general speak!" they called.

"Please don't do this. Please return to your homes," the priest yelled above the tumult. An unheeded supplication.

ON A SUNDAY MORNING IN LATE 1860, DR. FREDERICK Augustus Porter Barnard stood at a roughly hewn cherry lectern. He was conducting the service of Morning Prayer in St. Peter's Episcopal Church, Oxford, Mississippi, where he was rector. He began with these words:

Dearly beloved brethren, the Scripture moveth us, in sundry places, to acknowledge and confess our manifold sins and wickedness; and that we should not dissemble nor cloak them before the face of Almighty God our heavenly Father; but confess them with an humble, lowly, penitent, and obedient heart; to the end that we may obtain forgiveness of the same by his infinite goodness and mercy.

The sins and wickedness he talked about in his sermon that day were the growing alienation of the South from the rest of the country and the threat of war. The small congregation was far from united in its support of Dr. Barnard's views. (A hundred years later another rector of St. Peter's Church, Duncan Montgomery Gray Jr., would stand on the same spot, still wrestling with the fallout of that issue with similar sermons. And the congregation would still be divided in its support and opposition.)

F. A. P. Barnard was also president of the fledgling University of Mississippi and was on his way to turning it into one of the finest universities in the nation. But the resistance to his position on secession was as severe in the university circles as it was in the church. The most troubling of his problems was the resolve of the students to organize a company of soldiers to prepare for war. In the first place the chancellor was opposed to the war. In the next, it was difficult to run a school when the students had lost all interest in anything academic. The harder Chancellor Barnard tried at the university, and the more powerful his sermons at St. Peter's Church became, the more fierce local opposition became. When he sought to discipline two students who were identified by a faculty wife and another person as being the ones who had broken into his home and beaten and raped a slave girl, he was brought before the trustees where he was condemned for taking the word of a Negro over that of two reputable white boys. A matter offered in evidence of his being a Northern sympathizer was that he had contracted the printing of the university catalog with a non-southern company.

Increasingly Chancellor Barnard had trouble controlling the students. At first they called themselves the University Blues. Then when grey was adopted as the Confederate color they became the University Greys. Parades and drills took precedence over laboratory assignments and classroom lectures. The yells of battle in fancied romantic faraway places were stoking their passions now. Subjects in the curriculum such as Greek Prosody and Exercises, Arnold's Latin Prose Composition, and the Agricola and Germania of Tacitus became the source of yawns and campus jokes.

More and more Dr. Barnard was considered to be in the camp of the enemy; in the company of William Lloyd Garrison, Lucretia Mott, and Wendell Phillips. In a sense, when his time came, Duncan M. Gray Jr. was in the same lineage. Unlike Gray, Barnard would move on, leaving the

South to its own sad destiny. But before leaving, he would make a valiant effort to calm the troubled waters. Since John Brown's raid on Harpers Ferry in 1859, most Southern communities had been organizing militia, fearing slave rebellions and certain of armed conflict with the North. With the election of Abraham Lincoln those efforts had intensified, and the bluster of Southern chauvinism had outgrown reason. Still Dr. Barnard continued to try in his effort to administer what was becoming a great institution of learning. Because the hotheads prevailed and his best efforts could not bear fruit, the university, despite the striving of dedicated men and women, did not fully recover between the leaving of the Greys and the coming of federal troops to control a riot a hundred years later. Likewise, in 1962, following the failure of the state's power elite to give leadership in the inevitable outcome of *Brown* v. *Board* the university would again have to struggle immeasurably to prove that it was anything more than an ordinary little segregated academy in the nation's poorest state, excelling often on the football field but not to be taken seriously in the community of scholars. Twice in a hundred years, institutional greatness, in a state that in 1860 ranked near the top in total wealth, was stymied by the cultivated politics of racist swagger.

The university students did not wish to be left behind. In a sense, the mob that young Duncan Gray confronted in 1962 was an extension of the Greys' intent in 1861—the continued subjugation of those of African descent. The mob, like the University Greys, had been spawned in an atmosphere of hotheaded defiance of the federal system, fiery rhetoric and, after all other arguments had been exhausted, the view that one race of human beings was superior to another, entitled to special privileges.

With names like Lowry, McCaleb, Gage, Myers, and Kearney, those who joined the University Greys were considered Mississippi's finest young men. From an elitist judgment that might have been so. In terms of wealth, cultural exposure, and all the things by which young men were measured as gentlemen in those days, their sires could substantiate the claim. But a closer look at their deportment during the months leading up to their departure shows them to be, for the most part, what today would be called *spoiled brats*—fractious, belligerent, disrespectful, unyielding to authority, given to fighting and carousing, and neglectful of their studies. Wars seem to encourage the viewing of history in quixotic retrospect, and a lost war seems to supply heroes that never existed through the romanticizing of feats that might have been of the most ordinary dimensions when they occurred. That is not to say, however, that the University Greys were sluggards when the time for soldiering came. They did not

9

know where they were going, didn't like it when they got there, generally wanted to get out and come home, but in the heat of battle they excelled until the end. They were notoriously impetuous and undisciplined. Between battles, their whereabouts and activities were seldom known. But when the fighting started they were all present and accounted for. Up front. Stories abounded as to their appearance, boldness, and marksmanship. One conversation has become legend. A North Carolina colonel reported to General Whiting's headquarters that a hog had been killed by someone in the Eleventh Mississippi Infantry Regiment. When the general inquired as to evidence and was told that a gunshot had been heard, followed by a hog's squeal, the general replied that there must be some mistake: "When an Eleventh Mississippian shoots a hog, it don't squeal."

None of that mattered for Chancellor Barnard and his faculty during those months when the Greys were preparing to leave. They were a troublesome lot. William B. Lowry, for example, was a nineteen-year-old son of a planter when he was elected captain of the University Greys. He had arrived on campus with a slave, two horses, his guns, and hunting dogs. Reading accounts of faculty meetings of early 1861 is a study in Lowry's vanity. Dealing with him was sometimes an entire agenda. He was removed from the university for missing too many classes, then reinstated when he claimed he had excuses from the chancellor for many of the absences. He is generally listed as the original captain of the Greys. (Actually a Memphis boy named William Driver was elected first, although it is likely that he resigned before he ever received a commission from the governor.)

"You can't expel me just because I've been in a fight," Lowry told the faculty. When the faculty directed that he be expelled unless he left the campus and the town of Oxford within forty-eight hours Lowry's response was that he had been commissioned by the governor and elected by his company as captain and he must stay with his troops. When Chancellor Barnard asked Governor Pettus to remove Lowry from the captaincy of the university military company, Pettus responded that it was not within his power to revoke the commission. (One would think that because he had granted the commission he could also revoke it.) To demonstrate his prowess and express his anger, the newly elected captain rode his horse through the hallway of the Lyceum Building with a bullwhip in his hand threatening to whip the chancellor for treating a Confederate officer with contempt.

No less prominent a citizen than the Episcopal bishop of the Mississippi Diocese protested Lowry's command of the Greys. In a letter

10

to Governor Pettus, Bishop William Mercer Green requested that his son be transferred to another company. After explaining that his son had his tacit support to volunteer the bishop added:

> The present capt. of his co. is a very young man, is an expelled student of our univ. and is without that sedateness of character and sobriety of conduct which should distinguish a commander of your men.

To emphasize his objection to Lowry, the bishop stated that under a different captain he would be willing to bring his minor son from school in Maryland so that the two might be together. The bishop further stated that he would be willing to go to war himself to spare his son serving under William Lowry. Apparently the governor granted the bishop's request. His son was not among those who appeared on the Greys' roster. All three of Bishop Green's sons served, but none under Captain Lowry.

Jeremiah Gage, who later became the most famous of the Greys because of his dramatic dying letter to his mother, expressed his independence by whipping the slave he had brought to school. When he was questioned, he said the slave had been disobedient, was his property, and it was his responsibility to discipline him.

Although still university students, the members of the Greys were issued muskets and allowed to keep them in their rooms. When some of them used the muskets for hunting and random target shooting on campus, Chancellor Barnard attempted to restrain them. Again Captain Lowry's wishes prevailed. "My boys must be prepared."

At a few minutes before five o'clock in the morning on May 1, 1861, the frolicsome University Greys assembled and stacked their books on the spot that would later be the site of a monument in honor of the Confederates. From there they marched the short distance to the Mississippi Central Railroad depot and, amidst the sounds of drum and fife, brief speeches and well-wishes of loved ones, boarded the train that would take them to war. Not one would return. Only Professor L. Q. C. Lamar broke the spell of frivolity when he cautioned that they were not going on a holiday excursion, and that they would soon see hard service.

Only two students remained on campus and they were expected to withdraw within the hour. The university, with none left to teach, closed its doors. Many thought the closing would be but a brief interlude in the schooling of Mississippi's finest young white male minds.

The interlude continues.

What was happening on that fall night in 1962 was the beginning of another tragic military digression in the university's history. In the nation's history. The same issue that had spawned this gathering was the question then: are black people fully human, entitled to the same rights and privileges as everyone else? In 1862, black people were fought over as chattel. Now, September 30, 1962, they were citizens. Yet, theirs was a precarious belonging. Still dispossessed as a people, they fought the nation's wars with the bravest and paid the taxes assessed. With few white advocates. They struggled to sing the Lord's song in a strange land; ill at ease in Zion, waiting for those who had sown the wind to reap the whirlwind as their God had promised. But citizens nonetheless.

On May 1, 1861, the University Greys had marched off this campus to do battle with federal forces to preserve the status quo. Now federal forces, many of them the issue of erstwhile Confederates, were about to return to protect a black man who had been admitted to the University of Mississippi as a student. But until they arrived, the black man's patrons were few. Conspicuous among his advocates was the Reverend Duncan Montgomery Gray Jr. *Gray*. Not Grey. Though Gray was from the loins of the Confederacy as surely as were the Greys.

As the general and the priest clung to the monument and vied for a hearing, tear gas canisters landed nearby. A stiff south wind kept the disabling fog from engulfing the immediate area. The drift of the wind was a mixed blessing. The harsh fumes tended to shunt those milling aimlessly about toward the crowd gathered around the monument, swelling its ranks. Hostile shots fired from adjacent buildings, with no particular target, whizzing overhead, adding to the frenzy. Helicopters churning above the fracas darted low, zoomed away. One thing should be made clear. All the parties involved, those then gathered and their antecedents, Grays and Greys, were sincere in their behavior. Sincerity born of fear. The angular young priest feared for the plight of the soul of his people and the safety of his black brother. The tall Texas general feared what he thought was happening to his country: a communist menace. The angry students feared that their cherished symbol, Ole Miss, would never be the same. They were correct. It wouldn't. And certainly not even the most inflexible critic doubted Meredith's sincerity. Not all were morally right in their commitment, yet all felt called according to their purpose. The lonely parson knew it is sincerity caught at cross-purpose that makes for human tragedy. That was the greater burden as he contended for a hearing.

Suddenly a hand, thrust from the anonymity the mob provided, jerked the Reverend Duncan Gray from his makeshift dais and flung him to the ground. Then the general addressed the quietening mob, reinforcing the mischief of his following.

 IT HAD BEEN TWO MONTHS SINCE THE VAULTING YOUNG warriors left their books and caught the war-bound train. They had not yet drunk from the bitter springs of battle, death still unthinkable, as it generally is for the young.

"Where do you suppose we're going?" a boyish soldier asked another of the University Greys. The one he asked had been declared graduated along with the other seniors when they left for the war. The boy asking was in Company A but had not been a university student. He looked younger than the university graduate because he was smaller. Both were privates. They had been marching side by side since they left Harpers Ferry. They were told they were on their way to catch a train in Winchester, Virginia, that would take them to Manassas, but neither one knew that for sure.

"We're looking for the enemy," the second soldier said.

"*Looking* for the enemy? How can someone be my enemy if I have to look for him? If I don't know his name? Don't know what he looks like? What he smells like? What he thinks like? How can he be my enemy? Just you tell me that." The romance of the ill-fated junket was melting away.

"You'll know him when you see him."

"How?" They had been ordered to march at double quick time and they had to almost scream at each other to be heard above the noise of the trampling feet and rattling equipment. The second soldier didn't answer. "How will I know him?" the other soldier asked again, breathing in quick jerks.

"What color are your britches?" the second soldier asked.

"Grey."

"His will be blue. That's how you will know him."

Captain Lowry called Company A to halt, following the lead of the Eleventh Infantry Regiment commander, Colonel William Moore. The two soldiers who had been talking sat on the ground in the shade of a white oak tree that had been partially blown down. A low hanging limb almost hid them from the others. It was a colorless July day, overcast, with air so close deep breathing was a chore. Seductive orchards nearby were guarded by impenetrable briar fences. And by the captain's orders to stay out.

When they caught their breath the first soldier said, "Grey britches and blue britches. Is that what we're fighting about? Goodness gracious. Grey britches and blue britches. We're fighting about the color of our . . ."

"Skin," the other soldier interrupted quickly. "We're white. White people. It's God's will. He made everything. And He made us white." There was no answer so he went on. Condescending but firm. Like an inexperienced schoolroom lecturer. "You know that. God made us white. You know. Flesh color. And He made the Indians red and put them here to get this country ready for the white man. You know. To kill off the real bad wild animals, most of the spiders and snakes and all that." Still the other soldier didn't respond. "Of course, God expected us to be kind to them. He created us to be kind. That's why we found a nice place for them in the West. Or our daddies did. That was over thirty years ago. We weren't even born. And our soldiers helped them get to their new home and all that."

The sun was invading their shade so they edged closer to the trunk of the tree. Then he began again. "Be ye kind one to another, tenderhearted, forgiving one another, even as God for Christ's sake hath forgiven you."

"You oughten to talk like that," the smaller soldier said. "Remember what Reverend Witherspoon said in his sermon just last Sunday. He said we ought not to take the Lord's name in vain. Not ever. Said he had heard too much swearing around camp and that wasn't good with us right now fixing to go into battle for the first time."

"I didn't take the Lord's name in vain. What are you talking about?"

"Yes you did. You said, 'For Christ's sake.'"

The second soldier started to laugh, seeing the other boy confused. He tried to explain. "It's all a matter of punctuation. Now if I had said, 'Even as God comma for Christ's sake comma hath forgiven you.' But there wasn't a comma when I said it. So I didn't take Christ's or God's name in vain. I said, 'Even as God for Christ's sake hath forgiven you.' Anyhow, it's in the Bible. The fourth chapter of Ephesians, the thirty-second verse." He fumbled in his pack, found an almost new Bible and readily turned to Ephesians. He pointed to the verse he had quoted and held the book close enough for the other soldier to read.

"See. I was talking about how we were good to the Indians, finding them a good home out West and all that. I didn't take the Lord's name in vain. I wouldn't ever do that."

They began to march again, and the train to take them to Manassas was in sight. "You didn't answer my question," the first soldier said.

14

The other soldier went on as if he had not heard. "And the black people were put on earth to serve the white people. That's in the Bible, too. It's in Genesis. God turned Ham black and put a curse on him and said he would always be a servant. That's really what we're fighting about. The Word of God." The soldier's voice had a preachy, pontifical edge to it. With his left hand he slapped the musket stock for emphasis. "The Almighty, He created man to civilize and dominate the earth. To make his job possible He provided work animals of various kinds. Those with four legs he called cattle, and those with two legs he called beasts. See, that was God's plan. Man was entrusted to do the mental labor and beasts, Negroes, were to perform the manual labor."

"You still didn't answer my question," the smaller soldier said, not commenting on the lecture he was hearing. "Where are we going?"

The older Grey wasn't through. He began a long harangue about how the wife Cain took in the land of Nod was a Negro, a beast. He said she had to have been a beast because God had just created Adam and Eve and they had two sons and no other children. So Cain, after he murdered his brother, had no human to marry. Because of that amalgamation, God had to intervene. He said God did it first by the destruction of Sodom and Gomorrah. Then with the flood. "By Noah's time he and his family were the only white people left on earth and God decided to give man another chance by drowning all the soulless mongrels." The soldier explained further when he saw the questioning expression on his pupil's face. "There was a pair of Negroes on the Ark. See? Because there had to be two of everything, see. And amalgamation started all over again. Understand? Once more God found it necessary to intervene. This time by sending His son Jesus Christ to redeem man from atheism, amalgamation, and idolatry."

The smaller soldier tried to change the subject, tired of the pedagogical stance assumed by the self-appointed leader. And a little embarrassed for him. He had heard defenses of slavery, but never any quite like this. He talked about the time back at Harpers Ferry when a soldier brought a half-gallon of whiskey into camp inside a plugged watermelon. He buried it in the back of his tent with a straw sticking out. Boys would take turns sucking the straw for a drink. Only two swallows at a time though. The lecturing soldier was not deterred by the interruption. He soon resumed giving his own interpretation of the origin of black people. The younger soldier wasn't sure if what he was hearing was meant to be burlesque or if the university-educated boy actually believed what he purported. It really didn't matter to the young man.

15

"You didn't answer my question," he said again, his untidy backpack weighing heavily to his right side. "How can someone be my enemy if I have to look for him?"

"I don't think you understand about war," the other soldier said.

"No. I reckon I don't. And maybe if I don't understand hard enough they'll let me go home."

Nine days before the riot had been Gray's birthday, September 21. It was the Feast Day of St. Matthew, Apostle and Evangelist. Matthew, who in our day would have worked for the IRS. The Collect read from the *Book of Common Prayer* that day seems to have been a presage of Gray's future:

> O Almighty God, who by thy blessed Son didst call Matthew from the receipt of custom to be an Apostle and Evangelist; Grant us grace to forsake all covetous desires, and inordinate love of riches, and to follow. . . .

Duncan Gray had first become an engineer, not a tax collector. But he did become an evangelist and follower of Jesus; was never a lover of riches.

The Gospel reading that day spoke of Jesus having associated with the despised of the day and of how He had come to call not the righteous but sinners to repentance.

The Sunday Gray was accosted by the mob at the Confederate monument for his outspokenness regarding the evils of segregation was the day after the church's feast honoring St. Michael, the one who had fought the dragon, and his angels, leading to their being cast out of heaven:

> And the great dragon was cast out, that old serpent, called the Devil, and Satan, which deceiveth the whole world: and he was cast out into the earth. . . .

The Gospel for St. Michael's Day had been the story of Jesus telling His disciples that to offend one of the little ones offended Him and "it were better for him that a millstone were hanged about his neck, and that he were drowned in the depth of the sea. Woe unto the world because of offenses!"

Gray spoke to his people that morning directly from those Scriptures, applying them to the crisis of the university. He had publicly said Governor Ross Barnett was a living symbol of lawlessness. Like St. Michael who had fought the dragon before him, the Oxford priest gave no quarter to the dragon he was battling.

To quote from Gray's sermons is to dilute their power but the following is indicative:

> We do not have the right to defy and disobey the law when it is established and in force. In trying to do this, we have brought upon ourselves the threat of *anarchy*; and, as Christians, we cannot and must not support this alternative to the democracy under which we live. . . . We do not want troops in our state, and we can be thankful that the federal government has been as patient as it has in not taking this step so far. However, we may well see troops here in the next few days. But when this happens we will have only ourselves to blame. Ultimately, the federal government cannot be asked to withhold such measures if we refuse to give in, any more than a policeman cannot be told to avoid the use of force when a lawbreaker resists arrest and continues to break the law. . . .

> Our governor has said that the state's cause on this score is righteous and just; and I'm sure he is sincere in his belief, as are many other Mississippians who share it with him. But in the name of reason and in the name of Christian standards of freedom and justice, I ask you to consider the fact that no university in the world would defend this position rationally, and no Christian Church in the world would defend it morally. . . .

> Surely, most of us realize by now that there can be only one resolution to this crisis: the admission of James Meredith to the university. Our leaders have tried to make us think it could be otherwise, and they have succeeded in convincing many people that this is possible. This is especially tragic, because it will make our adjustment to the new situation all the more difficult. But we, as Christians, should now accept this fact, if we have not already done so. Not only is this the only practical and reasonable solution, but it is also the only answer that is just and right. It is our business now to get to work at once to do all that we can to make the adjustment

to this new situation as peaceful and orderly as possible on our campus and in our community.

For these are times which not only try men's souls, but also infect and poison them. The seeds of anger and hatred, bitterness and prejudice, are already widely sown, and as Christians, we need to do our utmost to uproot and cast them out. You and I have responsibility in the days and weeks to come. . . .

The prophets of old most often spoke with lips of thunder and eyes that threw flame, roaring their prophesies of the wrath to come, their bellicose ravings falling like the blow of a battle-axe on iron or the growl of a wolf. Mr. Gray stood with equanimity, calmly saying the most outrageous things as if they were ordinary ideas the listener surely shared. In his sermon that morning and on several previous Sundays he repeated some of the things he had already said to the community on radio. (There had been earlier attempts to register Meredith, efforts foiled by the governor who had had himself appointed registrar of the University of Mississippi. "And which of you gentleman is Mr. Meredith?" the governor had asked when greeting John Doar, a blonde-headed Republican assistant attorney general who had accompanied Meredith to the state capitol in Jackson, bringing a smile to the otherwise stony-faced would-be student.)

Most of the preacher's sermons were aimed directly at those who sat before him. After reviewing what was happening, not then knowing that the storm clouds that were brewing in the morning would bring the cyclone of evening, he brought the issue straight to the pews where they sat. It was not enough not to be among the physical detractors. Those who had not spoken out, had not worked to prepare themselves, the state and the community, for the inevitable were equally culpable.

And I do not believe that any of us here today could stand in the presence of Jesus of Nazareth, look Him squarely in the eye, and say, "We will not admit a Negro to the University of Mississippi." For it was He who said, "Inasmuch as ye have done it unto one of the least of these my brethren, ye have done it unto me."

He had preached the same sermon at the Church of the Holy Innocents at Como, Mississippi, a little town twenty miles to the northwest, and had served as priest-in-charge.

18

By today's reckoning the rector's words may seem tame. But with the populace stirred by eight years of hysteria, undergirded with centuries of anthropological myopia, the words were a flagrant testing of pulpit freedom and an uncommon violation of Southern mores. St. Peter's Church, with a preponderance of university people, many from outside the region, was by far the most open-minded of any congregation in town. Even so, the line in the sand drawn by the rector would lead to a schism long in healing. Some there that morning would be a long time returning.

When the little man with the turned around collar hit the ground he was not sure how, or if, he would escape. Though Professor Willis and a few other friendly faces were nearby, they were no match for the madness of the crowd.

The moment was lost in an aura of unreality. Evans Harrington, a professor of English at the university, remembers that moment with a foreboding that has not faded with the years. He saw Gray clinging to the Confederate monument. The throng surrounding the monument separated Harrington from his friend, who was in a life-threatening situation. Harrington didn't know what he alone could do, but knew he must do something. A broken jaw he had received years before when he was a student boxer flickered through his mind. As he was walking up University Avenue from where he had parked, he had seen dozens of young men walking onto the campus, each one carrying rocks, bricks, bottles. On the street was a long string of state trooper cars. Each of the uniformed officers had his window down with his head sticking out. As the students passed each patrol car, they heard the same words, as if rehearsed. "Kill the bastard." From car after car the same bidding. "Kill the bastard." From each officer, each custodian of the people's well-being, all in a row repeating the same words to susceptible youths. "Kill the bastard."

"That scene politicized me," Harrington says today. "Before that I was a James Joyce, ivy-tower sort." There, seeing his own students with rocks and bricks, he realized that even the finest academic training was not enough.

He describes what happened next. "I saw that hand reach up and then I saw Duncan disappear at the base of the monument, the troopers' words to the students still ringing." Without further thought the professor vaulted through the mob—he doesn't know how. Two massive young men had maneuvered Gray to the opposite side of the monument, facing the Lyceum. The larger one had him pinned to the ground, wrestler fashion. The other one was trying to dissuade the big one.

"No, no, no," he kept saying. "Let's don't hurt the preacher."

"You heard what he said on TV. Let's kill the son-of-a-bitch." Gray had addressed the admission of Meredith on radio and had been interviewed by television and newspaper journalists.

"I know, I know, I know. But he's a preacher. He really believes that stuff." They argued. "Well, who the hell are you? Maybe you believe it, too."

Gray recalls that the one who didn't want him harmed was a deputy sheriff from a neighboring county.

Harrington doesn't remember exactly what happened next. He remembers moving with Gray through the crowd and walking with him and some others away from the mob. Gray's point of reference that night was the Y Building on campus, a noble old edifice, no stranger to strife. Built in 1853 as a dormitory but never used for that, it had been, at different times, a hospital for both Union and Confederate sick and wounded. Following the war it had been a chapel, and in 1962 served as offices and meeting places for the various denominational organizations and their ministers. That usage, at a state university, if challenged, would probably have been found in constitutional violation of the First Amendment, unlike what the mob was challenging that night with force. By then the admission of Meredith had withstood every possible constitutional challenge.

Gray called his wife to assure her he was all right, then made his way back outside where he continued to ask those he met to surrender the bricks, bottles, and other weapons they held. Some did. He saw a shadowy figure coming toward him, then shift obliquely and move around the building. Gray would later learn that the person he saw was Paul Guihard, a French journalist. He was found shortly thereafter near the Fine Arts Building. He was dead, shot in the back of the head in execution style. Mr. Gray watched with sadness as the hearse hurried from the tumult. He would soon learn that what he watched was the first leg of a journey taking a foreign visitor home. Killed in action in Mississippi.

A few yards from where the old rebel statue keeps his vigil, and from which Duncan Gray had just been jerked down by the mob, stands the old Geology Building, a neglected but lovely relic of magnificence. Few knew that night that inside the burnished red brick building there was something worthy of protecting. If the mob had been a conscientious protraction of the claimed glory of the Lost Cause, it would have protected it. It is a memorial window to the University Greys. The old building, also called *Ventress Hall*, was in the beginning the university library, then the Geology Building, and by 1962 a place for painting and drawing. Standing silently, holding in its bosom the stained-glass elegy of the Greys, the Gothic cupola of Ventress frowned upon the crazed lemmings in their charge to end what they would eternize. For surely the riot in progress was chaperone for rapid Southern change.

The window had been placed there by the Delta Gamma sorority in 1889. Delta Gamma had been organized sixteen years earlier by three students of the Lewis School for Girls that was then located a few blocks from St. Peter's Church. Unable to go home to Kosciusko for Christmas because of bad weather and impassable roads, they organized a club to stay the boredom. On their way to becoming a national collegiate sorority, the Delta Gamma alumnae raised five hundred dollars and commissioned the Tiffany Glass Company to make the window that would be installed in the library. In the middle panel stands a gray-clad soldier, his left hand grasping a pistol, his right holding aloft a gleaming sword. In the background are faded figures in hand-to-hand combat, none approximating the ragged and dusty remnant that fell like wheat before a scythe when General Pettigrew sent them toward the Union line at Gettysburg.

> CUM PIETATE ALUMNORUM
> IN HONOR OF THOSE WHO, WITH ARDENT VALOR AND PATRIOTIC DEVOTION IN THE CIVIL WAR SACRIFICED THEIR LIVES IN DEFENCE OF PRINCIPLES INHERITED FROM THEIR FATHERS, AND STRENGTHENED BY THE TEACHINGS OF THEIR ALMA MATER, THIS MEMORIAL IS LOVINGLY DEDI-CATED.

Had the mob stood encircled in nonviolent protection of the ancient icon, Duncan Gray most likely would have stood with them. He was aware of its presence and on one occasion checked on it. He stood beside it for a moment amid the opaque stillness as the musty smell of longevity commingled with the acrid stench of gas from without. The battle outside was being waged by those who neither knew nor cared about the Tiffany treasure. Almost miraculously no flying object nor one of the thousands of stray bullets fired that night struck the University Greys' window.

THE OFFICERS WERE BEGINNING TO LOAD THE TROOPS onto the flatcars of the train that would take them to meet the Federal forces near Manassas. The University Greys had been marching slightly behind Company I, the Van Dorn Reserves from Aberdeen, Monroe County, Mississippi. The Van Dorn Reserves laid claim to being one of the wealthiest companies in the entire Confederate Army. Unlike many companies that required the volunteer to provide his own uniform, each soldier in the Van Dorn Reserves was furnished a finely-tailored uniform, a Colt revolving rifle, and a sizeable stake of gold. Also, the company had a treasury of several thousand dollars. The University Greys were of affluent stock, too, but Lafayette County had not invested in its soldiers like Monroe. Maybe because Lafayette had two companies to outfit, the University Greys and the Lamar Rifles. The young soldier who had been listening to his friend talk about racial hierarchy was disappointed when Colonel Moore said there was only room on the train for two companies of the Eleventh Infantry Regiment. The Mississippi Second Regiment was already loaded. The young soldier wanted the elegantly dressed Van Dorn Reserves to go into battle alongside the Greys. Somehow he thought the lavish uniforms made them better soldiers. In addition, their uniforms were the only thing that got the larger soldier's mind off his seeming obsession with black people.

"This is where we were headed," the lecturing Grey yelled to the smaller soldier as they arrived at Manassas. "And there's the enemy. The boys in blue britches. You don't have to look for them any more." Under the command of General Barnard Bee, the University Greys, along with Company F, Colonel William C. Falkner's Second Mississippi, the Fourth Alabama Regiment, Sixth North Carolina Regiment, and the First Tennessee Battalion had been posted in reserve behind the Confederate line along Bull Run. From there they were sent to meet what was thought to be a weak Federal feint. It was not a feint and for the first time the University Greys were facing battle. They could hear the noise of combat but no shot had been fired directly at them. Having just jogged four miles from the train, they were no match for the force they met and a retreat was ordered. In the retreat the Greys and Noxubee Rifles became separated from the rest of the brigade. They found themselves behind a newly formed line being held by the brigade of Brigadier General Thomas J. Jackson. Although the Greys were probably out of earshot, it was here that General Bee uttered the famous words, "See, there is Jackson, standing like a stone wall." Until he fell at Chancellorsville two years later, Thomas Jonathan Jackson would be known as Stonewall Jackson. The sobriquet remains in history and in lore. Within minutes, the general who uttered those famous words lay mortally wounded.

The boisterous, cocksure, spoiling-for-a-fight University Greys had now entered the war zone. No more drilling on the university campus. No more swaggering in dormitory rooms about what a short war it would be. No more shooting rabbits in Lafayette County with military muskets and pretending they were Yankee soldiers. This was war. With all its confusion, all its fear, crying out, swearing, praying, taking stock. The war itself was but three months old. Suddenly the soldiers here were far more than three months older than they were when Fort Sumter was fired on. Some were years older. Some were as old as they would ever be.

"Look out!" The soldier who had been immersed in his racial dogma yelled at the one he had chosen as pupil. Andrew Jackson Johnson, a University Grey and namesake of Andrew Jackson, was the first Mississippi casualty to fall in the Civil War.

> Visiting the iniquity of the fathers upon the children, and upon the children's children, unto the third and to the fourth generation. (Num. 14:18)

A short three decades earlier President Andrew Jackson's mischief at Dancing Rabbit Creek had given the whites the last of the rich Mississippi land, making the Cotton Kingdom a certainty, cinching the continued growth of slavery as an institution. Without the Choctaw and Chickasaw lands, Mississippi would not have been the leading slave-holding power it was. Without the riches of cotton, fortunes made possible by slaves— no war. Now, young Andrew Jackson Johnson was dead, his spleen pierced by a Minié ball. He was twenty-two years old, actually two years *older* than the one who addressed him as "young man" and had graduated from the university by fiat.

The romance of war was over. The University Greys were warriors.

Just across the bridge, where the campus ends and University Avenue leads to the town of Oxford, stood a lapsed communicant of St. Peter's Church and two of his compatriots; patricians all. They, of course, would not join the battle. Neither would they walk away. They stood in the fashion of the man of whom Chesterton spoke; one who would neither move inside the house nor put it entirely behind but stood forever grumbling on the porch. Their position spoke volumes—"See what they have done to our university." Like sulking possums they hurled no bricks, fired no shots, content to revel in the harvest of seeds they had planted with the young since Appomattox but taking no responsibility for the yield. They were not alone in their stance. From the governor's mansion to the farthermost boundaries of the state, huddled before radios and television sets, they secretly hurrahed, feeling "I told you so." It was to the likes of them the Reverend Duncan Gray had directed his most stinging indictment.

Gray had first come to the campus a little before six o'clock that evening. A mother had called and asked him to get her daughter and take her to the rectory for the night. As the coed was preparing to leave her dormitory, Gray checked the main campus. What he saw was a disquieting fulfillment of his own prediction. It was a riot in its infancy.

U.S. Marshals were ringing the Lyceum Building, the administrative lifeline of the university. The Lyceum is the only survivor of the five original buildings built for the opening of the university in 1848. With its six massive white columns standing with dignity and composure, fronting the red brick of three levels of time and history and contradictions, it seemed in stark contrast to what was happening. Already a crowd was gathering as more trucks rolled in with more marshals wearing arm bands, white helmets, gas mask pouches, sidearms, nightsticks, and tear gas guns, all standard riot paraphernalia; looking like ancient warriors to this campus unaccustomed to such displays of might—in all, 536 men.

Gray had followed the unfolding drama with determination, mounting sadness, and anger—the court orders, defiance by the governor and his underlings, the mounting hostility of people he loved but would not deceive with false prophesy. He had warned of the wrath to come. He had counseled, preached, and prayed. This was D-Day and he would not retreat from the battle.

The crowd was becoming increasingly restive but the parson thought savage violence might be avoided by having the marshals and several faculty members move throughout the gatherings advising the students that an agreement had been reached between the federal and state authorities. Some were already advancing on the marshals who formed a solid phalanx in front of the Lyceum Building, lilliputian under the tall white columns. Some threw lighted cigarettes toward the marshals who stood still, forbidding in their courage.

Duncan Gray got the student, drove her to his residence, then stopped for a short while with some students at St. Peter's Church. From there he picked up Professor Willis and together they went to Professor James Silver's residence to hear President Kennedy address the nation on what he thought would be a troublesome but not seditious transition at the University of Mississippi. Jim Silver, a guileless liberal and teacher of history, who claimed agnosticism as his religion but who held Duncan Gray in high esteem for his gutsy stand, was already on campus.

When Gray returned to the campus he found a pitched battle. The smell of tear gas filled the air, adding to the curses, shouting, and full-blown riot. He was sickened by what he saw.

Moving immediately into the crowd, along with the Reverend Wofford Smith, chaplain to Episcopal students, he began confronting students one by one, sometimes stepping in front of a rioter, grabbing his arms or his weapons. Some gave up their weapon—bricks, pipes, bottles, and the like—and drifted away. Others cursed and refused. One young man came at Duncan with a shovel, but backed away when the little man in clerical garb stood his ground.

Gray and Smith stopped a car with a deputy sheriff's insignia, begged the driver to get out and help them try to calm the riot. He said there was nothing he could do and drove away. The car was from Harrison, a Gulf Coast county.

It is not my intention here to relate an exact chronology of events during that long night. No one was keeping notes in the turbulence of the moment—except working journalists and by then many of them were intending survival. The word had spread that one of their colleagues was dead, and others had been attacked. I do not know precisely at what point marshals began firing tear gas canisters into the mob, nor who gave the order. It is, however, known that Edwin O. Guthman, in charge of public relations for the Department of Justice, Deputy Attorney General Nicholas Katzenbach, and John Doar, attorney for the justice department, were present, as was Chief Marshal James McShane. A direct telephone line was open between the justice department officials on the scene and the White House.

Nor is it my purpose to detail the sequence of discussions between the governor of Mississippi and federal officials and assess blame for Mr. Meredith's being brought on campus Sunday evening rather than Monday morning as the university administration had expected. Volumes, hearings, and courts have thus far failed to settle all that.

Smith and Gray decided to separate, feeling that more individuals and small groups could be addressed. Those Gray could identify as students were generally more receptive to his appeals than were outsiders. He succeeded in temporarily stopping a small group from breaking out all the lights around the Lyceum with bricks and bottles, although someone later completed the job. In addition to trying physically and verbally to dissuade the rioters, he sought to dispel the rampant rumors. One was that the marshals were firing into the crowd and had killed two coeds and seriously injured many others. Another was that Director of Student Activities Tom Hines had died on campus of a heart attack. None of this was true.

As Gray moved about the circle, an area extending from the Confederate monument to the Lyceum Building, he began hearing a common remark in the small groupings. "We have a leader now." At first he didn't understand. Then he spotted the tall Texan and realized they were talking about General Walker.

Walker was surrounded by an entourage of young to middle-aged men, none appearing to be students or local citizens. Mr. Gray approached the gathering, introduced himself to the general, and began to plead with him to try to bring order among the rioters. General Walker said he wasn't there to do any such thing, that the students had a right to protest and that he was there as an observer only.

When Mr. Gray continued to walk along with the group, talking to General Walker, pleading with him to use his influence in the situation, a heated exchange developed. The general stopped walking, turned on the priest and with anger in his voice demanded, "Just who the hell are you, anyway? And what are you doing here?"

"My name is Duncan Gray. I am the rector of the local Episcopal Church," the priest replied. "This is my home and I am deeply hurt to see what is happening to the university and to the state. I am here to do anything I can to stop the rioting and keep any more people from getting hurt or killed."

The general became even more angry, moving toward Mr. Gray and exclaiming, "You're the kind of minister that makes me ashamed to be an Episcopalian!"

Mr. Gray, realizing that he was on the verge of losing his own temper, tried to remain calm, explaining that he was on home ground. "I have a proper concern and interest in keeping law and order. You, sir, are a Texan and have no business here. Your very presence here is making matters far worse. You should have stayed in Texas. We have enough problems of our own."

General Walker turned to walk away, the others following. Duncan Gray moved with them, addressing the other men. "You fellows aren't from around here either," he told them. "You have no business here." No one claimed to be local. One man, who spoke in the vernacular of a lawyer, tried to justify the students' defiance, talking about constitutional law and the judicial process, but really said nothing.

Mr. Gray headed back toward the Y Building, then noticed the crowd around the monument. That was when he mounted the monument alongside General Walker but was prohibited from speaking.

By this time the area of the campus known as the circle was a jumble of chaos. Duncan Gray knew the marshals were no match for the mob that was still growing. He would remember later that of the scores of cars he saw streaming onto the campus, not a one was from Oxford or Lafayette County. Also, as the night wore on, more and more of the rioters were non-students. Of the students, however, there were about as many women as men, screaming and cursing as loudly as the boys. "They kept comparing themselves to Hungarian Freedom Fighters," he remembers.

"Me and my daddy drove up there from Jackson," one of the rioters told me recently. (He was a teenager at the time.) "Daddy kept drinking Crown Royal all the way up there. Right straight out of the bottle. Chasing it with Seven-Up. Warm Seven-Up."

Now age fifty, the rioter spent seven years in prison for something he says he didn't do, although he will acknowledge many bombings and burnings in the sixties for which he was never charged. He was an active Klansman at the time, and later a leader in the White Knights, by far the most violent of all the Klan groups.

"Did you feel like a Hungarian Freedom Fighter that night?" I asked him.

"Man, I was seventeen years old. I never heard of Hungary. I just knew about Mississippi. And niggers."

He said his daddy was bad drunk by the time they got to the campus. Said they got separated early and he was glad because as a rowdy teenager, he had come there to do some damage.

"The last time I saw Daddy that night he was handcuffed to a fire hydrant. Kept mumbling something about a brook rumbling over pebbles in Smith County, and something about a springtoothed cultivator in a newground field pulled by a spirited mule and how one of the spring teeth would get caught in a root, making the plow handles kick him in the belly and how it hurt and how he wished he was at a Klan rally in Smith County making things right like they used to be instead of being chained like a dog in this big ole city, and he kept mumbling about how he would suck eggs when he was a boy to prove he could pick as much cotton as any nigger."

Interesting metaphor I thought, the one about the springtooth cultivator and the newground. "Did you know what your daddy was talking about?" I asked.

"Not then I didn't. No, not then. Man, there was so much going on. Daddy started crying and I got the hell away from there and went on back to fighting."

"Fighting?"

"Hell, yes, fighting. Man, this was war. Me and this other ole boy got on a fire truck that was there and drove it right toward the marshals. Man, we was going to knock them flat with that water pressure. The sumbitches shot the tires and then they shot the hoses. I got wetter'n hell. They got the other boy. Dragged him in the building but I got away."

I asked him if he was just there having fun. "Fun? We didn't go all the way to Oxford to have fun. We could have had fun back home. We was there to fight the feds."

He said he fought until the army got there and chased everybody off.

"One of my daddy's Klan buddies had told us there was a Confederate cemetery right on the campus. Said if we got in trouble we should go there. Said the Greys would look after us. Damned if that wasn't where I found myself when the soldiers ran us off. I wasn't even looking for it neither. Just happened up on it."

The story he told me of the cemetery was not all correct. Actually both Union and Confederate soldiers had been buried there since the Y Building was used as a hospital by both sides. The Magnetic Observatory was used as a morgue and called the *dead house*. Bodies would be taken there each night to await burial in the little plot called *God's acre*. Although there are several hundred bodies buried there, only a few names are listed on a monument that was erected by the United Daughters of the Confederacy in 1939. The inscription on the plaque tells part of the story:

> Here rests more than seven hundred soldiers who died on the campus of the University of Mississippi when the buildings were used as a war hospital 1862, 1865, most of them Confederates wounded at Shiloh, a few federals of Grant's Army, a few Confederates of Forest's Cavalry. Even their names, save these, known but to God.

I told my Klan reporter the story I had heard regarding the unnamed soldiers. A few years after the war the university opened again, and the caretaker sent some Negro workmen to clean the cemetery. When he returned, he found the workers had pulled up all the markers and stacked them to the side so it would be easier to cut the weeds and grass. There was no way to determine which cross went where.

"Now ain't that just like a nigger," the Klansman exclaimed. "And then they want to go to school with us." He said he had a small Confederate flag with him that night in 1962 and stuck it at the base of the monument before leaving.

Lord, Lord.

I asked him if he saw the priest on the monument with General Walker. "Yeah, I seen him all right. But I woudn' the one that jerked him down. I would of though. He didn't have no business even being there."

I didn't argue.

"Next thing I knowed I was ten miles out in the county somewheres with five of them fellows I met at the graveyard where our boys had been buried. Must have been two, three o'clock in the morning by then. One of them said he knowed where some dynamite was. We went and got the dynamite and had us a plan. Some state troopers stopped us and give the driver a ticket because he didn't have no driver's license. Me settin' there with my feet on a case of dynamite. The trooper didn't see it though. Maybe didn't want to see it. Anyhow, he let us go.

"My daddy never did get over the feds chaining him to a fire plug when all he was doing was trying to keep the white race pure, and anyway he was drunk and didn't mean no harm. Daddy's dead now though."

The time I spent with the middle-aged Klansman, who was seventeen years old when it all happened, haunted me—the things he was still saying after all these years! Amortization of history? Sins of the fathers? What has shaped him to the thing he is? I recalled some words of Gray when the riot was over. He said that since many of the rioters had been ten years old they had heard nothing but venom directed at Negro citizens. Who could blame them for what they were doing? he asked.

The St. Peter's rector continued his efforts into the night. A building under construction provided a plentiful supply of ammunition for the rioters; bricks, board and pipe pieces, broken cinder blocks. The partial construction also provided cover for those firing rifles and shotguns; sometimes firing aimlessly, at nothing in particular, and sometimes with scope accuracy. Professor Willis asked a man firing a rifle in the general direction of the Lyceum, without aim, if he didn't think he might hit someone on his side. "I hadn't thought about that," was the reply.

Mr. Hugh Clegg, who had been a top assistant to J. Edgar Hoover until he retired and came to the University of Mississippi as director of development, was frantically trying to get a change of orders from Washington. Mr. Clegg, a tough ex-federal agent who had once traded shots with John Dillinger, had been assigned to the Meredith case early because of his connections. Certainly he enjoyed a close, first-name relationship with Mr. Hoover. That night the connection wasn't helping. The once nearly all-powerful director of the bureau had already begun a steady decline.

Marshals were falling but no doctor in Oxford had come to the campus. Finally George Street, a university official who was serving as spokesman for the university, got in touch with Dr. L. G. Hopkins. He was an alumnus and opposed desegregation. But he remembered his oath. He was a physician first and said he would be there as soon as possible. By then the injured were lining the wide corridor of the Lyceum. It was the same hall William Lowry, captain of the University Greys, had ridden his horse down to intimidate Frederick Augustus Barnard, chancellor of the university and priest of St. Peter's Church. And the hall frolicsome Union soldiers had ridden through just for the fun of it.

With the aid of George Street, Dr. Hopkins set up a first aid station in the women's rest room, with facilities no more elaborate than those of Dr. Joseph Holt's field hospital in an old barn on Seminary Ridge on the third day of Gettysburg where the Greys fought until not one was left to fight. Like the Confederate surgeon, Dr. Hopkins worked throughout the long night, doing what he had committed himself to when he took the ancient Oath of Hippocrates. When Dr. Hopkins arrived, U.S. Marshal Graham Same was lying on the floor gasping for life, a bullet hole in his throat. Doubtless the doctor saved his life. Twenty-eight other marshals were shot that night, plus 160 marshals were hurt with bricks, pipes, bottles, and timbers.

There were two that Dr. Hopkins could not help. Paul Guihard, the European journalist, and a local man named Ray Gunter. Charles "Peas" Graeber of Yazoo City remembers the scene well. He was starting his junior year at the university and had returned to the campus just as the trouble was beginning. He was sitting on a ledge with some friends, not participating in the melee. They were looking in the direction of the Lyceum where the major action was taking place. Suddenly he saw a man about fifteen feet away slump to the ground. "I helped put him in a car,"

Mr. Graeber recalls. "I noticed a little hole, almost directly between his eyes. I had no idea what had happened." Mr. Graeber said that as soon as he helped get the man in the car, "I got out of there. It could have been me . . . any one of us." The man who had been shot was Gunter, a local jukebox repairman who was standing on a cinder block to get a better view of the battle. He was dead.

Duncan Gray was still in the midst of the battle, ducking occasionally into the Y Building where the air was slightly clearer of tear gas. There he checked on the family by telephone. Gray was concerned about his wife, Ruth, and their new baby. Catherine, the Gray's fourth and last child, was supposed to have been born on September 30, the night the riot occurred. Instead she had arrived exactly one month earlier. She is still known as an exceedingly thoughtful person.

On one of those trips into the building, Gray was stopped by the commandant of the university ROTC who questioned him on the activities of General Walker. Gray reported in detail all he had seen and heard, then rushed back to the maelstrom outside. He did not know at that point that the marshals had repeatedly asked for permission to use their guns. Permission was being denied. He watched with consternation as the highway patrolmen moved around the circle, leaving the campus. He had felt their presence was at least a mild dissuader to the more violent rioters (though he had seen no evidence that that was their intention). When the state troopers pulled out, there was no symbol of authority left that the rioters respected. Now it was just they against the marshals.

At one point Wofford Smith tried to effect a truce. One student had been hit in the hand with birdshot, another in the stomach. The students convinced the priest that they had been shot by marshals. Reverend Smith advanced on the marshals to beg them not to use shotguns on boys. The marshals quickly convinced him that they had not brought a single shotgun.

The marshals said they would quit firing tear gas canisters into the crowd if the rioters would stop throwing missiles at them. Smith, with a marshal beside him frantically waving a white handkerchief and shining a flashlight directly on the wilting clerical collar, moved forward as the crowd gathered around. General Walker hovered nearby, saying nothing. When Smith made the offer, a spokesman, a senior student, replied, "We aren't after the marshals, really. We want to get Meredith." Smith convinced the student that Meredith was not in the building. The war, however, continued. Although few knew it, Meredith was in a room in Baxter Hall, a dormitory a quarter of a mile away. He had been secretly brought there hours before the riot began. The marshals had a last-ditch plan. If completely overpowered, they would all make a dash for Baxter Hall and try to prevent the lynching of James Meredith. That was Gray's greatest fear—that Meredith would be murdered.

The circle was now a furious conflagration. Burning cars, Molotov cocktails that had been hurled at the marshals and vehicles thought to be unfriendly, and burning debris cast ghostly shadows through the roistering haze. The whole world seemed on fire. The sounds were those of a thousand hyena: howls of defiance and strength and blood-thirstiness. Loud, resounding, splitting up the darkness into a deeper midnight. Could the pernicious words of one governor have brought us to this? Gray wondered.

Billy Ellis, now a banker in Holmes County, had graduated from the university but was still in town waiting to be inducted into the U.S. Air Force. He knew Gray and feared for the rector's life that night. He and a friend decided to reconnoiter the area and got to the edge of the campus in time to see a rickety old vehicle, long out of service as a Louisiana school bus, ease in behind Hemingway Stadium. From inside they heard the blaring of a tape player and lyrics they had never heard before:

> You niggers listen now/ I'm gonna tell you how/ To keep from being tortured/ When the Klan is on the prowl/ Stay at home at night/ Lock your doors up tight/ Don't go outside or you will find/ Them crosses aburning bright.

They later learned the song was called "The Cajun Ku Klux Klan." Five burly men made a speedy exit from the bus, one carrying a beer cooler, another what they took to be picnic supplies, as if setting up a Mardi Gras or football game tailgate party. "Ah'm gone tole you, my frien, we're looking fo du action?" one of the men said with a distinct Cajun accent.

"Those guys said they had machine guns," Ellis says today. He thought it strange coming from a group whose ancestors had fled persecution in Acadia.

As Gray continued his peace-making efforts he could overhear men on CBs and radios calling for reinforcements. A man in a white sheriff's car was heard talking to someone in Tennessee. "Send reinforcements right away." Others talked on two-way radios to Alabama, Georgia, and down state. More trouble was on the way. Gray was picking up bits and pieces as he moved through the mob. The FCC monitor reported a bus carrying fifty armed men was on its way from the coast. A convoy of twenty cars, each one with four heavily armed men, was approaching the campus on Highway 6. The highway patrol was making no effort to stop them.

Gray noticed that fewer and fewer of the rioters could be identified as students of the university. More and more wore the marks and decorum of the hill country. He heard that the marshals were running out of tear gas. More was on the way from the airport less than a mile away but could the driver get through. He watched helplessly as some of the newspersons were roughed up or beaten by the mob, their various equipment destroyed. Ironically, most of the journalists were Southerners—just doing their job.

A bulldozer with the vertical scoop erect for a shield made its grinding way toward the broken line of marshals. It had been commandeered by the same young man who had tried his luck with the fire engine. When he was knocked off the machine by a direct hit from a canister, the dozer hit a tree, spun around and continued its merciless journey, narrowly missing some dodging marshals until one jumped on it, steered it away, and stopped the engine. Thereafter the dozer served as a bastion for the marshals.

By then Gray knew troops were on the way. But where were they and when would they arrive? He did not know the first soldiers to arrive would be the local National Guard unit, Troop E of the 108th Armored Cavalry Regiment, commanded by one of his parishioners, Captain Murry Falkner, nephew of the Nobel Prize winning novelist, William Faulkner. Had Gray known, he might have had mixed feelings. Falkner was an ardent segregationist and vocal critic of his rector's sermonizing on race. The priest, however, need not have worried. Military regimen prevailed. Murry Falkner was no longer Mr. Falkner, insurance executive of Oxford. He was now Captain Murry Falkner, ordered into service by the commander-in-chief himself, perhaps the only soldier in military history to so short-circuit the chain of command. President Kennedy, his brother Robert, and Burke Marshall, assistant attorney general for civil rights, were still in constant touch with Katzenbach and McShane.

The captain, with fifty-odd men, had brought rifles and bayonets but no ammunition. Gas masks though. When they roared across the bridge in trucks and jeeps and onto the campus, they were met with a hail of bricks, planks, bottles, and bullets. Seeing a barricade of concrete benches ahead, they lunged through, sending broken concrete flying and rioters scampering for safety. No vehicle was left undamaged. The lead jeep had six bullet holes in the windshield. Captain Falkner's arm was broken when he shielded his face from missiles directed at him. These were his people, but his orders were to protect life and property and with his limited resources that was what he intended to do. Trying to ignore the pain of his broken arm, he continued to command his troops until early morning when the campus was cleared of rioters, agreeing finally to let George Street drive him to a nearby hospital so the bone could be set.

After thirty-five years the debate as to who saved the night still goes on. Was it Captain Falkner and his tiny band of National Guardsmen or was it the 503rd MPs, an advance party that marched through Molotov cocktails with fixed bayonets, a hail of bricks, bottles, books, and boards and took their place beside the beleaguered marshals whose ranks by then had been reduced by one-third? Not long before he died, George Street, who missed not one minute of the action on that fateful night, assured me emphatically that the marshals, out of tear gas and with no more on the way when Captain Falkner arrived, would certainly have been overrun and suffered innumerable casualties without him as ally. Mr. Street further felt that had Captain Falkner not arrived when he did there would have been no way to stop the mob from storming Baxter Hall and lynching the defenseless James Meredith.

What had it all meant? Gray wondered as he made his weary way home, feeling that he had been at the base of Mount Vesuvius. Was he correct that it would not have happened had there been bold leadership given on the racial issue? From President Dwight Eisenhower to Governor Ross Barnett, the direction given had been paltry. Was it ignorance that thrust the young men and women into the fracas? Or is the human soul so shallow that it will throw itself beneath any juggernaut that promises glory and triumph? These were Christians all. Christians fighting Christians. What had happened? Where the hark of herald angel? *Peace on earth and mercy mild, God and sinners reconciled?* Did Gray believe this? Yes, he really did believe this. He was certain of it. God and sinners are reconciled.

If only they had known.

The registration of James Meredith at eight o'clock the morning after the riot was not the end of the crisis for the university, James Meredith, or Duncan Gray. It was more a beginning.

Chapter Two

BE OF
GOOD COURAGE

The following Sunday, the Reverend Duncan Gray was back in his pulpit. Despite the sizeable number of the congregation that had deserted the fold, the sanctuary was packed. The faithful were there as usual. In addition, there were journalists from around the globe, curious onlookers, White Citizens' Council spies, students, supporters and opponents from other denominations—many for no other reason than to see what the little giant would do for an encore. At the altar with the rector was Chaplain James Emerson. He was a Mississippian, ordained in the diocese in 1942 and was attached to the 503rd MP regiment, the first contingent of soldiers to enter the campus a week earlier. To have a member of the enemy assist in the service was about as bold and defiant as facing the mob the Sunday before. The troops had been asked not to attend services in town but Chaplain Emerson's assistant was present, dressed in full battle uniform.

Because the troops were not to come to church in town, Gray and some of the other local clergy had conducted services at the armory. At Christmas, with the troops still occupying the campus, he got permission from the army to have a special service for the military at St. Peter's Church, with Oxford-University Methodist Church choir furnishing the music. He would be a good neighbor to all.

If his detractors thought he would be frightened to silence or pious platitudes they were mistaken. Instead, the first Sunday after the riot, he stood in his pulpit, once again offering himself as a target for retaliation. Looking out over the silent sea of faces, all wondering what they would hear, he again lashed out at the governor, the legislators, most of the press, and not least of all those present who deemed themselves guiltless.

"The first thing we can do," he began, "is to face up to our own guilt in the situation. You and I didn't go out there and throw the bricks and bottles. You and I didn't go out there and fire the guns. Yet you and I along with every other Mississippian are responsible in one degree or another for what has happened."

He noted in his sermon that most freshmen at the university were ten years old when the Supreme Court had first said this day would come. "Theirs is the generation that has been exposed to textbook and library censorship, mandatory essay contests on white supremacy and a massive propaganda campaign against the federal courts," he reminded the worshippers, his voice soft as snowflakes, his message as troubling as the tornadoes of spring.

Ole Miss students took a major part in the rioting a week ago, he pointed out, but "who could really blame them when the governor of the state himself was in open rebellion against the law—a living symbol of lawlessness?"

What could be expected, he asked, "when supposedly responsible legislators were saying, 'We will never surrender.' . . . What could you expect when so much of the Mississippi press was voicing the same sentiment?" He added that all white Mississippians must share the blame for the impossible climate in which the violence erupted. There was the cruelty of silence and the cruelty of lies and apathy. While the fire-streaked campus should remain forever etched on their conscience, "True repentance means more than just remorse." Not just grieving but turning, knowing, living the truth of the Gospel. "We must now give our all to salvaging the situation; to bringing order out of chaos; peace out of strife."

Mississippians must, he summed up, "accept the fact that the color of a person's skin can no longer be a barrier to his admission to the University of Mississippi."

He added that he had hoped this might be accepted "because it is just and right." But he said, "If we are not able to do that, we can be realistic enough and patriotic enough to accept this as the law of the land."

In those days of hate and fear, those were strong words for so gentle a man. But fear continued to be something to which he was apparently immune. He would not retreat, no matter the attacks directed at him.

Visiting journalists took note of the American flag that flew outside the rectory, seeing it as a contradiction of his iconoclastic words. Then, moving around the town, they saw that most others were flying the Confederate stars and bars. Mrs. Gray, on the surface a winsome, demure Southern belle, but underneath an indomitable champion of justice equally as tough as the man she married, had suggested that they post the American flag as further extension of their position.

His sermon made headlines throughout America, bringing with them condemnation and approbation. The *Los Angeles Times* commented in a signed dispatch:

> It took more than a small amount of courage to talk that kind of Christianity in that neck of the woods. I don't know Rev. Duncan M. Gray, but, on the basis of his name and his act, I feel free to picture him as a resolute, stubborn Scotsman with an inability to remain still when he feels that somebody is tampering with justice. And I wish I did know him.

Denver's *Rocky Mountain News* reported:

> ... The Rev. Mr. Gray has a conscience. Because of it, he finds himself engaging massive forces in battle with weapons no more substantial than eloquence and the *Book of Common Prayer.*

It is doubtful if Dickson Preston, who filed his story with Scripps-Howard papers, knew just how substantial a weapon the *Book of Common Prayer* was in the life of Duncan Gray.

Other Oxford ministers had delivered similar messages to their congregations the Sunday after the riots, sharing some of the heat directed at Duncan Gray. Murphey Wilds of the First Presbyterian Church, Wayne Coleman of First Baptist, and Roy Grisham of the Oxford-University Methodist all joined in what they called "a day of repentance." But the denunciations against Gray were growing by the hour. He must be silenced. But how? That was the question. If one will not run, he cannot be chased. To flail an anvil is to confirm your weakness. To post unsigned threats is but to argue your own cowardice.

Hundreds of letters poured in, some friendly and others exceedingly hostile. Gray answered all of them with candor and courtesy. If they spoke in error, he graciously but explicitly stated the facts. An irate letter from Alabama said the writer had been there that night, that his car had been searched and thus his constitutional rights had been violated. Gray wrote him about a neighbor on his street watching a Thunderbird with an

Alabama license plate driving to and from a vacant house a few doors from the rectory. Gray's children often played in the old house. Later, in the basement garage of the vacant property, Gray found a cache of .38 caliber ammunition, the kind with which the two men had been killed on the campus. He heard no more from the Alabama carper.

WILLIAM BENJAMIN LOWRY, THE IMPULSIVE, SELF-VAUNTING teenage captain of the Greys, was in an animated conversation with William Raines, his third lieutenant. Lowry was telling Raines to move around the left flank and try to maneuver the bluecoats into a ravine. More precisely, though, Captain Lowry was trying to figure out what role he was supposed to play. He knew no more of battle strategy than the most unseasoned footman. It had been easy enough giving routine commands on the drill field. There, a foolish command amounted to no more than minor embarrassment. Now it could mean life or death; victory or ignominious defeat. Despite his hard-as-nails veneer, Lowry was facing his first battle test near panic.

"One of your men's been shot," a corporal from Company F called to Captain Lowry. The corporal, firing from behind a tree, said it casually, as one reporting the time of day.

At first Lowry did not answer. Just went on talking to Lieutenant Raines. Then, whirling to face the corporal, moving to him and grabbing his arm he yelled, "Who, who, who shot him? Did, did, did you shoot him?" Lowry had a stuttering problem when he was a child and now it was back. "Wha, wha, what did you shoot my man for? You'll pa, pa, pay for this you sorry ba, ba, bastard. I'm in charge here and I'll kuh, kuh, kill you right now."

"Settle down, Captain," the unruffled corporal said. "We're on the same side. But you'd better get a litter over there. I think your man is bad hurt."

The excited and angry young captain tried to control himself. He remembered that if he would hold his breath for a few moments the stammering would subside. While he did that he began loading and firing his musket. He fired at no particular target, simply aimed in the direction of the Federal troops moving toward them in droves.

The Greys were fighting valiantly but without direction, each man his own leader.

When the number of General McDowell's Federal troops became overwhelming, a Confederate retreat was ordered. Captain Lowry had calmed down and was gathering his troops like a mother hen, calling for a report from each squad leader as they moved along. He had not remembered to ask the Company F corporal which of his men had been shot. Not until the Confederates got reinforcements and reversed the retreat, putting the bluecoats to rout, did he feel that perhaps part of his responsibility was to find the wounded or dead soldier. Even then it was after the other companies of the Eleventh Mississippi arrived and the two Rebel companies that had fought together in the battle were showing them the battlefield.

Suddenly the reality of war hit him. He saw his fallen soldier. There, lying on his back, eyes wide open, his lower body caked in an enormous quantity of drying white and red pulp, organ tissue, mixed with blood that had flowed from his left side, was Private Andrew Jackson Johnson. The spleen, at various times considered the seat of mirth, caprice or melancholy, had been robbed of any purpose at all by a missile no bigger than the soldier's thumb.

The bewildered young captain had never before seen a dead person. Dealing with the dead was something they did not practice in their training. He did not know what the appropriate, the expected thing was. He didn't know what he was supposed to feel. Nor could he describe what he was feeling. A lot of things rushed through his mind: the fight he had on campus that got him expelled from school; disagreements with Chancellor Barnard and the faculty; riding through the Lyceum with a bullwhip intending to whip Dr. Barnard.

Johnson was not a university student when the company was formed but he was popular with the students; all except Lowry, who thought Johnson was prissy and vainglorious. Now, standing there, looking down at his dead body, Lowry knew that was not the real reason he disliked him; he knew he disliked him because Johnson was so popular. Lowry had overheard several of the students whispering that a taciturn outsider such as Johnson would have been their preference for captain over a loudmouthed stripling like Lowry. He had resented that and had kept Johnson from getting any of the noncommissioned positions, fearing that Johnson might be elected captain when the company was reorganized.

Hunkering beside the dead soldier, leaning forward and embracing him was a Negro man who appeared to be at least sixty years old. The soldiers recognized him as Malachi, Private Johnson's body servant. He had arrived less than a week before Company A left Harpers Ferry.

Malachi. Last of the prophets. Last of the Old Testament men. The climax, the seal, the end of things.

A dozen or so of the Greys stood with their captain and formed a circle around the dead man and his slave, each holding his musket at a mannerly position of attention. They glanced inquiringly at their boyish chief, looking for a signal. But the captain's eyes were fixed on the Negro, observing his response to death but not joining him in that response. In that moment, what had once been implacable wrath seemed to be giving way to an amalgam of regret and gentleness as, for the first time, Lowry beheld the inevitable fruit of warfare. Suffering and death. And perhaps at that moment he felt firmly at the head of his troops for the first time. For a minute the only sound they heard was their captain, mumbling what words he remembered of the Lord's Prayer, words he had not said since early childhood.

Then they heard sounds they did not recognize. They were a lamentation, a fracturing of the human spirit the soldiers could neither appropriate nor comprehend.

"Lawdy, lawdy, lawdy. Dey done kilt young massa. What fo to kill young massa. Young massa a good boy. Neber hurt nobody." His voice trailed off into indescribable wails, moans, whoops, sobs—calls of seeming despair. Or perhaps calls of ecstasy. The soldiers didn't ponder which. Whatever the sounds were they were from a world the young boys thought they knew and owned but neither owned nor knew.

The grieving servant shooed the flies that crawled in and out of the dead soldier's mouth. Blood from his nostrils had already dried, and the Negro tried to wipe it away with his thumb and forefinger. He moved to sit directly on the ground and pulled the heavy corpse onto his lap, cradling it in his arms like a baby. He gently patted the firm but motionless chest while at the same time vigorously kissing the cheeks and forehead. He rubbed the eyelids until they remained closed.

"Lawdy, lawdy, lawdy. Young massa. My sweet young massa. Big massa give me to you day you was bone. So he sed. Give you to me way I figured. I raised you that day on. Raised you good. Learnt you everthing I knowd. Lots a time jus me and you agin the lot of um."

The former servant sat as still as the rocks around them, gazing intently at the silent figure he held, as quiet now as the corpse itself, thinking what thoughts the soldiers could not imagine.

Suddenly and without warning the former servant bluntly, almost contemptuously, pushed the body from his lap, leapt to his feet and ran screaming into the gathering darkness. The sounds they heard now seemed to have a ring of celebration. Not the gloom of helplessness they heard before. The new sounds drowned all other sounds: the rattling wagons picking up the dead and wounded; the anguished cries of the Blues and Greys lying together, no longer enemies; military commands from the immediate area; a band with its doleful sounds in the distance. His own sounds drowned them all.

The soldiers listened until the sounds faded and died away. They thought it was in the direction of the North Star. They couldn't tell for sure.

A woman from the most powerful political family in the state (and whom the Grays had known well in the Delta) had met with a group of women in Jackson calling themselves Women for Constitutional Government, and a statement had been issued saying, among other things, "Before the marshals fired tear gas into the crowd of unarmed students at the university, not one act of violence had occurred. The students had not attacked the marshals or threatened violence against them." Gray's terse reply was, "This simply is not true and I'm sure that no one who was actually present that night would say that it was." He added, "If the women really want to know what happened on that awful night, they should press for a full-scale, free, and open investigation by a responsible group with all the witnesses *under oath*. However, I'm afraid that would be most embarrassing to our beloved state, and I'm sure this is why the legislature, Sen. Eastland's committee, and Sen. Stennis' committee all dropped their preliminary investigations so quickly."

When Elmore Douglas Greaves, an Episcopalian and then editor of a scurrilous segregationist paper called the *Gulf Coast Gazette*, published a gnarled chronicling of events during the riot entitled "Eyewitness Account," Duncan fired off his own account in which he came as close to calling the man a liar as I ever found him to do. Duncan had known Greaves since high school but the greeting was a blunt but formal, "Dear Sir." The lengthy letter corrected many points of the article and asked that the true account be printed which, of course, was not done.

A clandestine newspaper calling itself *Rebel Underground* was distributed widely on campus and sent by mail around the South. The masthead said simply, "Champion of Students Rights at Ole Miss," along with the epigram, "Disobedience to tyranny is obedience to God." It was a strange emendation of a supposititious epitaph found in the papers of Thomas Jefferson. Most of the copy was given to attacks on the "Party pinks, comsymps and libbies" alleged to be among the administration and faculty of the university. Referring to Meredith as "the Coon," students were encouraged to keep up the attacks and harassment on him. "We have an ample supply of pure blooded Brick and Bottle Greys and 'Blue-Ticks' on hand to keep him under control."

James Silver, professor of history, was a favorite target. "We understand that Jim 'Thirty Pieces' Silver likes to discuss the Fall of Rome over the telephone after 2 A.M. with any interested Rebs who care to call." The phone number was listed.

Gray never escaped full coverage. One issue stated:

> Speaking of blasphemers, how about this Cool Padre Gray in town? Said the Bible "was just a fairy tale." Can't you just see that wily viper rockin' in the Rectory, suckin' on those weeds, sippin' on that brew and perusin' that ol' Manifesto, while that Good Holy Writ gathers dust in the corner.

The evermore clement rector laughed it off, took it all in stride, and went on. A mutual friend, a New Yorker and zealous liberal, once asked me, "If Duncan Gray is serious about the race problem, why does he find it so funny?" I tried to explain that some things become so utterly preposterous laughter is the only appropriate response. Laughter is sometimes a form of protest of the absurd. Or a way of dealing with it. Like Sarah and Abraham, when she was ninety years old and he was a hundred, and a messenger said she would have a baby. According to the Scripture, Abraham laughed so hard he fell on the ground. And "Sarah laughed within herself, saying, After I am old shall I have pleasure, my lord, being old also?" As well they might have laughed. "O sure, fellow! We're going to make love and have a baby. Gimmie a break!" Then Sarah lied about it, said she didn't really laugh standing there in the tent listening to the menfolk. But she did have a baby: little Isaac. (The name means laughter.) Duncan Gray laughed a lot in those days. Sometimes there was nothing else to do. Black people learned that a long time ago. The contradictions and inconsistencies of "the Southern way of life" were often so absurd, if they hadn't laughed, they wouldn't have made it. Like the planter's diatribe about compliance with *Brown* v. *Board* leading to inevitable race-mixing when his black tenants knew the white planter had already sired five children by one of his croppers. Just . . . funny. Duncan Gray laughed a lot. And sometimes wept.

Invitations to speak flooded his office. Virtually all were declined with the response that his ministry was a local one. Even when the national forensic society, Tau Kappa Alpha, gave him their annual speaker-of-the-year award, he found his local duties too pressing to attend the banquet where the honor was presented.

Still he exulted in the Faith, never felt martyred, never felt alone. Not one letter in his files suggests that he ever felt at all sorry for himself. Most of his fellow Episcopal priests were for him and he knew it. The Reverend Alex Dickson, then Rector of St. Columb's Church, Jackson, preached a powerful sermon of affirmation. The Right Reverend John M. Allin, bishop coadjutor of the Mississippi Diocese also added his blessing in the diocesan newspaper. Despite the fact that the Natchez vestry was correct when it said Gray was costing the diocese money, he still had the support of his bishop, who was also his father. The Right Reverend Duncan Montgomery Gray Sr. had been elected bishop of the Diocese of Mississippi in 1943.

Friends of the past rallied. Gray heard from his former teachers at Sewanee. The Reverend Emile Joffrion, Gray's predecessor at St. Peter's, kept in close touch from his church in Huntsville, Alabama. People like Jim Silver, Russell Barrett, Evans Harrington, and Nolan Fortenberry of the University of Mississippi faculty remained solid supporters. The Reverend Duncan Hobart of Meridian, a friend and liberal ally, was never far away. Later, when the smoke of insurrection was clearing, friends and devoted parishioners would try to get Gray away from Oxford for short periods. Even then, it most often had to do with the work of the Church. For example, in the summer of 1963 his old seminary friends, Davis and Mary Carter, insisted that the entire family come to Washington, D.C., for two weeks. Carter was administrative assistant to Congressman Jack Brooks and a non-stipendiary priest at Washington Cathedral. Knowing that Gray would not leave his duties at St. Peter's for sheer rest and relaxation, Carter arranged to have the rector of little St. Peter's preach at the magnificent and prestigious church of the mighty—Washington Cathedral. Preaching from the prophet Amos, his message was the same as to his own congregation: a prophetic word of judgement upon a stiff-necked generation, capped with the good news of redemptive grace.

It was a needed but short-lived reprieve. Their visit ended at the same time Dr. Martin Luther King Jr. gave his historic "I Have a Dream" speech at a mammoth civil rights march on Washington. When the Grays returned home they found the local press had confused the Washington Cathedral with the Washington Monument. Gray had not even witnessed the civil rights march but the damage was done. The nocturnal threats which had previously plagued the Gray household following Meredith's admission began anew.

When the General Convention of the Episcopal Church was meeting in St. Louis the following year, Gray, because of his still pariah status in the diocese, was shunned as a delegate. Dr. Robert Holley, a prominent physician in Oxford and a loyal parishioner, gave Gray one hundred dollars and told him to go. Gray rode the train with the other conventioneers, stayed in the YMCA for four dollars a night, attended the sessions as a guest, and still managed to see the New York Yankees defeated by his beloved St. Louis Cardinals in the World Series. All for a hundred dollars. During one of the long debates on the convention floor, he was photographed by a joker friend in one of his rare off-guard moments in the posture of Little Boy Blue; fast asleep.

On a trip with his two boys, Duncan M. Gray III, and Lloyd Spivey Gray, to see the Cards a few years later, the Gray's fun was vandalized by Lloyd coming down with acute appendicitis. That remains a source of family banter in that the father and a St. Louis physician diagnosed the lad's bellyache as too many stadium hot dogs, popcorn, and soda. By the time they got back home Lloyd's appendix had ruptured: a close call.

Erosion along the shore of St. Peter's Church continued and the rector tried to keep pace with damage control. When a student, Phillip Patterson, hosted some students from Rust College, a Christian college for Negroes in nearby Holly Springs, Mississippi, at an address by Howard K. Smith, Patterson was ostracized, his room trashed, and campus life made unbearable. Duncan and Wofford Smith took him in, and Mrs. Gray (affectionately called *Ruthie*), fed him and looked after him until he could graduate. Today the student is Dr. Phillip Patterson of Tullahoma, Tennessee, a town close to Gray's alma mater, the University of the South at Sewanee. As a way of thanking the Grays for what they did, Dr. Patterson, an optometrist, never charges Sewanee School of Theology students, faculty, and their families for his services.

Although Gray would not agree that his stand at Oxford bolstered the courage of others, there is ample evidence that it did. Twenty-eight young ministers from the Mississippi Methodist Conference issued a statement in early 1963 in support of keeping the public schools open and asserting freedom of the pulpit. While most of them did not survive the fallout that resulted from their manifesto, and although they did not mention Duncan Gray by name, their stand served to divert some of the vehemence that was being concentrated on him. On the other side, old adversaries began to resurface. According to an article in the *Jackson Daily News*, entitled "Lawmaker Says Marshals Should Not Go Unpunished," Representative Charles C. Jacobs Jr. of Bolivar County attacked Gray along with Robert Farley, dean of the university law school, for their remarks during the crisis. Jacobs, chairman of the powerful house Ways and Means Committee, had been a member of Gray's first parish in Cleveland and had been a major critic. Mr. Jacobs, according to the newspaper, advised university Chancellor J. D. Williams to ignore Gray and Farley "as the voices of fuzzy-thinking Kennedyites who advocated integration and surrender many years ago."

The vestry of Trinity Church, Natchez, sent a three-page letter to Gray's father, then bishop of Mississippi, expressing their extreme displeasure with the words and actions of the younger Gray and Wofford Smith. The letter stated that the vestry feared the two men were creating a feeling of ill will toward the Episcopal Church. Further, they were in a position to influence the young people.

> When they are instilled by ministers of their own church with ideas repugnant to those of their parents, the result must, in many cases, be unpleasantness, that might result in discord and strained family relationships.

Most of the letter was given to a defense of what the white race had done for the Negroes and criticism of the federal government:

> The attempt by the federal government to impose this ridiculous concept upon people by force, as in the Meredith case, and to enforce so-called "civil rights" of the minority without any regard whatsoever to rights of the majority, has led to nothing but unhappiness, discord, and violence among those who are most concerned. When our own ministers advocate submission to this form of tyranny, we are shocked and dismayed. . . . We feel that if Mr. Gray from his pulpit referred to the Governor of our state as a 'living symbol of lawlessness', as was reported, his action in doing so is extremely reprehensible.

The letter conceded that Gray had a right to his opinions but that he should seek "a more congenial climate in which to express them." Again, after berating the bishop's son for three pages, Southern manners of the gentry were not neglected: "The members of the Vestry have asked me to convey to you our continued feelings of respect and affection." The elder Gray took no action.

Controversy continued to swirl in Oxford. Deputy U.S. Attorney Katzenbach, who remained on the scene for some time following the riot, was an Episcopalian and, because the two were seen together, Gray was roundly criticized for "fraternizing with the enemy." Two weeks after the riot, the Delta Kappa Epsilon fraternity still had breastworks of hay bales flanked by Confederate flags in front of their fraternity house, indicating that they had not yet surrendered. Somehow Katzenbach knew Gray was a DKE at Tulane. When Katzenbach expressed his feelings about the symbol of defiance, Gray talked to his young fraternity brothers and they promptly dismantled their little fortress, explaining that they really meant no harm.

Through it all Gray insisted that good would come out of this evil. Again, he was correct. Within days of the riot almost two hundred of the state's business and industrial leaders met in Jackson to devise a strategy of damage control. They were the power elite of the state. They wisely chose not to invite a single elected official to their meeting. Whether wisely or not, they also chose not to invite a single educator or clergy person. None was an integrationist, but a consensus that violence was not the way was quickly reached. Who would move a business into an area of civil unrest? Who would bring a manufacturing plant into a community where there were no public schools for the workers?

Meeting without fanfare in the Crown Room of the King Edward Hotel in Jackson, the gathering unanimously adopted a statement that was precisely what the lonely parson of Oxford had advocated: compliance with federal court orders. "No matter how unpalatable any breaching of Mississippi's segregation laws might be to them." It was to these citizens that Duncan Gray had directed his strongest indictment, for it was they who had stood silently by as the rhetoric of their governor and most elected officials had set the stage for mob action. Now the business community had had enough and was ready to take a stand. W. H. "Billy" Mounger, head of a major insurance company and television and radio station and one of the most influential men in the state, was first to offer a modest balm as he said,

> I am not in conflict with the governor's purpose of trying to protect the legal and sovereign rights of our state. But I think it should be done legally, not by violence. And the governor is the only one who can stop the violence. We must obey federal laws.

It was a strange sector for such words to come from. Although Mounger would prove to be an honorable man, and his leadership of moderation would prove costly, the television channel owned by Lamar Life Insurance Company of which he was president had been the mouthpiece of the White Citizens' Council. The station lobby was a bookroom of Citizens' Council literature. The station manager was a zealous council leader. A senior newscaster had a regular program that he used to refute any network news segment or program with a racially progressive slant. Sometimes there would be "cable trouble" (blank screen with captions of excuse) if a program offensive to white sensitivities was being shown from the network. Interviews and speeches of General Edwin Walker in which he invited the citizens to join him in Oxford were given prime time and coverage. Their commanding signal transmitted the general's words across the state with the urgency of a tornado watch, urging his listeners to prepare for battle. "Ten thousand strong. . . . Bring your flags, your tents, and your skillets. It is time. Now or never." And they obeyed his command. With anger, weapons, and fire. Now Mounger was doing what he could to extinguish the conflagration started in part by the rantings from his studios. (The television station would later lose its license for its imbalance, the license awarded to a black-owned and operated corporation. And Mounger would lose ground in the world of insurance and broadcasting and move into the investment business.)

The *Wall Street Journal* carried the names of those attending the King Edward meeting and identified them as "moderates," a perilous label in 1962 Mississippi. They had come from every town in the state, large and small; Hernando in the north to Brookhaven and McComb in the south; Vicksburg and Port Gibson of the west to Columbus and Meridian in the east. Alphabetically, the listing ranged from Louis Alford of McComb to D. R. Yandell of Jackson.

Each man in the Crown Room that day committed himself to work publicly for law and order, and together they called upon "all mayors and public officials in every city, town and community to advocate forthrightly and immediately the maintenance of law and order." There was agreement that the incendiary statements made by Governor Barnett made the violence inevitable. At the time, the governor was a man of enormous popularity and power. He was criticized publicly at one's own peril.

The men at the gathering were obviously worried, afraid that since violence had been loosed by the state's highest official it would spread. One spokesman said, "When they are frustrated by the troops at Ole

Miss, some extremists are apt to turn elsewhere in the state. Some crackpot is apt to try to bomb a Negro school."

Speaking out was a bold thing for the group to do. But, just as Gray had predicted, they had waited too late. There was indeed a wave of bombings, murders, church burnings, and widespread lawlessness that swept the state for a decade. The men had learned what they should have known from the beginning. The brackish waters of hate they had poured into the bayous and back eddies with rhetoric designed to maintain the status quo could not be contained. It had seeped into every stream and spilled over into the mighty rivers of the body politic, polluting the commercial as well as the spirit. Bigotry, they were learning, is a pox with a costly antidote; more contagious than compassion. Nonetheless, the significance of the meeting was indisputable. It did mean an end to defiance by the state's highest officials. Federal jurists at the district level became more compliant with higher court directives. But if defiance through violence was not the way, well, what was left? Those in the Crown Room were aware that remedies through the courts had been exhausted. Legislation at the state level had proven fruitless. The major tactic of the White Citizens' Council, economic sanctions to coerce Negro citizens to accept the status quo, was less and less effective. Even the Gestapo-like work of the State Sovereignty Commission was failing. They knew that nothing was left except some degree of compliance. They were also aware that gradualism had been frowned upon from the beginning, and the signers of the statement were now advocating gradualism. "How can one be a little bit pregnant?" had been the rejoinder to any such suggestion. The argument was that a little desegregation would result in a lot of integration. In *that* the resisters were correct. That is precisely what happened and that was why the dark night of rioting in Oxford and this meeting were the harbinger of dawn.

Unfortunately, by the time the state business leaders gathered at the King Edward Hotel, that portion of the citizenry that had heard and heeded the inflammatory oratory since *Brown* v. *Board* could not now be turned off by a mild manifesto of the affluent—the plebeians had never trusted them in the first place. The citizenry was seen by the gentry as plowboys, woolhats, and rednecks to be used for political and economic purposes but not to be brought into the signing of the truce. And because they were not represented that day, there would be no truce. Not really. They had been primed for violence and it would take more than words of calm from the Crown Room patricians to stop them. To those who gathered, there was nothing left to do but comply. Not so with the man with the hoe. He knew what was left. More violence. But, he too would finally be stopped. He would be stopped when his whirlwinds of rebellion shook the commercial shores and became a greater threat to the economic well-being of the state than desegregated public schools. In the while, what Gray had warned would be reality. Sweeping violence.

Back at St. Peter's Church Gray took comfort in the report of the Jackson meeting. In his sermon the following Sunday, he mentioned it as a sign of hope. Still he knew they had missed something. He knew they were afraid; knew well it took courage to do what they had done. Yet they had not heeded his real message. A week earlier these same men had been silent as their governor threatened to arrest and put in jail any federal officials who tried to enforce desegregation decrees. Now, face to face with the fruit of the poison seeds they had allowed to be planted and, yes, helped to plant with their silence and support of the status quo, they were fearsome of the harvest.

Other seeds had been sown as well, by sowers the King Edward confluence had real economic reason to fear. On the same day the governor was spewing jingoistic madness about jailing federal agents, the Congress of Racial Equality was meeting in New York. From the meeting, the organization threatened boycotts against manufacturers locating any new plants in Mississippi and said they would challenge in court the state's right to federal tax exemptions on its bonds. Ah, that's the rub. The heat lightning the business community had ignored as being too far away, signifying nothing concerning them, struck now the very infrastructure of their empires. Since the 1930s when Mississippi began its program to balance agriculture with industry under Governor Hugh White, Mississippi had attracted major industries to the state with industrial development bonds. Suppose Ingalls Shipbuilding wanted to build a $100 million plant in Pascagoula. Instead of borrowing in the name of Ingalls, they borrow in the name of Pascagoula. If Ingall fails, tax the citizens. Not a bad risk. So with a cheap and eager labor force, mild winters, a citizenry generally hostile to organized labor and tax-exempt financing by industrial development bonds, the state had moved a long way from the cotton economy of the past. Even the mere possibility that the federal tax exemptions on those bonds might be cut off was not to be taken lightly.

So Duncan Gray knew the fear was not of Divine wrath to come. The fear had to do with filthy lucre: the thing his Bible told him was the root of all evil. The morality of *Brown* v. *Board* had been addressed not at all. With Gray, Christian theology and ethics were the dominant arguments for compliance and those were *not* on the agenda of the Crown Room conference. In the Crown Room, compliance was not just and right according to Christian principles. It was simply necessary for continued economic growth. Even so, the priest of St. Peter's was not despairing. He could even laugh at their unawareness of the real key to the problem, remembering that the Lord works in mysterious ways. Duncan Gray's laughter, however, was never sardonic. His laughter was always a reflection of ultimate hope. Grace still abounded. He would go on preaching. This was not the *eschaton*.

Despite the omission of righteousness in the response to the mob's sabotage of reason, Gray felt that in a real sense the riot at the University of Mississippi on the night of September 30, 1962, was the turning point of massive resistance to *Brown* v. *Board*. He was right. There would be more violence, many more altercations, and more deaths, just as there had been after the high-water mark of the Confederacy at Gettysburg. But from the night of the riot on, every rational person knew the outcome of America's greatest social crisis since the Civil War. Massive resistance against the inevitable was dead. The high-water mark had been reached at Oxford. And the King Edward assemblage was like Lee's retreat into Virginia from Gettysburg. Lee's war would go on too, despite the known outcome. So would Barnett's war go on in Mississippi, with years of guerrilla warfare that by then was on automatic pilot.

In addition, the Crown Room colloquy was analogous to the meetings that took place between Union and Confederate emissaries following the defining Gettysburg battle. Even Albert Gallatin Brown, Jefferson Davis's fellow senator from Mississippi and a fire-eating secessionist, began to press for an end to hostilities, knowing how the war would end. In praise of a Cuban expatriate named Narciso Lopez, who led an earlier version of our Bay of Pigs, Brown had said, "I want Cuba, and I know that sooner or later we must have it." (Gray would certainly have taken him on for that.) Then, in an extravagant rendering of that ill-considered American notion called *Manifest Destiny*, Brown added, "I want Tamaulipas, Potosi, and one or two other Mexican states; and I want them all for the same reason—for the planting and spreading of slavery." Despite that posture, following Gettysburg he led a sizable Mississippi movement for stopping the violence. Such feelings were not uncommon, leading up to the famous Hampton Roads peace conference where President Lincoln himself came down to hear the Rebels' terms for peace. But, like Barnett a century later, Jefferson Davis would not risk a loss of face by bowing to the inescapable. And, like the Crown Room conference, it was too late. Too many words had been spoken in indurated haste.

That is why the juxtaposition of Duncan Montgomery Gray Jr. and the University Greys at Gettysburg is a valid consideration. The University

Greys fought passionately for more than two years. They vowed never to call retreat. *Never!* was the watchword for the University Greys and *Never!* was the motto for the bulk of white Mississippians a hundred years later. But never is a long time. It ended for the University Greys on the third day of Gettysburg when they fought their most costly and final battle and came closer to Union lines than at any time during the war. If Pickett and Pettigrew had succeeded in that charge, historians tell us the final outcome might have been different. Though there were a lot more lives sacrificed after July 3, 1863 (more than had been lost prior to that encounter), the carnage *should* have ended there because from that day forward every knowledgeable person knew what the outcome would be.

Never ended, Gray believed, for the diehards of the South in that small area between the Confederate monument and the Lyceum Building on the campus of the University of Mississippi when Captain Falkner and his little company of troops roared over the bridge that separated the campus from the rest of the globe. Gray knew that before Falkner arrived, the new confederates were on the verge of defeating the federals, by then a besieged minority. That was as close as the resisting South ever came to turning back the tide that *Brown* v. *Board* had set loose. The irony was that it was Gray, a native Mississippi priest, unquestionably of the gentry class socially, and his colleague, Wofford Smith, who did more than any other civilians present to harness the mob's intent until armed help arrived. The greater irony was that a Mississippi citizen-soldier, Murry Falkner, himself a segregationist at odds with his parish priest, whose great-great grandfather fought the Federals at First Manassas and whose uncle, novelist William Faulkner, was a voice of prophecy on the racial scene, is credited with staying the mob's mischief.

AFTER EARLY REVERSALS AT MANASSAS, THE GREYS' FIRST encounter, there was a solid victory. The battle would come to be called *First Manassas*. Or *Bull Run*. Even in victory, however, the University Greys learned that war was not the frolicsome outing they imagined when the train left the station that rainy Mississippi morning, leaving their kinfolk and sweethearts standing in the smoke along the tracks, assuring them they would be back in two months. Two months were now behind them, and the war was just beginning. The two companies of the Eleventh that engaged in the fighting at Manassas, the

University Greys and Noxubee Rifles, would move on without seven of their comrades. Another twenty-one were wounded.

One of those who had been injured by a bluecoat, Private T. E. Tucker of Marshall County, was later killed by an officer of the Eleventh after the battle was over. The soldier was lying on the ground awaiting medical attention when the officer's pistol fell from its holster as he was mounting his horse. It discharged, killing the already wounded soldier.

In addition, their brigade leader, General Barnard Bee, was dead. Their regimental commander, Colonel William Moore, who had remained behind when the train could not carry the entire regiment, had shot himself in the foot, presumably an accident, and was furloughed home where he would be discharged.

The Greys' baptism of fire was a calamitous one. Their troubles did not end with the last shot. A steady downpour of summer rain began as the battle ended. For two days the men huddled with no tents and no food. Many of them were already weak from the awful and ever-present affliction of camp life—diarrhea—and an outbreak of measles weeks before at Harpers Ferry. Their fortune would not improve as the war dragged on. Through it all they were never accused of being slackers or cowardly.

The remaining eight companies of the Eleventh were envious because they had been left out of the fighting. Never again would they be sorry to be left out of a battle.

There was something else weighing heavily on Gray's mind and heart as the leaves of October fell on the university circle, casing the spilled blood of marshals, citizen soldiers, and civilians, as if concealing it would mean that it never happened. He was troubled by what appeared to be certain military action involving the island of Cuba. He had spent a summer there while he was in seminary and had deep feeling for the Cuban people. The revolution against Batista had come (as Gray knew it would) before he left Santiago ten years earlier. Now, with Fidel Castro in command and with Russian missiles pointed at American cities in the fall of 1962, there was cause to worry. Gray knew the line in the sand had been drawn and that President Kennedy would not back away. Gray was a loyal American, yet he feared for his people he had left in Santiago and

Oriente Province. Torn between working assiduously to mend the tattered coat of Christ in his own parish and his deep uneasiness about the safety of his people in Cuba, Gray found October to be a long month. When October 28 came and the Cuban crisis was resolved without the hurling of atomic missiles from both shores, he felt he had much for which to give thanks. It was the Saints' Day of Simon and Jude. Simon, first to confess Jesus as the Christ; Jude, who preached divine judgment against those who departed from truth. The epistle assigned in the *Book of Common Prayer* that day declared that "we are no longer strangers and foreigners, but fellow-citizens with the saints, and of the household of God." The Gospel reading began with a quotation from Jesus: "These things I command you, that ye love one another. If the world hate you, ye know that it hated me before it hated you" (John 15:17–18).

It had been five years since Gray left the Delta and moved to Oxford. The years of ministry had been both routine and fervid. The White Citizens' Council was always at his heels, watching, spreading discord within the flock. Even so, the church had moved to full parish status, meaning that it was self-supporting, not dependent on the diocese as a mission station. A second priest, Reverend Wofford Smith, had been brought on board as chaplain to Episcopal students at the university. He was formerly a teacher of speech at the university, and was Gray's close collaborator during the campus riot.

Gray's interest in a ministry with and to Negro citizens had not lain dormant. Until then there had been virtually no communication between Negro and white clergy. Partly because it was the proper thing to do and partly because everyone knew the day would come when the University of Mississippi would have to desegregate, long before the riot, Gray began convening as many clergy as possible across racial lines.

He had been active in the summer training school at Okolona College, the two-year college for Negroes associated with the diocese. It was little more than an hour away from Oxford. Under the deanship of Mrs. James Raspberry, mother of the now noted columnist William Raspberry, Duncan served on Okolona's summer faculty as teacher, chaplain, or daily lecturer. This gave him contact with most Negro Episcopalians in the state as well as an opportunity to get to know virtually all Negro priests in the nation. Although the White Citizens' Council took note of his presence on the Negro campus, no one ever physically tried to stop him from being there. "Those were fun times," Gray remembers. "I looked forward to it. It was serious work all day but at night we partied." It was a time when most white moderates in Mississippi were remaining conspicuously silent. Duncan Gray knew them all, sought them out. And although he never thought of himself as being lonely in Oxford, he must have been. He really needed the camaraderie, the interracial comfort and openness of Okolona.

Prior to the riot he had become an actor and consultant for a major movie. *Home from the Hill*, starring Robert Mitchum, Eleanor Parker, and George Hamilton was being filmed in Oxford. Vincente Minnelli was directing the film and wanted to use St. Peter's Church for a baptismal scene. He told the rector that he wanted it to be as authentic to the period as possible. Gray looked at the script and told Minnelli that if he wanted authenticity he must first get another *Book of Common Prayer*. The time period called for the 1890 revision, not the 1928 edition. Apparently the director was sufficiently impressed to ask Gray to play the part of the priest. "And that's how I became a movie star," Gray laughs. "My role was to baptize an illegitimate baby." He remembers the director had selected two infants, in case one screamed during the filming. But he doesn't recall whose babies they were. "I remember they both stayed in the parish hall all day." He recalls he had a stand-in so his vestments wouldn't wilt under the hot lights.

"Did they pay you well?" I teased.

"Oh, sure. Of course. I got a hundred dollars for one day's work." (That was more than he got for a week's work as a priest.) "And St. Peter's got rafters cleaned of dust and cobwebs left over from the Civil War." He also got a lot of joking from his friends about his Hollywood image and new career. Duncan joined in the fun. The movie can still be seen on late-night reruns and on video cassette.

The father was not the only family member to get in show business. Arthur Krentz of the University of Mississippi music department, with Zoe Lund Schiller as librettist, composed an opera called *The University Greys*. It had first been performed in 1954 and was shown on Memphis television ten days prior to that year's historic Supreme Court decision declaring segregated public schools illegal. In 1962, in celebration of the centennial of the departure of the Greys from the campus on May 1, 1862, the opera was again produced in the university theater. Anne Gray, ten-year-old daughter of Duncan and Ruth Gray, was in the cast of the opera. This production was just five months before there would again be troops on campus. Not departing. Occupying. At least in the minds of most white citizens. Not Confederates, although most of the local members of the National Guard would have been sympathetic to the Confederate cause. The occupying troops were federals. Unlike the Greys, these troops would be victorious. The campus and town would be cleared of rioters and James Howard Meredith would remain to graduate. Although father and daughter had only cameo roles in the movie and opera, and that would be the sum total of their acting careers, it was needed diversion for the family at a time when fun was in short supply.

Opposition to Gray within the parish had begun long before the admission of James Meredith and the national publicity Gray's efforts to still the storm generated. The court cases surrounding Meredith's application had gone on for nearly two years and Gray had been consistent in his criticism of the political games played to thwart Meredith's acceptance. Gray did not court the media, never held press conferences, and did not see his behavior as of epic dimensions. But the interest of the media in an Episcopal clergyman standing in the face of death for his convictions was inevitable. His activities and sermons were reported assiduously by newspapers, magazines, television, and radio. Opposition within the parish and beyond grew with the coverage and was unrelenting. In religious circles there is rejoicing when the sun of growth and harmony is pouring its splendor through stained glass windows. Discord begins when the preacher's views and pronouncements are in violation of the things held sacred by the congregation and larger community. The stand of Duncan Gray on the sacrosanct subject of racial segregation was not in keeping with the notion that those who pay the piper are entitled to call the tune.

Church members have several major weapons when they are vexed by the preacher. One is to simply get rid of him. In Anglican circles, where politeness is a self-conscious virtue, this is cumbersome. A more acceptable practice is to empty both the offering plates and the pews. Gray had a loyal and tenacious cadre of support at St. Peter's. There was a sizeable group, however, whose grasp of the Gospel was quickly preempted by their glandular understanding of what it means to be a Southerner. Empty pews had been conspicuous for months prior to the riot. Following the night of rioting and the subsequent military presence of thousands of federal troops, Gray became the easy target of all who felt betrayed and defeated. Urged by the fervor of bigotry and sustained by overwhelming political unanimity, the undulant opposition he had experienced following each development of the "Meredith case" became a ground swell. At the university, Ole Miss football was in its heyday. Virtually the entire athletic department staff were Episcopalians, parishioners of St. Peter's. Winning football coaches get big salaries and bowl-game bonuses. Most were heavy contributors. The withholding of their pledges was substantial. Their absence was noted by those who continued to attend. While the athletic department was not unanimous in its defection, the number was significant. Nor were they alone. Approximately one-third of the congregation stopped attending, canceled their pledges, or both.

Duncan Gray did not waver in his pastoral duties to anyone, no matter their views toward him. One well-known communicant who had publicly criticized his rector was at death's door in a Memphis hospital. The rector had spent many midnight to early-morning hours with the man who had a serious problem with alcohol. The man's adult son, who along with his father no longer attended services, stood at the door of his father's hospital room and physically barred the parish rector from entering. The saddened priest prayed in the hallway for his apostate parishioner:

> Hear us, Almighty and most merciful God and Saviour; extend thy accustomed goodness to this thy servant who is grieved with sickness. Visit him, O Lord, with thy loving mercy, and so restore him to his former health, that he may give thanks unto thee in thy holy Church; through Jesus Christ our Lord. Amen.

And added this absolution:

> The Almighty and merciful Lord grant thee pardon and remission of all thy sins, and the grace and comfort of the Holy Spirit. Amen.

The dying parishioner had earlier written that he would not ask forgiveness for any personal responsibility for the riot. After Gray and other Oxford ministers had called for a service of repentance, the parishioner, writing in the *Saturday Evening Post* had said:

> Now our preachers have gotten in on the show. We have been called to our churches for penitence meetings. We are to ask forgiveness for our parts in bringing on the riots. I shan't go. If all the sin I have to answer for is my part in bringing on what happened here that Sunday and Monday, then I relinquish my place to someone more needful of forgiveness than I.

When the man died his family, though lifelong Episcopalians, forbade that the requiem be conducted by Gray or in St. Peter's Church. Because the deceased had earlier placed instructions for his burial in the care of St.

Peter's rector, someone had to come to the church and get the rector to open the safe. The service was conducted by a Presbyterian preacher on the university faculty.

Oscar Carr, a distinguished Episcopal layman from the Delta, knew of Gray's parish afflictions. Oscar Carr was old family, Naval Academy graduate, former Cotton Carnival King, and big Delta planter. He was also involved in diocesan stewardship. He called Gray and asked if there might be something he could do. They had been friends since high school days. Gray was not a devious priest. Neither was he stupid. Time was approaching for the annual stewardship dinner, when pledges for the church year were made, and he knew that it might mean St. Peter's would have to revert to mission status. Even then, a petition to dismiss the rector was being circulated by a prominent layman. The picture was a bleak one. Gray accepted his friend's offer and asked him to speak to the stewardship banquet.

Carr was not stupid either. But unlike his priest friend, he could be devious when he felt it was indicated by the work of the church. He informed the rector that he would share the speaking with his friend and colleague Farley Salmon.

Salmon was remembered in Oxford as the best and most colorful quarterback Ole Miss had ever fielded. Carr did not mention the defection from the flock of the university coaches. Nor did Gray. But both men knew the athletic department would not boycott their legendary quarterback. They might not renew their pledges but they would be there. "So there we were," Gray says today. "With a Cotton Carnival King and a football king. The hall was packed."

Neither speaker mentioned race, the riot and Duncan's role in it, or difficulties in the parish ranks. They talked only of stewardship. The proposed budget was $26,000 and it was subscribed in that one evening. Gray laughs when he recalls that the pledge of one man, Dr. Robert Holley, the local physician and loyal friend of the church and its rector, was five thousand dollars, almost one-fifth of the total.

"Who the two men were made all the difference," Gray says. "They saved the life of St. Peter's as a parish."

Many of those who left St. Peter's Church because of Gray's actions and preachments were well-known. He refuses even to list them by name. But he will talk at length about those who stayed, some who were not in sympathy with his personal position but who understood that the sacraments of the church did not depend upon the priest for their efficacy. Men and women like Robert and Jean Holley remained because they agreed with their rector as well as because of their commitment to the church. Junie Hovious, popular Ole Miss backfield coach, bucked his colleagues and stayed on. His wife, Kitty, never wavered. Murry "Chooky" Falkner, the man who led his National Guard troops and contained the mob until regular army soldiers arrived, did not leave the church, though at the time he was critical of the priest. Loren and Patricia Young stayed the course. And, of course, there was the family of Professor Willis, the man who would not deny his priest at the Confederate monument when such fealty was not cheap.

Some of the parish dissidents began meeting in a nearby restaurant as a congregation of the Anglican Orthodox Church, a schismatic group founded by a North Carolina Episcopal priest that espoused racial segregation and other extremist political causes. They never had a resident priest and eventually faded away. The roots of St. Peter's were too deeply embedded in Lafayette County soil to sprout alien shoots.

The best known parishioner of St. Peter's Church during Gray's tenure was William Faulkner. His attendance was sporadic but his presence was a diversion from the perpetual strife. Such pastoral chores as performing the wedding of Faulkner's niece, Dean, daughter of William's brother who was killed in a plane crash and for whom the writer served as surrogate father, meant they were together often. William Faulkner was no more popular in Oxford and Mississippi at the time than was Duncan Gray. There was an understood, though unspoken, bond between the two men.

A woman who was cook and maid for Faulkner also worked for the Grays one day each week. It was during the time Faulkner was writing *A Fable*. He regularly wrote the gist of the story on a wall in his home and the maid kept the Grays informed on the progress of the novel.

On July 6, 1962, three months before the tragic night that brought twenty thousand soldiers to Oxford, William Faulkner died. The service was held in the parlor of Rowan Oak, the Faulkner residence. Only the family and a few friends were there—Bennett Cerf, Shelby Foote, Joseph Blotner, and William Styron among them. Wearing a white surplice and holding nothing except his *Book of Common Prayer*, Duncan Gray stood before that company and solemnly intoned the same words he used for those the world knew not at all. "The Lord is my light and my salvation, whom then shall I fear? The Lord is the strength of my life; of whom then shall I be afraid?" As he read, the sprightly song of a mockingbird, its medley of sounds a seeming summation of creation, mixing and melding with the stifled sobs and droning of overhead fans stirring the summer air, seemed a fitting and parallel requiem. All things the now silent laureate might have been appropriating for the morrow's tale. When the brief rite was over, Gray followed the slow-moving hearse down the long lane of ancient cedars, leading the cortege through the town of stories and into St. Peter's Cemetery. At the grave his words were the familiar ones, whether beside the mausoleum of kings or in potter's field: ". . . earth to earth, ashes to ashes, dust to dust."

Ironically, thirty-three years earlier Duncan Gray's grandfather, the Reverend Dr. Edward McCrady, had declined to perform the wedding ceremony for Faulkner at St. Peter's Church because his bride, Estelle Franklin, was divorced, and church canons forbade a priest to officiate at the wedding of a divorced person. Faulkner was a struggling young writer of thirty-two for whom success had been an elusive and unpromising thing. Now McCrady's priest-grandson, the Reverend Duncan Montgomery Gray Jr., was laying to rest an illustrious Nobel laureate. Faulkner's death brought almost as many media people to Oxford as the riots would bring three months later, serving as a sort of rehearsal for what was to come.

At St. Peter's Church there hangs a collection of fine art as testimony to the kindness and good manners of Gray. The bequest of the art pieces came through a strange set of circumstances. Miss Theora Hamblett, daughter of a Confederate veteran, was a country schoolteacher whose avocation was painting. Like most artists who move on to recognized greatness, she was not taken seriously by many in the local community. Although her work was in the primitive mode she had studied sporadically under others, developing her own inimitable style. Many of her paintings were on biblical and religious themes. Miss Hamblett was a Baptist. One day she called Mr. Gray and asked if he would come to her house to talk about something that was troubling her. He, of course, went. Miss Hamblett showed the visiting priest a number of her paintings, all on biblical themes. She asked if he thought her paintings were idolatrous. "Am I guilty of producing idols?" the worried and pious artist asked.

The priest consoled her, encouraged her to continue her work, and wisely counseled that questions of idolatry might have been raised about all religious art of the ages by those who did not understand that art was an expression of the painter's religious commitment. He found no fault with this idiom of proclaiming the Gospel.

Miss Hamblett was visibly relieved. When Gray inquired as to why she was troubled, she said that someone, or some group, within her church had accused her of painting idols, of violating the Second

Commandment. She was a devout person and was deeply troubled by the accusation. After talking to Gray, Miss Hamblett gave two pieces to St. Peter's Church. Later she came to see Gray and said she had painted a series on the miraculous escape of St. Peter from prison as related in the Book of Acts. It was her wish to donate them, six in all, to St. Peter's Church, Oxford. The rector and congregation graciously accepted.

Today Theora Hamblett is recognized as one of the great artists of her time and the paintings belonging to St. Peter's Church are worth a great deal of money.

Gray remembers his years at Oxford, Mississippi, as never boring. There had been a brief interlude as a screen actor; his dealing all the years with attacks from the White Citizens' Council and the KKK, leading up to a night of severe civil disruption; the failed effort to establish an apostate congregation; ministering to and burying one of America's best known writers; and his beloved Ruthie giving birth to their fourth child. All parts of the Oxford years of Duncan M. Gray Jr. All awash with the things of his calling. It had been what seemed a short eight years.

And then a search committee came calling. St. Paul's Church, Meridian, wanted to call him as their rector. His reputation among many in the diocese was that of a troubler whose very presence preempted harmony, that most desired property of the established church. Those who bothered to see him through unbiased eyes knew him as a joyous, kind, and gentle shepherd whose flaw and excellence were synonymous: integrity. He was astonished that they had come. But, yes. If they wanted him he would go. It was time to move on to fuller fields of service. But what field, he must have wondered, could be fuller than Oxford, Mississippi, in the mid-part of the twentieth century?

Gray was no stranger to St. Paul's Church. He had many friends there, among them Judge Billy Neville, then senior warden of the parish. Three years earlier they had issued a call for him to become their rector. At the time, storm clouds were gathering over the anticipated admission of James Meredith. The violent upheaval lay in the future. No one knew that the riots that came in the fall of 1962 would be as calamitous as that wretched night proved, but the Grays knew there would be trouble. "We didn't know what was going to happen," Gray says, "but we knew something was going to happen."

The 1962 offer to move to the historic and prestigious St. Paul's Church and escape the impending crisis must have been tempting to a young couple expecting their fourth child. The salary was better and so was the ambiance. Today Mrs. Gray says,

Duncan and I were never believers that God directs us to the best parking place; things like that. But after taking serious counsel together on that occasion we had no doubt that the Lord wanted us to remain in Oxford.

She laughs heartily and quickly adds, "But three years later we were just as sure God was ready for us to go."

So the Grays moved on. The eight years they had been there, longer than they had lived anywhere since their marriage in Canton in 1948, had been some of the most tumultuous years Oxford, Mississippi, had known since the University Greys went away and the Civil War came to the campus and to the nave of St. Peter's Church a hundred years earlier. The Grays, especially Duncan, had faced and survived the most insolent indignities: slurs, insults, humiliations, hurts from within and without the congregation. A priest in a denomination noted for its civility and deference to its clergy had been shunned, maligned, cursed, and treated to bodily harm at the base of a monument purporting to honor honorable men of other days. Now he was departing without rancor. Waving no banner of self-righteousness; wearing no placard of self-pity. Dwelling instead on the good times, the faithfulness of the faithful, and the love of their four issue who would recall when they were adults that they never realized their family was any different from others. Even so, the Reverend Duncan Montgomery Gray Jr. and his wife, Ruth Miller Spivey Gray, were ready to move on to another field of service.

Another priest in the Meridian area received a telephone call from an over-zealous Northern bishop, berating St. Paul's Church for getting rid of their recently departed priest, saying that it was a blatant, blasphemous racist deed.

"Do you know the man they have called to replace him?" the priest replied.

"No, I don't know. But I can imagine what he's like."

"They've called Duncan Gray Jr."

"Excuse the ring," the embarrassed prelate replied. "I owe you an apology."

Chapter Three

HOLD FAST THAT
WHICH IS GOOD

Duncan Gray had not entered the battle of Oxford unprepared. His three years at the University of the South at Sewanee, Tennessee, had been basic training. His first parish, Cleveland-Rosedale in the Mississippi Delta, had further seasoned him. When he entered the University of the South School of Theology in 1950, he was an engineer with a BSEE degree from Tulane University. While there he had been in the navy and was commissioned an ensign upon graduation, about the time World War II ended. Now he was a postulant, preparing to be a priest in the Episcopal Church.

He would learn much from books and good teachers at Sewanee. He would also be well tutored for what lay in store for him. The three years spent there would be a training ground for a priest whose ministry would be spent in a time of serious social unrest. In the struggle, he would be deemed by many a hero; tribute he never acknowledged nor took seriously. By others he would be considered a knave. The seminary students were, for the most part, from families of the median league. At least financially. The young men in the college, on the other hand, were more apt to wear family-crested blue blazers under their academic gowns and have triple or quadrupled names followed by III, IV, and sometimes V, setting them apart as well-connected; of Southern carriage trade. Duncan Gray was a junior and his son was Duncan III, but the Gray family, though from a line well-thought-of and honorable, did not see itself as inordinately privileged. Duncan's sole purpose was to be a faithful priest. For that he took no personal credit. Those along the way, on the Mountain and later, who saw him as a traitor and a scoundrel, he took no more seriously than the accolades; laughed it off, rendered no one evil for evil.

In July of 1950, Gray, his wife Ruth Miller Spivey Gray, and son Duncan Montgomery Gray III, left Shreveport and the Westinghouse Corporation behind them forever. Gray had been with Westinghouse since graduating from Tulane in February 1948. The Grays had also lived in New Orleans and Pittsburgh. They traveled to Mississippi to visit their parents in Canton and Jackson. From there they would continue to Sewanee, Tennessee. In the vernacular, it was called *St. Luke's* but the official name was the School of Theology of the University of the South.

Duncan Gray recalls no second thoughts about the decision to become an Episcopal priest. (He had grown up the son of a priest and by then his father was a bishop.) He does remember some rumblings of conscience regarding the hardships he knew lay ahead for his family. He was consoled by the thought that it had not been a unilateral decision. His wife, Ruth, was not a subsidiary character in the drama that was unfolding. Nor, in the years to come would she stand uninvolved on the sideline. Though she had left the University of Mississippi shortly before graduation to join her husband in Pittsburgh, in what was to begin as a career in electrical engineering for Duncan, she was well-grounded in the liberal arts. Her father, a Canton attorney, had insisted upon an excellent education. Gracious, exceedingly bright, quick-witted and competitively beautiful, Ruth Spivey Gray was prepared and ready to take her place on the team. Still, despite his wife's support and participation, when they left Madison County, Mississippi, in a borrowed car, before the days of air-conditioning in automobiles, made their way through the muggy, red clay hills of Alabama with fast-growing kudzu gnawing the edges of the narrow, two lane highway, a certain uneasiness gripped the young husband and father. Sewanee, Tennessee, was holy ground for Mississippi Episcopalians, but to ask his family to spend three years of sacrifice was more than a bit daunting for the young husband and father who was leaving a secure profession.

Heavy clouds, the final exertion of a seasonal hurricane that had passed menacingly but hurriedly over the Gulf Coast, had tracked them since about four o'clock when they started the climb up the incline leading to the university. As the car made the curves and turns through the campus, the clouds let loose an abrupt deluge. Duncan had hoped the first sight their one-year-old son would see of their new home would be the facade of All Saints' Chapel, and the first sounds he heard would be the melodic Westminster chimes of Breslin Tower proclaiming to his firstborn son that he was on holy ground. Duncan would point to St. Luke's Hall, where the School of Theology was housed, and tell his son that was where his daddy would unlearn being an engineer and learn to be a priest. Instead, a violent thunderstorm was commanding the entire landscape, threatening everything in its wake. Claps of thunder drowned the slapping cadence of the windshield wipers and the sputtering of the car's engine as it resisted the swashing pools on every street. Lightning had struck one of the giant oak trees shading historic Rebels Rest, a large log house built one year after the Civil War ended (so named because it was built on land originally granted in 1860 to the bishop, later general, Leonidas Polk), scattering huge boughs in all directions. Roofing shingles from nearby buildings danced in the wind and trashed the ground, a portent perhaps, of things not yet imagined. Instead of cooing with awe at his first sight and sound of Oxfordian splendor, Gray's son, already feverish from a slight head cold, was sobbing with fright.

As they made their way past the football field, out of the village of Sewanee and onto the graveled Alto road leading to the housing for married students, the rain stopped as suddenly as it had begun. The last of an overcast sun cast an eerie glow on the wet leaves of maple, sweetgum, and tupelo trees as Gray eased to a stop in the shadow of a row of World War II buildings. The black tarpaper covering all sides of the rectangular barracks, native coal piled in high rows along the front, and deep muddy ruts in the yard made for a bleak and ablative welcome to academe. For a fleeting moment the young engineer-turned-postulant considered the dividends of Pittsburgh and Shreveport. Life for a while, he knew, would not be easy.

The new home was an apartment in a World War II army barracks, bought by the university for a dollar each from government surplus and moved to Sewanee from Camp Forrest, an army base near Tullahoma. Each barracks was divided into three apartments. For heat, each one contained a cast iron coal stove in the living room. The kitchen had a wood burning cook stove. A small ice box, the kind an iceman would supply with a twenty-five pound block of ice twice weekly for fifteen cents, stood on the scant front porch. There was a small, unheated bathroom with a shower, commode, and lavatory. There was no tub and the only hot water was from a hot plate fastened to the bottom of a small water tank that sometimes caused steam to rise from the commode in the mornings. Baby baths would be in a galvanized washtub, filled by hand and emptied outside. The walls and ceilings were made of beaverboard, thin, compressed wood pulp that easily let in all but the softest whisper from the neighboring apartments. Floors had cracks ample for mountain vermin.

The Diocese of Mississippi had sent a moving van with the belongings of the Grays and two other postulants, Peyton Splane and Michael Engle. The movers had not arrived. That night the Gray's bed would be a blanket on the living room floor. Food was what remained of a picnic basket Ruth's mother had packed for the trip. Ruthie thinks it was deviled ham in a can and saltines.

Their livelihood for the next three years would be the subsistence allowance from the veteran's Bill of Rights, plus a small supplement from the diocese. Ruth's parents offered to send a regular subsidy but the young couple gratefully declined. They did, however, gladly accept presents of snowsuits for young Duncan—he slept in them—boots, and heavy clothes instead of frills and toys at Christmastime. Tuition, books, and supplies would also be paid for by the G.I. Bill.

When the first morning came, Ruthie suggested there should be some kind of a ceremonial, a celebratory break with the past. Something that would establish forever that Gray was no longer a Westinghouse engineer but was on his way to becoming a priest in the church of his people. At their breakfast of fruit and coffee, Gray offered a prayer of thanks for what had been. Then asked for guidance and grace for the new life before them. As if he wasn't aware already of what the ceremonial was that Ruthie had in mind, Gray announced that his swan song to the world of Westinghouse and engineering would be to wire their apartment for two-twenty voltage so they would have electric heat when the cold winds blew upon the Mountain. Without comment, Ruth leaned over and kissed the already balding head of her lifemate.

With the electrical wiring done, further scrubbing of the walls and floors, furniture arranged, and other household chores accomplished, Gray was ready to turn to the rigors of Ecclesiology, Soteriology, Greek grammar, Tertullian, Cyprian, and Liturgics. Theological education. No one complained. No one took thought for the morrow.

As seriously as he took the curriculum, none of it would prepare him for the discord that would claim his energies before his time on the Mountain ended. In 1950, the mightiest tempest ever to hit Eagle Mountain at Sewanee (what many called the *Holy Mountain* or simply *The Mountain*) was on its way.

Ruth quickly involved herself in the responsibilities of homemaker, making children's clothes by hand, washing and ironing for the family, cooking and cleaning. In Shreveport there had been a maid who came in once each week to help her. Not on the Mountain. There was little time for involvement in the cultural activities of the university community. Dealing with frozen diapers, asthmatic bronchitis attacks, and household chores claimed her days and evenings. It was, Ruth recalls, "survival time." However, in this veritable veteran's village, called *Woodland*, or *The Woodlands*, but later nicknamed "Fertile Acres" because it was said there was a baby born each week, a spirit of cooperation and community did exist to ward off any feeling that they were drifting in a sea of squalor and aloneness. The Woodlands was actually a distinct neighborhood, not resembling the university campus proper.

The first year was routine but never boring. Gray was an exceptionally bright student, steeped in the Anglican tradition and did not have to study as hard as some. Still he found the courses exciting. The second year was more demanding. In addition to a more intense course schedule, Sundays took him to his field work assignment, a small church in, ironically, South Pittsburg, Tennessee, twenty miles down the Mountain. He remembers the assignment as also a place and time of learning; in some ways more profitable than the classroom. His duties were to preach occasionally, assist with Sunday School, conduct Morning or Evening Prayer and parish business, and perform tasks not specifically reserved for an ordained priest. The field work bonus was that his supervisor was Dr. Robert McNair, who taught Ethics and Moral Theology, Gray's major interests. As priest-in-charge at the little church, McNair generally rode with his student to the field work assignment. A bond developed between the two far surpassing a faculty-student relationship. A favorite visitation for the pair was the home of Judge J. T. Raulston, whose wife was an active Episcopalian. It was he who had presided over the celebrated Scopes trial in Dayton, Tennessee, in 1925. The old judge, in declining health, regaled his visitors by replaying the courtroom antics of Clarence Darrow and William Jennings Bryan, one an atheist, the other a biblical fundamentalist. The stories were funny. They were also enlightening. Seventy years after the famous Monkey Trial, evolution was then, and still is, a volatile subject in Gray's Mississippi.

Gray was not reared as a fanatical racist, but it was a subject not discussed much when he was growing up in Mississippi and attending college in New Orleans. As a young man, he was aware that the status quo was not right and would not long endure but it was not yet a cause with him. He was a dutiful son of a conservative tradition that exacted of him few new ideas.

A few unrelated incidents sent him on the road to a greater awareness of racial injustice. In Shreveport, Gray's once-each-week maid had come to work one day highly disturbed. Her teenage son had been put in jail for allegedly making an unacceptable remark to a white woman. She feared for his safety and Gray went to the jail to assess the situation. Finding that the lad was being held and would be charged, he decided to discuss it with his boss at Westinghouse, knowing him as a kind and considerate man. Instead of a sympathetic hearing, the man snapped, "They ought to kill him. Right now!"

Duncan was shaken by the response. "For the first time," he says today, "I knew that race relations in the South were on a perilous course. Much worse than I had ever imagined."

Ruth had had an earlier experience that had set her on the same course as well. When her first child was born, in Canton, Mississippi, there was a minor respiratory problem. The doctor saw it of no consequence but said he would place the child in an incubator as a precaution. The doctor was a family friend to whom Ruth was deeply beholden. When she was born, her mother's milk was very limited and little Ruth was allergic to all available formulas. This same doctor went to great length to develop a special formula that saved her life. Now that Ruth was grown, he also took heroic measures with the birth of her own child.

Ruthie had only the highest appreciation and respect for both hospital and physician. Notwithstanding that, something happened that would open her eyes to what she had lived with all her life without challenge. She learned that a newborn Negro child was in a life-threatening condition in the same little hospital. Overhearing the nurses discussing the child, she asked if he was in an incubator. The nurse told her there was not one available. Ruthie asked that her son, then out of danger, be taken from the unit so that the other child's life might be saved. She was never told whether her request was honored. She recalls that the incident turned a light on; that she was deeply aware of the preferential treatment she had received in the past without questioning.

With those experiences and similar observations, the Grays arrived at the seminary with their hearts and minds seasoned for the consciousness raising that was to come. Dr. McNair was a major influence in that process. As he and his young charge made the weekly drives to South Pittsburg, racial injustice was a regular topic. "Also," Gray laughs, "the good professor liked football. I really liked the man." McNair was but ten years older than Gray and the two became pals and colleagues in their quest. That relationship would deepen when the gathering clouds turned ugly in the not too distant future.

A routine of study, work, and family rearing was established and the first eighteen months saw no serious difficulties. They looked forward to

Gray completing the bachelor of divinity degree, ordination, and assignment to a parish in the Diocese of Mississippi.

In February of 1952, Anne Miller Gray joined the family. Gray's son, Duncan III, missing the initial introduction to Sewanee his father had intended—All Saints' Chapel and the chimes of Breslin Tower—enjoyed instead watching the band from Sewanee Military Academy leading the procession of cadets in full dress uniform every Sunday morning as they marched into All Saints' Chapel. "Onward Christian Soldiers," they played. Every Sunday without exception. It was a family ritual. An added incentive never to miss was that Ruth's brother, Lloyd Spivey (Uncle Sonny), was banging the drums as they marched by where the Grays stood. During the three years Gray was a student at the University of the South School of Theology, Spivey attended Sewanee Military Academy just a few hundred yards away. Adding to the family presence of life on the Mountain was the McCrady name. Dr. Edward McCrady was at the time doing research with the Atomic Energy Commission in Oak Ridge, Tennessee, but from 1937 until 1948 he had been professor of biology at Sewanee. He would soon return as acting vice-chancellor and then be elected vice-chancellor and president by the board of trustees. McCrady was Gray's uncle, the brother of his mother, Isabel Denham McCrady Gray. McCrady, "Ned" as he was called, was born in Canton, Mississippi, where his father was rector of Grace Church. Gray Jr. was also born there when *his* father was rector of Grace Church. Canton, Mississippi, was an incestuous presence at Sewanee. It had also played a major role in the life of Gray Jr. and the Episcopal Church in Mississippi.

At the end of Gray's middle seminary year, he had an experience that would further strengthen his commitment to social change. The overseas department of the national Church sent seminarians to various overseas mission stations. Gray had a chance to go to Santiago de Cuba. With two small children—Anne was four months old—he hesitated. Both he and Ruth knew it would be a growth experience in addition to the good he might do there, but Gray pondered the fairness of leaving Ruth to care for the children alone.

It was she who made the final decision. She felt it was an opportunity that would not come their way again. She could handle the children on her own. "I'll make it a vacation," she assured him. "I need some time out of the barracks. We'll go to Canton and Jackson and the grandparents can enjoy the children." Ruth felt as comfortable with Gray's parents as she did with her own. They sublet the university apartment and Gray left for Santiago in early June. Accustomed to the material comfort of most

Episcopalians in America, he was stunned by the poverty of the Oriente Province of Cuba. Although at Sewanee Gray and his family were living at a survival level in a tarpaper barracks with few comforts, he realized that compared to what he was seeing in Santiago they were rich. One of the stations he served was a chapel on a sugar plantation, much like the antebellum plantation chapels found in Mississippi. At the plantation he observed Cuba's sharp economic variance; ostentatious wealth alongside the most abject poverty. Whites were the rulers, managers and owners; blacks, the workers. He recalled that his native Madison County, Mississippi, was once a land of wealthy planters hoisted to their station by slave labor. He wondered how long the arrangement would last and when the seething cauldron of infection would erupt.

His most important role in Cuba was simply to live with the people, eat what they ate, learn their language. By the end of summer Gray was able to preach in Spanish, a skill he has retained, though he says he needs a refresher course occasionally. The seminarians had been supplied with various medications to combat food poisoning. While the other student missioners tried to avoid suspect food, Gray ate whatever he was offered, no matter how distasteful or unsanitary. All the others got sick. Gray never did. That led his jesting father-in-law to say that it said a lot about Ruthie's cooking.

Fulgencio Batista y Zaldivar (Batista), who had been a dictatorial power in Cuba since 1933, making and breaking presidents, always had the support of the United States. He had returned to power with his coup against the elected president Carlos Prio Socarras three months before the seminarians arrived. Already, populist buds of revolution were beginning to flower. In this city of a quarter of a million people, Gray found some pro-Batista sentiment among a few clergy, especially those who served churches of the gentry class, but those who served in the slum areas opposed him. One priest Gray got to know well, Father Alonzo Gonzales, was a gun-runner for the growing movement of discontent. As something of a folk hero to the military because he was widely known as one of the finest marksmen in all of Cuba, Gonzales had easy access to the island garrison. On frequent visits inside the base, he loaded his Jeep with rifles and ammunition, covered them with a tarpaulin and made his way into the Sierra Maestra mountains. On occasion, Gonzales would show Gray his cache of weapons or take him far out in the jungle where he demonstrated his expertise with them, snapping faraway twigs blowing in the wind, or shooting fish in a swiftly flowing stream.

Gonzales was later killed by the same forces he had helped put in power. After he learned of Fidel Castro's close ties with the Soviet Union,

Gonzales became an ardent counter-revolutionary and was arrested and executed. Gray rejected the tactics of violent political revolution, feeling that his religious faith, when taken seriously, offered a better way. He learned much, however, of revolutionary zeal and tactics. It was also being confirmed in his mind that one league of humanity holds another down at its own peril. He would not forget it. It was a lesson about home, learned in a strange land. He had grown up hearing the petitions of patricians. Here he was participating in the supplications of the hurt whose cries were an important factor in his decision to become a priest. Gray would never be a political revolutionary like his Cuban colleague. But the discernment would serve him well, as well as bring him personal grief. It wasn't being taught back at the University of the South, although a social revolution was about to erupt there in which Gray Jr. would be a major warrior.

While in Cuba he learned that the faculty of the Sewanee School of Theology had protested the position of the board of trustees and board of regents discouraging the admission of Negroes to the seminary. Duncan was not surprised by the position of the trustees. Confederate influence abounded at Sewanee. Robert E. Lee had declined the vice-chancellorship but the ghosts of such Confederates as Ellison Capers, William Porcher DuBose, Josiah Gorgas, and Leonidas Polk watched doggedly from the shadows. It was inevitable that the trustees would resist this kind of change on their watch. On the other hand, with James Hervey Otey, first chancellor and bold opponent of secession never far away, it was certain there would be those to say them nay.

Nor was Duncan surprised at the bold stand of the faculty. One thing he had admired about the Sewanee theological faculty was their diligence in trying to raise the consciousness of their students on the evils of racism and segregation. It was a difficult and delicate matter to consider. Difficult because most of the students, born of gentility and good manners, equated racism with bigotry. And they were not bigots. The faculty, especially Professor McNair, knew that racism and prejudice are not the same. Racism is a condition: the structures, the institutions in which we move and breathe and have our being that give whites, especially white males, ascendancy. Because the Anglican Church in America was historically the church of the more affluent, McNair reasoned that it was potentially more truly racist than the sin shouters of the sects. Racist, and racialist as well.

He discussed the difference between racism and bigotry, and the difference between racism and racialism. He explained that just as the elite of England and the Continent held the Stoic classist notion that the power to rule inhered naturally in the best man, that is, the upper class, there evolved in their descendants in the new country the notion that one race was best prepared to rule. In America's new aristocracy the further Stoic notion that those who ruled were expected to behave decently and honorably toward those they ruled led to the fallacy that "we are the best friend the black (inferior) race has." This kind of classism-become-racialism made McNair's task all the more significant. He heard, and disputed the usual argument:

> We are decent and honorable. We do justly toward those of an inferior rank. We are therefore and thereby behaving in a Christian fashion. We do not lynch, rape and pillage. The "Rednecks" do that. And we are not Rednecks. Therefore, we are not racists.

Gray was aware that the faculty had been criticized in some quarters for placing too much emphasis on race. But with McNair and the others, it was a theological issue. Not to emphasize the doctrine of oneness in Christ was to neglect a major tenet of the faith. And thus heretical. They were not hired, they reasoned, to teach mythology. Nor to perpetuate a social stratification in the name of the faith. Gray applauded their teachings.

When Gray read in the church press of the controversy at the seminary, he assumed it would all have blown over by the time he returned at the end of the summer. He reasoned that the trustees, especially the bishops, once at their private prayers, and facing the possibility of losing the strongest theological faculty the University of the South had ever attracted, would reconsider, and reverse their ill-considered action. It would be the last time Gray would underestimate the depth of classism, racism, and racialism in his beloved Anglican household. All three influences would burgeon in the months ahead. And sexism, lying dormant in expression at the time, as well.

The board of trustees consisted of the bishop, or bishops, a priest, and two laymen from each of the then twenty-two dioceses owning the University of the South. Although Gray did not know all of them, he assumed they were all high-minded men. After all, his own father, Bishop Duncan Montgomery Gray Sr., was among them.

The seeds of discord, intended as seeds of compromise, had been planted in the fall of 1950 at a meeting of the executive council of the Diocese of Florida. That gathering passed a resolution requesting the delegates to the Provincial Synod, a body consisting of all bishops of the fourth province plus six priests and six laymen from each diocese, to study the desirability of re-establishing a theological school in the province to train Negro clergy. The Bishop Payne Divinity School in Petersburg, Virginia, that had formerly trained Negro priests had been closed in 1949 because there were so few students; the assets turned over to the Episcopal Seminary of Virginia. The doctrine of separate-but-equal had been usurped by separate-but-none, a tactical error that would later work to the detriment of those pressing for continued segregation. It could not be said that "They have their own school."

By steps, the resolution made its way to the fall 1951 synod meeting in Birmingham, Alabama. There the department of Christian social relations, chaired by Bishop Moody of the Diocese of Lexington, reported that in its thinking it would not be advisable to establish a segregated seminary. And then the other shoe fell. "But it (the department of Christian social relations) thinks it desirable and advisable that we should open existing seminaries in the South to students of all races."

With routine institutional caution the matter was sent back to the panel for further consideration. Next day the department of Christian social relations of the fourth province was still of the same mind. By a vote of 66 to 25 the report was adopted, with instruction to the secretary to inform the University of the South.

Although it is hard to believe today that such a tame action would create the slightest ripple or even make the local news, in 1951 it chiseled new craters in the slopes of the Mountain. The sky was falling.

The generally judicious regents and trustees maintained their composure but they were not unmindful of the impending crisis. Answer must be given to the synodical action. A decision in the famed Supreme Court case, *Brown* v. *Board of Education*, was still two years in the future. But warning shots had already been fired across the bow of legal segregation. In 1950 the U.S. Supreme Court had ruled that G. W. McLaurin, a Negro, must be admitted to the graduate school of the University of Oklahoma. In the same year it had ordered Heman Sweatt admitted to the University of Texas Law School. As early as 1938 the court had decreed that the University of Missouri School of Law could not deny admission to Lloyd Gaines simply because he was not white. Few thoughtful people questioned the final outcome of *Brown* v. *Board*.

On June 6, 1952, the board of trustees met and elected Dr. Edward McCrady as the eleventh vice-chancellor and president of the University of the South. Uncle Ned, blood of Duncan Gray. Then, in executive session, the board turned to the major item on the agenda: race. The air was filled with a medley of exhortation and gainsaying. Grace and Law. Charity and tinkling cymbals. Words of Jesus, sayings of the Prophets and vaunting chauvinism.

A resolution was adopted by the trustees saying that Negroes could not be admitted to any institution of learning chartered by the State of Tennessee because of the laws of the state. When a trustee began naming colleges and universities that were wholly or predominantly Negro but chartered by the state the resolution was reconsidered and defeated. The men of Grace were encouraged. But Law was not finished.

A year earlier the trustees present at commencement had met with the seminary faculty and discussed the matter of admitting Negroes to the School of Theology. The faculty and many of the bishops agreed that it should be done. But that was unofficial sentiment. Now the die was cast. Both sides were playing for keeps. But forever is a long time.

The deliberations then took on more a flavor of tactics—evasion and delay—than compliance. There was little discussion of what to some of the trustees was the basic question: the nature of the church; Sewanee as *communitas* and *universitas;* ethics; morality; and whether Grace or Law was chief among them. The resolution that was finally adopted addressed none of that.

First, the trustees stated that ". . . there is nothing in the ordinances of the University to prevent the admission of Negroes, or men of any other race." Had the trustees stopped with those words it would have settled the matter. At least for the while. Until a black man applied. (Application of a woman would have been a separate matter.) Instead, they added that ". . . the Trustees are of the opinion that the encouragement of the enrollment of such students now is inadvisable. . . ."

The two reasons given had to do with Law and Culture. No biblical nor theological "whereas" was offered.

1. We are informed by several legal authorities that such action would be in violation of statutes of the State of Tennessee.
2. The School of Theology at Sewanee, unlike most of our theological schools, is not a separate and self-controlled institution, but is part of the university both in administration and in social life; and therefore must consider the whole life of the university community which is located in an isolated domain.

And then the usual: "Therefore . . . furtherance of the Church's work and the happiness and good will of both races will not now be served by the action requested by the Synod."

And then the rage. The faculty of the School of Theology huddled immediately. Incensed and disappointed, they approached the next day's meeting with the bishops with resolution and abandon. The trustees' statement was completely and unconditionally unacceptable. Seeing the resolution as one of expediency, with no consideration for Christian principles and Christian ethics, and untenable in the light of teachings of the Anglican communion, they stated their case. Vociferous and resolute they whittled away at every point. Words were spoken. Names were called. Allegations, often unsubstantiated, were made. Anger prevailed. It was an extraordinary encounter. Teachers were on the campus at the sufferance of those they were now contesting. Hired servants contending with the boss man. Utterances and conduct unbecoming in a company of gentlemen.

The news story missioner Gray read in Santiago had the passion filtered out. While at first he saw it as of no grave consequence, still he was troubled by the action of the trustees. The invitation of Holy Communion was especially poignant to him that morning:

> Ye who do truly and earnestly repent of your sins, and are in love
> and charity with your neighbors, and intend to lead a new life. . . .

Yes. Love and charity with neighbors. A new life. For his church. His country. He thought of his father. It came to him that bishops and trustees were sinners too. It was the twelfth Sunday after Trinity. The Collect: ". . . Pour down upon us the abundance of thy mercy; forgiving us those things whereof our conscience is afraid. . . ." My God!, Gray thought, our very conscience is afraid. Of what? Apparently of Oneness in Christ. He felt a disappointment. He remembered the bishops and other trustees who had voted against admitting their brothers to altar and edification on what was called the *Holy Mountain*. He pondered its holiness. He remembered the people to whom he had been sent to Cuba to minister. Some were light-skinned. All right. Perhaps God would call one of them to serve at His altars and Duncan could take him home with him. What of the West Indian acolyte? He is dark. Black. Very black. Suppose he was called of God to the priesthood as Gray had been? What must he tell him? Not to Sewanee? God does not want you at Sewanee? Not yet? The trustees have spoken? Those were troubling questions. *These* are my people. *They* are my people. *Who are my people?*

Duncan Gray, about to return to his third and final year leading to ordination, was learning to pray in a fashion he had never prayed before. And feeling something of the profundity of liturgy he had lived with since the day he was born.

On his return to the Mountain, he learned that there had been no repentance by the board of trustees. His friend and mentor Robert

McNair briefed him, detailed the frustration and anger of the seminary faculty, and read him the statement of protest against the trustees' action they had sent to Bishop Richard Bland Mitchell of Arkansas, chancellor of the university, who had presided. They had requested a reconsideration by the board, pointing out that the position undermined their effectiveness as teachers of the Christian faith and way of life, and compromised them as priests.

The last paragraph of the faculty's statement pained Gray deeply but enhanced his respect for these men as they demonstrated their willingness to make a personal sacrifice for a principle in which they believed. It was an ultimatum:

> If our request is ignored or if the assurance sought is refused, we are without exception prepared to resign our positions and terminate our connection with the University in June 1953.

It was signed by F. Craighill Brown as dean, followed by Robert M. Grant; R. Lansing Hicks; Robert M. McNair; J. Allen Reddick; Claude E. Guthrie; Frederick Q. Shafer; and Richard H. Wilmer Jr. Howard Johnson, professor of theology and a Kierkegaard scholar and one of Gray's favorite lecturers, was on leave in Tokyo. Johnson added his name when he learned the facts. Wilmer's name on the list was especially ironic for many. His great-grandfather, a Virginian by birth, had been elected bishop of Alabama in the Protestant Episcopal Church in the Confederate States of America during the war and had been one of the last to hold out against reunification when the war was over. He insisted that Southern clergy and the Confederacy were a small remnant anointed to maintain the supremacy of the Word of God and the teachings of universal tradition. Now one of his own issue saw himself as part of a remnant to repudiate the Confederacy.

Gray was grateful that, through consideration for the students they had nourished for two years, the faculty would see them through to graduation. But the thought that the seminary he had come to love was being destroyed by something he saw as terribly wrong was overwhelming. Many observers of the theological landscape thought that the faculty at Sewanee was the strongest in the nation at the time; the best teachers, the finest scholars. Their subsequent careers have borne that out. Gray and the other students considered themselves exceedingly fortunate to be under their tutelage. The thought that students coming after him would be denied that privilege was appalling. The Episcopal

Church in the South, he felt, would suffer irreparable harm in the near future when the region would cry out for dedicated and well-equipped leadership.

Gray was incredulous. "All of you? The entire faculty? You really mean this, don't you?"

"All but one," McNair replied. "Jones refuses to join us. And yes, we really do mean it. We must go if this thing isn't resolved." Dr. Bayard Jones was in California when the upskuttle developed but he soon made it clear in caustic rhetoric that he was not in sympathy with his colleagues. His father and grandfather had been Baptist ministers and he had become an Episcopalian when he was twenty-four. He taught liturgics.

"We really didn't expect Jones to be with us," McNair went on. "Too bad. It should be unanimous."

Slowly it began to dawn on Gray what the year would be like. He had been elected president of St. Luke's Society, a title that meant he was president of the theological student body. His uncle was vice-chancellor and president of the university and a seeming defender of the status quo, and Gray would be pitted against him. As president of the student body he would represent the students, most all in strong sympathy with the faculty, to the vice-chancellor, trustees, the press, and the national Church. As the son of a bishop and trustee some would see him as opposing his own father.

The conversation with McNair continued. "They'll eat you alive," the professor said, not teasing. "You're caught in a trap."

"I guess so," the soft-spoken candidate for holy orders sighed. "I'll do what I have to do."

They talked through the afternoon and into the night. Gray wanted every detail: the sequence of events, who said or did what and when. He must learn the dynamics of the situation. Exactly what had happened. No controversy, he knew, was all darkness or all light.

Some of his assessment would have to wait until morning. Back in the apartment he found both children awake and crying, with Ruth frantically fighting an infestation of fleas. The tenants who had sublet their apartment had a dog and a cat. They would soon learn the dog had slept in little Duncan's youth bed, the cat in Anne's crib. When Ruthie put the children to bed they had started crying almost immediately. It was unusual. When she couldn't get them quiet, she undressed them and found measle-like welts all over their little bodies. Then she saw their clothes and bedding were crawling with fleas. She had both children in the galvanized wash tub when Duncan came in. She had put half a box of baking soda in the water. Trying to tell her husband what had happened above the crying, she stumbled over the tub and almost fell. "Run next door and get something," she said, going back to the bathing.

Gray started for the door, turned back smiling. "Get what? You didn't tell me what to get."

"I don't know. Just something. The neighbors must have had fleas while we were gone. Oil. Butter. Liniment. Whatever's good for fleas. Just something." She was having to yell above the screams.

"Good for fleas or bad for fleas?" Gray asked, trying to be funny.

"Good for flea bites, Duncan," Ruthie snapped, adding, "Oh, for heaven's sake, Duncan. This isn't funny. Hurry." Instead of going next door he dashed in the bathroom and came back with Johnson and Johnson baby oil, Johnson and Johnson baby talcum, and a bottle of Dr. Tichenor's antiseptic.

"Thou anointest my head with oil," Gray said, still trying to calm his wife with his characteristic banter. He took little Duncan and started massaging his body.

"And my cup runneth over," Ruthie added, sighing deeply, laughing lightly for the first time and sponging Anne with a soft cloth.

"They were covered with them," she told her husband as they worked. "Hundreds."

When the children were finally calm, they made a careful search of their bedroom and didn't find fleas. They made a pallet beside their bed and Duncan sang, patted, and cooed the children to sleep.

"It's going to be a long year," he said as they shared a glass of wine. He would wait until morning to report the other scourge. Ruth didn't answer.

"At least we can get Otto the Orkin man to handle this one," Duncan mumbled as they settled down in the living room.

"What?" Ruthie asked. "What did you say?"

"Aw, nothing," he said, snapping on a reading lamp and reaching for a book.

They were both too keyed up to think of sleeping. Instead of reading, Gray told more stories about his summer in Cuba. Ruthie talked of the cute things the children had done that he had missed.

"We have a serious problem," Ruthie said. He could tell by her tone of voice that she didn't really mean serious problem.

"No kidding," Duncan answered, but thinking, "We surely do."

"We do. I thought about it a lot while I was in Mississippi. You know, your folks and most of your friends, when they refer to you, it's always, Little Dunc. Or Little Duncan."

"Always have," Gray said. "What's the problem?"

"Now I know he won't be confused when every kid in the parish calls you Father because you won't let them call you Father Gray." Gray, like his sire before him, disapproved of the title "Father" for Anglican priests, preferring Mister or simply Duncan. "What I mean is, well, what are we going to call our little man-child? You'll be Little Dunc as long as you live. How many Little Duncs can there be out there?" She peeked in the bedroom to make sure the children were asleep. "So what do you say?"

"I say that's too important a decision to make tonight."

She changed the subject. "Say, Duncan. Do you think the Orkin man will get rid of the scorpions too?" Since they had come to Woodland, they were pestered by those horrid little beasties with their segmented bodies and menacing, venomous tails; they found their way through the cracks in the floors when the weather turned cool. To protect the children Ruthie kept them in the play pen a lot.

As they sat there, talking of Cuba and babies and spiders and scorpions and mice and now fleas, Ruthie began reciting, then singing the commercial jingle: "I'm Otto the Orkin man. I'm Otto the Orkin man," then couldn't remember the rest of the words.

Gray finished for her, in harmonizing alto: "When termites are swarming, be sure to take warning, call Otto the Orkin man." They sang it over and over. Like little children.

"But we don't have termites," Ruthie said. "We have fleas. And scorpions."

"We never will have termites," Gray said. "Termites don't eat tarpaper." "Lucky us," Ruthie said playfully. "We're something else, Duncan Gray. You know that?"

"You beat all I ever saw," Gray teased, a Mississippi idiom he had not used for a long time. Then he repeated it in Spanish, not sure of his syntax. "*Tu eres el mejor que yo vi.*" They got the giggles. A Mississippi candidate for holy orders and an Ole Miss Tri Delt. Both already far more than that. Two people. Much in love. Much exhausted.

When his wife retired for the night, Gray turned off the lights and sat alone in the darkness, listening to the sounds outside. The wind, the chirping of crickets, and croaking of bull frogs in the distance, calling for rain, reminded him of the Delta of his youth. Maybe a storm, he thought. Yes, for sure a storm is brewing on the Mountain. He thought about all the things Bob McNair had told him. He remembered his young friend, the West Indian acolyte back in Santiago; could see his beautiful black face. Already he missed him and wondered if they would ever see each other again. For a moment he recalled the children of their neighborhood, Woodland, how, when they came in from playing on the rows of coal piled high along the road, their hands and faces were always as black as the acolyte. What is race? he mused. Guess if what God has given won't wash off, then you're black. If it will, well, we'll declare you white. He was believing voices he could not hear. A power he could not see. He thought about the scorpions, and that he had never admitted to Ruthie how he feared them. Actually she knew it; had noticed his pasty white face the day he crawled from underneath the barracks apartment when he was wiring it for two-twenty current.

Suddenly Duncan remembered a passage from Ezekiel.

> And thou, son of man, be not afraid of them, neither be afraid of their words, though briars and thorns be with thee, and thou dost dwell among scorpions: be not afraid of their words, nor be dismayed at their looks, though they be a rebellious house.

Indeed. A rebellious house. The trustees have made the house of St. Luke's a rebellious one.

He remembered also another passage. From the Gospel of St. Luke. Ah, St. Luke again. Professor Grant had talked about it.

> Behold, I give you power to tread on serpents and scorpions, and over the power of the enemy: and nothing shall by any means hurt you.

But precisely who, he wondered, is the enemy? The world of a young man who had come in routine innocence to a theological school considered to be of the carriage trade had become complicated. And he was expected to be a leader in that world. President of St. Luke's Society. That will be tomorrow, he thought. It will have to wait. Now he had to struggle with today.

The Orkin man was called early next morning. "A professional exterminator was our primary luxury that year," Ruthie laughs today. But the scorpions of discord tarried with them.

AFTER THE MANASSAS BATTLE IN LATE JULY OF 1861, THE Greys had a respite from combat the remainder of the year. The tedium of camp life, however, was little preferable to the perils of battle. Discipline was a constant problem and the murmurs of the unranked soldiers kept the officers troubled. This was especially true within the Greys' ranks where officers and men had been of equal standing at the university. Resentment at being disciplined for a minor transgression or being assigned arbitrary chores by one who was a roommate or close pal two months earlier was inevitable. Adding to the unrest among the rank and file were the personal habits of General William Henry Chase Whiting, General Bee's replacement as brigade commander following Bee's death. A Mississippian, he was by training and profession an engineer. (As was Robert E. Lee and as Duncan Montgomery Gray Jr. would be a century later.) Other similarities, however, were few. Letters from Whiting's soldiers indicated that he was ". . . nearly all the time drunk." The paucity of numbers among his supporters was made up for by their zeal, and history has not dealt as harshly with Whiting as the foot soldiers at the time.

The Confederacy had not provided separate uniforms for summer and winter and the Greys had to get by on their summer uniforms plus what their families back home could send. On the lower Potomac, with freezing wind and snow invading the hastily built and unchinked cabins in the harsh winter of 1861, it must have been easy to find fault with peers claiming ascendancy. Acrimony was the given.

To preempt the boredom of camp routine, the soldiers had an uncanny ability to subvert the system with frivolity. While most of the officers equated solemnity with duty, many of the soldiers chose to clothe the unpleasantness of army life in an aura of unreality. They concocted fun and games that would both entertain themselves and irritate the officers.

Near the winter quarters of the Mississippi Eleventh there was a slaughter pen. Only bored but ingenious soldiers could make creative sport of a butchery. Each time a soldier was detailed to go for meat he came back with as many horns as he could carry in a poke. These were cleaned and carved into blowing horns like most of the boys had used to call the hounds at fox, raccoon, or possum hunts back home. Eventually almost every soldier in camp below the rank of sergeant had a horn. Sometimes, late at night, the mischievous Greys would, in unison, begin a continuous peal of their horns. Another company would answer, then another, until the night was filled with the blare of horns from all ten companies of the regiment in a cacophony of "let's get even with the officers." They came to be called *the horned regiment*.

Their fun and games ended in early March when General Johnston, fearing General McClellan was going on offense, moved his troops west to Fredericksburg and then immediately southeast to the mouth of the

the York River. For the next month the living was easy. Even in time of war the Chesapeake Bay had much to offer and the University Greys exulted in it all. It would be the last good time they would have as rough-housing college boys. Manhood would soon overtake them with hyperbolic wrath. Such are the ways of war. To make old men of children.

Gray's courses for the fall would be Systematic Theology, Ethics, Church Music, American Church History, Liturgics, and Homiletics. He decided to add an advanced course in New Testament under Professor Grant. As president of the seminary student body he could skip one required course but decided against it, choosing the heavier load.

Although he would not neglect his academic studies, the curriculum was not the drumbeat in his head. He knew he could excel in the class-room. The pestering question of how an institution that wore the sign of the cross could, for any reason, refuse to admit another Christian was more elusive than high marks. He had known of the case before the Supreme Court challenging segregated schools and had hoped the church would lead the way by volunteering. He knew now that was not to be; that, once again, the keeper of the Law and the Prophets would munch Caesar's crust with toothless gums. Still he never considered leaving the household for a more promising ship or pleasant voyage. He had answered a call to be a priest in this house. He would work in its renewal without self-righteousness or despairing aloneness. He was sure the resources for righteousness were there.

As student body president he felt his first obligation was to find out what his fellow students were thinking. He had already talked informally with the seniors and felt most were with him. They were a good class, with solid undergraduate training. Several were graduates of the University of the South and Gray gave certain and early attention to them. Others had come from Vanderbilt, Syracuse University, West Point, Columbia, William and Mary. He was especially concerned with the first-year class. Most of them were just out of Deep South communities and had not been exposed to the influence of the seminary's liberal faculty.

On campus the talk had been of one thing. Generally returning students compared summer experiences and vacations, while seniors talked of ordination and first parish assignments. Now every conversation opened with what some were calling the trustees' *whites only* policy.

School would open as usual, and with the same faculty, for they had agreed to remain until the seniors graduated. But the pall of what Gray saw as ecclesiastical racism hovered over St. Luke's Hall like the heavy fogs that often blanketed the Mountain. Early in the school year, at a regularly scheduled meeting of St. Luke's Society, Gray and some of the student leaders decided to present resolutions they had prepared to encourage the students to express their feelings. Following Evening Prayer, the St. Luke's Society convened in the Commons Room of St. Luke's Hall. After a few matters of routine business the group turned to what had happened during their summer absence. Unlike what had been reported of the meeting between the faculty and trustees on the day after the resolution was passed—heated debate—this discussion was without rancor. It was more like what would, in some circles, be called a *testimony meeting*. Hearts were opened; deepest feelings shared. The first resolution introduced had to do with the students' views on the faculty:

> RESOLVED: That this society expresses hereby its full confidence in the professional competence and integrity of each member of the faculty of the School of Theology as constituted September 17, Ember Wednesday, 1952, and in the Chaplain and in the head of the Department of Religion of the University as of that date.

Fifty-nine voted for the adoption of the resolution. Two voted against, fifteen abstained, and six were absent. Gray was discouraged by the abstentions. To him the competence and integrity of the faculty were beyond question. Yet he could understand why the rumors making the rounds concerning one of the faculty members might have left uneasiness in the minds of first-year students who did not yet know the faculty.

Gray saw the litmus test as being the views of the students themselves on the admission of Negroes to the seminary. A second resolution was submitted:

> RESOLVED: That this society fully favors admission of applicants approved by the Diocesans to the School of Theology on the sole basis of merit and preparedness for study leading to the sacred ministry, regardless of race or color of either the applicant or the sponsoring bishop.

This vote was seventy-two favoring adoption, none against, six abstentions and four absences. This was the reassurance Gray wanted. No matter that the action of the trustees, and the reaction of the faculty had been muddied by allegations of imperfect timing or methods, it was clear where the students stood. Without exception they had no hesitation about studying Soteriology, Greek grammar, or the Patristic Fathers beside a black man.

A final resolution having to do with approval of the position of the faculty was less encouraging to the student body president. Although only two voted objections, against forty-six approvals, there were thirty who abstained and four who were absent. Perhaps some of those abstaining were voting against losing the faculty. Others might have been influenced by their bishops, or others back home, or at that point were not well enough informed to vote intelligently.

As news of the meeting spread, Gray received praise from the larger campus community for the calm, rational leadership he had shown at such a tense time. He felt better prepared for what he had known was inevitable—a confrontation with his Uncle Ned, something that had been gnawing at him since he had heard of the trustee's stand. He dreaded the thought of a direct encounter with the newly elected vice-chancellor.

Now he must talk again with every member of the faculty, including Dr. Jones, who had not signed the statement of protest. Gray had already spent long hours with his friend and faculty advisor, Robert McNair, and knew generally what the others would say. Gray spent three days and evenings talking with the others.

The Very Reverend F. Craighill Brown, dean of the School of Theology, was first on his list. Dean Brown had grown up in South Carolina. He had attended the College of the University of the South, graduating in three years. While a student, he had helped found the Sewanee chapter of Phi Beta Kappa, was president of a literary society, the Neograph Club, and was Latin salutatorian of his class. From the Virginia Theological Seminary in 1925 he went to China where he taught in Yangchow, Shanghai, and Nanking. Before coming to Sewanee in 1949 he had been rector of Emmanuel Church, Southern Pines, North Carolina. A thin, fragile-looking man with horn-rimmed glasses, a sparse black moustache, and dark, beady eyes that sparkled when he was aroused, his carriage and countenance portrayed the scholar he was. He quickly expressed to Gray his anger and frustration over what had happened. The two men turned quickly to discussing similarities between what was happening on the Mountain and their experiences in China and Cuba. Similarities that had to do with the repression of dissent.

Next, talking with Robert Grant, Gray heard an animated lecture on the teachings of Jesus, obviously meant for the bishops and other trustees. Robert Grant would prove to be one of the greatest scholars ever to grace the Sewanee faculty. With earned degrees from Northwestern University, Union Theological Seminary, and Harvard, with further work at the University of Leyden, he was twice a Guggenheim Fellow. From Sewanee he went on to become one of America's foremost scholars in biblical literature, church history, and biblical research. Being in his classes and presence had been an exciting blessing for Gray. Hearing him face to face in his own tiny office, listening to him drawing on the radical teachings of Jesus as they related to a Christian seminary refusing entrance of any for whom Christ died was an overpowering bonus.

In the office of Professor Lansing Hicks, Gray listened with awe to an exegesis of the elegant poetry of Isaiah. "Isaiah was as cultured and refined a man as any son of Canterbury," the generally moderate of word Professor Hicks said, referring sarcastically to Sewanee's reputation of gentility. "Isaiah warned of the judgment to come, calling the people of God back from their blasphemous, hollow prayers and to genuine justice and humanity."

The professor repeated the question of the prophet Micah asking, ". . . what doth the Lord require of thee, but to do justly, and to love mercy, and to walk humbly with thy God?" Teacher and pupil pondered where was there justice, where mercy, where the humility in what the elders of the Mountain had said? Gray was learning more in crisis than a sterile, unrelated classroom lecture could ever yield in comfort.

The inquiring candidate heard again the dull rumble of thunder rolling out of the desert of Tekoa as a bearded, brawny, flame-throwing man named Amos shouted God's hatred for their solemn feasts, impotent rituals, grand processions, and sacred ceremonies. Shame to those who live at ease in Zion, untroubled in the face of arrogance. "Let justice roll on like a river and righteousness like an ever-flowing stream." From Hosea to Malachi, prophets who were speaking as surely to this Mountain as they did to the unfaithful of Israel. "Where is the soul of religion?" the teacher asked his student, and then answered his own question "It has fled; it has divorced itself from morality. The outside of the cup is gleaming in the altar candles. The inside is tarnished and foul."

Gray was drained when he left the office of Lansing Hicks, feeling that he had viewed the past as unheeded augury; the future as pits of empty skulls. He recalled words from St. Matthew's gospel: "A prophet is not without honour, save in his own country, and in his own house."

Conversations with the other seminary faculty, Allen Reddick, Claude Guthrie, and Chaplain Richard Wilmer Jr., and Frederick Shafer, head of the college department of religion, went the same. It was indignation such as Gray had never seen before. It was clear to him that they intended to resign unless their terms were met.

The common thread among the faculty was that the trustees had hidden behind law, with no consideration given to justice and grace, reducing the issue to the level of expediency.

As Gray began circulating in the wider university community he found that the matter had become so bedimmed by extraneous trivia that the real issue—whether or not to admit Negroes to the School of Theology—was hardly discussed. In the first place, it was being said, the faculty had released their statement of protest to the press before Bishop Mitchell of Arkansas, chancellor of the university and therefore president of the board of trustees, had received their wire. It was an undeniable but innocent mistake. Following their meeting with the trustees the faculty had met most of the night, then wired their message to the bishop's office in Little Rock. The bishop had not gone to his office after the long automobile drive and did not know of the faculty statement until calls about it began reaching him at his residence. In the second place, the faculty statement had said, ". . . are deeply disturbed by the statement in the public press reporting the negative action taken by the board of trustees on the resolution from the Synod of the Province of Sewanee, asking for the admission of Negro students to the School of Theology."

As the flash fires of controversy spread and feelings heated, everyone felt they had to be on the side of the faculty or on the side of the trustees. Detractors used the timing of the faculty in releasing their statement to the press, plus the fact that they were responding to published accounts and not to the original text of the resolution, as a basis for siding with the trustees.

To say the faculty acted in an inappropriate and disrespectful manner because they did not have the original text before them was a weak argument. In the first place, no one denied the position to which they were reacting. In the next, the original text was brief—sixteen lines, most of which had been quoted in the newspaper articles. In addition, many saw the faculty statement that they would resign as an ultimatum, a threat not in the Sewanee tradition of gentlemanly good manners. Gray knew such reasoning was a rationalization and tried not to discuss anything except the central issue—racial prejudice.

The argument that Sewanee had no ordinances against the admission of Negroes carried no weight at all with Gray. The ordinances had been written in the 1850s. It was ludicrous to suppose that bishop, then general, Leonidas Polk would have seen fit to exclude chattel by written ordinance. Actually, there had been changes made in the ordinances since the beginning. None of the changes, however, addressed the matter at hand. Rumors were being used to subvert the facts. A member of the faculty was said to be an excessive user of alcohol, a strange allegation for a tradition hardly known as staunch prohibitionist. It was true, however, that Chancellor Mitchell, bishop of Arkansas, was as inflexible on the subject as the most inflexible Baptist. The fact that the incident was admitted to by the accused but had happened six years earlier seemed to make no difference.

Gray could still think as an engineer. The turbine was being sabotaged by defects he could identify but not correct. A Christian irrelevancy, race, was short circuiting the system. The waters were being muddied. He would do his best to get the current flowing and the waters cleared of pollution. Keep the issue clear and simple.

It was a grievous burden for the young candidate to carry. "I have to talk with Uncle Ned," he thought. It could not be postponed much longer. They were a close family. He felt a certain sympathy for his uncle. His first day as formally elected vice-chancellor and president and he had to face the most serious crisis the University of the South had known since the postponement of its establishment in 1860 by the same issue: "What are we going to do about the Negro question?" In that case the answer was war. At least that was not a consideration this time.

Gray and Uncle Ned had enjoyed a close friendship as well as kinship. Gray did not wish to offend him. But he knew the position he was going to take and was sure Uncle Ned's position would not be the same. Generally the two visited informally. They met on the walkways, at Morning Prayer, or Gray simply dropped by his uncle's home for an unannounced visit. It had always been friendly chit-chat, talk of family or Mississippi friends. Perhaps, he thought, the estrangement he was feeling was a projection on his part. Maybe Uncle Ned would laugh it off, assure him that it was no more than a schoolyard scuffle that would all be cleared up at the next meeting of the trustees. Or maybe, since the trustees had said there were no ordinances against admitting members of other races, Uncle Ned would tell him he was by his own authority instructing the registrar to consider any application on its merit.

Gray knew that was wishful thinking, for he had seen the vice-chancellor's statement of June 11 in which he said, "After as conscientious and prayerful consideration of the subject as I was able to make, I feel deeply convinced that the action taken was in the best interest of both races." Gray also knew the McCradys were a strong, tenacious lot, imbrued with Old South ways, and not given to vacillation.

Instead of waiting for a chance and casual meeting on the sidewalk, Gray decided to make a formal appointment with the vice-chancellor as president of the School of Theology student body. It would be a man-to-man discussion, based on mutual respect, strengthened by family ties. Gray would not present himself with an air of arrogance as president of the student body but neither would he be a third grade boy in the principal's office.

McCrady was a scientist. He was also a man of the arts: a classical violinist and a competent architect. On the Mountain he was known as the Renaissance man. Although of medium height and build, his brushy hair and massive eyebrows that he regularly combed seemed to reach out and speak before he did, giving him the appearance of a strong, unapproachable Trojan. Many who knew him remember him as gentle, cultured, courtly, quiet and caring. Some remember him as delicate, even sickly looking, though he was in excellent health at the time. Three upstairs rooms of his residence, Fulford Hall, were reserved for students, with whom he related with good manners and beneficence. His undergraduate degree was in classics at the College of Charleston, South Carolina. His doctoral dissertation at the University of Pennsylvania had to do with the effects of a gene for albinism in mammals. In a post-doctoral program, he had spent three years studying the embryology of the Virginia opossum. His research was later helpful in studies of the human ear that led to more advanced treatment of deafness. The allegorical and metaphorical irony of his uncle's research did not elude Gray's mind. A man whose erudition could help thousands hear the pindrops of the present could not himself hear the roaring thunder of past prophesy. Yet he believed his uncle to be an eminently decent, spiritually knowing human being.

Others are not so sure. Some still on the Mountain, as well as some who were on the scene in 1953 but have moved on, believe that as vice-chancellor and president McCrady played a far more active role in the trustees' action to deny the admission of Negroes to Sewanee than was publicly acknowledged. For that, they, unlike Gray, have never forgiven Ned McCrady. No one questions that he was gifted and talented: the Renaissance man described above. But there is an undercurrent of lore at Sewanee which describes him as hard-headed, willful to a fault, and, upon occasion, less than self-restrained in terms of some of the steps he took to advance his own personal interests. It was further believed by some that keeping Negroes out of the University of the South was a major interest at the time. None who expressed those opinions asked not to be identified. I do not name them here because I believe, at least in this case, a smoothly healed scar is preferable to a seething cauldron of infection. Moreover, not even his most vocal detractors question that McCrady took a struggling liberal arts college and converted it into an institution with great potential.

McCrady had grown up in an academic community and knew the terrain. His father, Gray's maternal grandfather, had been professor of philosophy at the University of Mississippi and rector of St. Peter's Church, Oxford, the same parish Gray would later serve. (Still later, beginning in 1985, Gray's eldest son, the Reverend Duncan Montgomery Gray III would also serve St. Peter's Church.) All of McCrady's siblings were people of superior intellect and cultural acumen. One was John McCrady, the celebrated American painter. An earlier John McCrady, a famed scientist who left a position at Harvard and came to the University of the South as a professor of biology in 1877, was Ned McCrady's grandfather.

According to most people I interviewed, the essence of Dr. Edward McCrady was refinement and good-manners, someone steeped in matters of the mind. He would have been outraged at any allegation of bigotry. Such a trait would be considered common, beneath the dignity of a gentleman and a McCrady. Especially a Sewanee McCrady. However, when the incrustation of excellence was penetrated, the urbanity and pedantry swept away, underneath it all his young nephew knew there would be found a helping of the Gothic purposes of the Old South. It was that awareness that most troubled Gray.

Despite the jokes he had heard as a lad about Uncle Ned and the sex life of the Virginia opossum, Gray knew that he would have a formidable opponent when he stepped into the ring with McCrady, vice-chancellor and president of the University of the South. Still, it must be done.

The appointment went as Gray expected; polite, formal, and unbending. There was not a hint of condescension; no patronizing on the part of the vice-chancellor. At least he is meeting me man-to-man, Gray thought. For that he was grateful. From his chair the vice-chancellor simply reviewed the action taken by the trustees, stated his agreement with their position and said it was the solemn vow taken at the installation of the vice-chancellor and president of the university to abide by the decisions of those at whose sufferance he presided. When Gray appealed to matters of the spirit; principle, theology, ethics; or tried to talk about his experiences with nonwhite Episcopalians in Cuba, he was parried by answers about institutional responsibility and integrity. That and what the vice-chancellor saw as the wrongful way the faculty had dealt with the press were the only things McCrady allowed on the agenda.

This put Gray at a disadvantage. Their difference was not one of methodology; had nothing to do with poor judgement of the faculty. They disagreed on the basic issue. Gray knew there were some financially strong, politically powerful men among the trustees. Men capable of bringing the university to its knees or of removing the vice-chancellor from his post. Some felt McCrady was unduly influenced by those considerations. Others saw the purse strings of Mrs. Jessie Ball duPont, who promised to be one of the university's most generous benefactors, and who was a close friend of Bishop Juhan, a staunch advocate of the status quo, as a threatening presence. Duncan did not agree. He knew that McCrady, for reasons of his own, simply did not think it was a good idea to admit Negroes to the University of the South. He also knew his uncle well enough to know that once they were admitted by order of the trustees McCrady would do everything within his power to make it work. That was why he tried so hard to change the vice-chancellor's mind. Gray had not, he thought, wanted their meeting to be one between a nephew and blood uncle. Yet the kinship was real and, although he did not want to use it to personal advantage in the discussion, he did not wish to deny the kinship. But he had not reckoned that their meeting would be quite so ordered. He left the office more discouraged than when he went in. Like a mouse in a newly shredded nest.

Something else, even more troubling, was pressing in on him. It was something that had worried him back in Cuba when he first heard of the board's action. He had tried not to think about it since returning to Sewanee; to not consider it as a factor in the equation. It was so burning he had not even discussed it with Ruthie, his confidant and best friend. But, it would not go away. Just where had his own diocesan bishop, his father, stood when the issue of admitting non-whites to the seminary came to a vote?

At first he had felt disloyal even thinking about it. The Fifth Commandment had been an important one in the Decalogue when he was growing up. Was he violating the command of honor even to question his father? Was it any of his business? What bearing did it have on the personal role he knew he must play? There was also the matter of church discipline: obedience to one's bishop and all others in authority. But there comes a time. Some words of Jesus came to mind: "He that loveth father or mother more than Me is not worthy of Me." And the words that followed: "And he that taketh not his cross, and followeth after Me, is not worthy of Me."

Those were hard sayings. He was not positive that his bishop, his father, had even been present at the meeting of the trustees. The news accounts had said it was well attended. That told him nothing. He had thought of asking for the minutes of the meeting, to which he was entitled, and checking the list of those present and voting. That would not tell him how each bishop had voted for there was no roll call votes at trustee meetings. Roll calls were considered ungentlemanly at the University of the South in 1952. His engineer mind devised a compromise. He would learn if his bishop was present but not know how he voted. At least not now. But was that not what the resolution had said about admitting Negroes to the seminary? Not now? He decided to live with his tidy little compact. Know if his father was present. Not know how he voted. "Sufficient unto the day is the evil thereof." Whatever that means, he thought.

Suddenly Gray's mind was cleared of the thoughts that had been plaguing him; thoughts he saw now as overzealous fantasy. He recalled that on the day of the trustees meeting, his mother was recovering from surgery and he was with both parents in Jackson, on his way to Cuba, so his father could not have been present at what he considered the day of infamy on the Mountain. It was a glorious unburdening for him. Things were bad enough without letting his own thinking run afoul of reality.

By chance Gray got an opportunity to go outside the compound in search of allies. Or answers. A classmate, Woodland neighbor, and close friend named Davis Carter asked Gray to ride to West Tennessee with him. Carter, a U.S. Marine Corps veteran, University of Texas graduate, and Texas newspaperman who would become a priest, was presiding at the little Episcopal church in nearby Alto, Tennessee. Carter would also go on to be everything from administrative assistant for Congressman Jack Brooks, to lobster fisherman in Gloucester, Massachusetts, to sculptor, to Civil War historian and author. Tom Roberts, a candidate who had entered seminary in 1950 but had been ordained after doing two years in seminary and was in Germantown, Tennessee, had offered Carter some discarded church windows for a parish hall he was building in Alto. Carter asked Gray to go with him to help haul the windows. At first Gray declined, wanting to remain ringside for the fight raging on the Mountain. When Carter reminded Gray of the many hours Roberts, joined by another Texan, Joe Routh, and he had spent playing pinochle under Woodland trees, a cooler that would barely hold eight cans of beer at their feet, Gray decided that it would, after all, be good to see Roberts again. It proved a serendipitous journey.

Roberts, before becoming a priest, had been a business man in Chattanooga and was a friend of Edmond Orgill, merchant prince of Memphis, prominent member of Calvary Church there and chairman of the board of regents of the University of the South. Roberts arranged for Orgill to meet with Gray and Carter. Gray, meaning only to express his disagreement and distress over what was happening, was surprised at how freely Orgill talked. He launched into an excursive monologue on everything from the early Church of England to the Monroe Doctrine, his digressions often filling in wide blanks for Gray, who had not known, for example, that there were three faculty members, not one, on the hit list of some of the trustees. He had known that Robert Grant was a target. From Orgill he learned that McNair and Reddick were in the crosshairs of the detractors' scope as well. Apparently Orgill assumed the students knew everything that had gone on and did not hesitate to talk freely. He explained that the alleged offenses of the three men were discussed at the last meeting of the board of regents, at least informally, and it was his recollection that the meeting had adjourned with the understanding that the administration would deal with it. That is, investigate the charges and get rid of all three if the charges could be documented.

Carter had known little of what was going on back at Sewanee. A few years earlier, he had married the former Mary Busch, a native of Pennsylvania, whom he had met in 1945 in Quantico, Virginia, when he was hospitalized with pneumonia and she was a navy corpsman. Although many such wartime marriages did not last, this one is still blooming after more than fifty years. In the fall of 1952, when they returned to Sewanee for Davis's final seminary year they had agreed to stay clear of the controversy, graduate, and go back to Texas. However, after the session with Orgill, Carter quickly revised the plan. The dean and faculty had done him two special personal favors and he felt morally obligated to come to their defense. The previous year, when Jack Brooks, his college roommate and godfather to his older daughter, was running for Congress in Texas's old Second Congressional District, he had asked Carter to come and help with the campaign. The faculty gave him permission to take his exams early. Brooks won by three hundred votes and never forgot Carter's coming to help. Carter also got the dean and faculty's permission to be assigned to assist at the Alto church for a second year so he could assist in building the parish house at the little church. Generally the mission assignments were for only one school year. He felt that he owed the faculty on both counts. That, and his ire at hearing what some members of the faculty were facing, got him involved. Just back from a heated Texas political campaign, and still with marine ardor, he felt that he might be helpful. He saw the ruckus on the Mountain as much a political battle as a theological one. It was his kind of fight. Thus, after listening to Orgill and as Gray filled him in on the details, he was ready to enlist for the duration.

In the pickup truck on the long drive from Memphis to Sewanee, the truck overloaded with secondhand church windows, the two men talked of how to use the information they had to the best advantage. They knew that if Grant, McNair, and Reddick were fired for alleged moral improprieties, the leverage of a united faculty was of little account. The word would be that the faculty did not resign in righteous indignation over racial exclusion; rather half of them were fired upon being accused of carousing and violations of their sacred vows. The advantage the two students had was that they now had information considered top secret by the administration, things unknown to the faculty, students, or others on the Mountain. The question was just what to do with that intelligence.

Carter saw it as a checkmate find. "We've headed them off at the pass," he grinned. "We'll put 'em in the position of being petty, devious, desperate, uncivil, and plumb low-down. That's the last portrait a Sewanee cavalier wants to have painted of himself." He was moving up Highway 64 just outside of Memphis, driving as fast as the loaded pickup truck would go, the moist fall wind blowing through the windows almost drowning his voice. He rapped the outside of the pickup, his hand a riding crop.

Gray, never given to histrionics, wasn't so sure. "You're talking like a cowboy, Tex," he said, smiling and motioning for Carter to slow down and stay on the road. "The folks we're talking about ride to hounds, not in rodeos."

Tex was not a sobriquet Gray normally used for Davis so he was mildly jolted, feeling that perhaps his friend was getting impatient with him. Maybe felt he wasn't taking the whole thing seriously. "Well, you know I'm really not much of a cowboy," Carter called back over the roar of the engine and the wind. "I'll talk some like a marine. I know when it's time to lay down a heavy artillery barrage. I know when it's time to fix bayonets. And every Longhorn poker player knows when to hold and when to fold and we aren't fixing to fold, my friend."

"I'm not talking about folding," Gray said. "I'm talking about the best use of the hand we've been dealt." He knew that they had some vital information that they were not supposed to know. He also knew that his uncle, as vice-chancellor and president of the university, was going to be upset when he found out that they knew about the petty things that were coming down; the shameless things some of the trustees wanted to pull on three good men, including his friend Bob McNair.

"You know what, Dunc?" Carter said. "I don't understand why Orgill told us all that. I'm not sure he meant to. Gray, we're just a couple of neophytes. I think he just got carried away and let information slip. Maybe he had a martini for lunch. Your father is a bishop, and maybe Orgill thought you knew all that. But he didn't have to spill as much detail as he did."

"Of course he meant to tell us," Gray said. "Don't you see the picture?"

"I guess I don't."

Gray explained. The two of them had gone in talking of nothing but integration. Gray reasoned that Orgill was telling them that the melee raging on the Mountain didn't have anything to do with racial justice. He was implying that they all wanted that. But first they had to purge the bad apples. "So, yes," Gray said, "I think he meant to tell us. And I think he meant for us to spread the news."

For a long time Gray gazed out the window, trancelike, saying nothing. Finally he sighed deeply and said, "But no one can ever convince me that Uncle Ned has the least thing to do with all that. He's too gentle a man."

Davis told Gray that he knew he had his Uncle Ned, kinfolk, to think about. "I understand. But don't forget the Blue and the Grey were sometimes brothers and. . . ."

"I'm not talking about Uncle Ned," Gray interrupted, his voice slightly testy. "I'm not thinking about Blues and Greys. I'm thinking about getting my black Cuban acolyte into the School of Theology. And some Negro priests into the Diocese of Mississippi." Carter didn't answer. "And I'm thinking of what is the honorable, the appropriate way to do it."

Carter differed on that. "I don't have any Sewanee blood in me," he said. "I don't think about nobility, about dignity. I think about winning."

"So do I," Gray said. "So do I." Although Gray had gone to Tulane and not Sewanee as an undergraduate, he did have long time ties to Sewanee in addition to his uncle being vice-chancellor. His father was a graduate of the School of Theology and was then a trustee; his mother's father was an alumnus and had met his wife there. Gray's great-grandfather, John McCrady, was a distinguished professor of biology at Sewanee. In addition, it was still remembered that early in the century, when the first Edward McCrady, Gray's grandfather and the vice-chancellor's father, while still at Grace Church, Canton, had lectured at Sewanee on "Scientific Evidences of the Divinity of Christ." His well received book, *Reason and Revelation,* in which he attempted to reconcile Christian theology with science, a risky undertaking for a churchman at the time, was still remembered at Sewanee. It was the exception for a Mississippi Episcopalian not to have close Sewanee connections. Carter knew that. Gray had been invited to join the Red Ribbon Society, the eminent super fraternity of old line Sewanee vintage. The flower of Sewanee society. Davis Carter was Green Ribbon. So was Professor Bob Grant. All right, but not quite up to Red Ribbon.

They passed more time in silence, passing fields with black people picking cotton, unpainted shacks, mule-drawn wagons, and houses with fancy cars in the driveways. In Bolivar they passed a little Episcopal Church. Neither man commented. "Maybe we're a little like marines and Seabees," Carter said, stopping at a small roadside cafe. "The marines took the beaches."

"And then the Seabees built the runways," Gray said, checking the ropes holding the windows in place.

"One thing is certain," Gray said as they stirred their coffee and watched an old black man sweeping the floor.

"What's that, Padre."

"We have about two hundred and fifty miles to think about it."

When I shared with Davis Carter my account of this conversation during that long ride and asked for his comments, he said that the truth was there but he couldn't remember the exact wording. "Neither do I know precisely," I assured him. I wasn't there. "Just the facts, ma'am," I added, mimicking Jack Webb, the television detective of *Dragnet* fame. "Or maybe I should say, 'Just the truth'," I continued. Carter agreed that fact and truth are not always the same.

When he talked about that trip after so many years, Carter freely admitted that he was looking to Gray for leadership, letting him call the shots. "In the first place," he said, "Duncan did have Sewanee blood in his veins and I didn't. He knew those people. And don't ever forget . . . Duncan is incredibly bright." Gray was of the genus all right. His father was a bishop, and neither Gray nor Davis wanted to put the bishop in an embarrassing position by not having both the facts and the truth. They were in the fight together, both were willing to play hard ball. But they had to be right and they had to be good.

The two men decided they owed it to the faculty to tell them what they had learned from Edmond Orgill. Early next morning they went straight to Dean Brown. The dean didn't seem surprised. "Did you know that already?" one of them asked.

He said that he didn't, but nothing surprised him any more. A guilty conscience has no bounds. He asked them to tell the other faculty, that he wanted them to hear it from the two students. First hand.

When confronted, Grant merely shook his head, at first not responding. Then he said he knew they were after him, that he had acknowledged a couple of occasions of over-indulgence. "Boys, the hang-over wasn't worth it." But he had not thought they would go after the others. Then, for the first time, he told them that he was accepting a teaching position at the University of Chicago, that he would insist that the vice-chancellor accept his resignation before the end of the academic year, but that he would arrange his classes so that he might commute back and forth until the class of '53 graduated. (Despite vehement protests from some of the regents, the vice-chancellor honored that agreement.)

Grant's mood was one of utter sadness, the anger gone. "They can't prove the charges they are making," he told the two students. So far it had all been innuendo and inference. Adding ellipses to mask evil. Apparently those out to get the faculty felt the time had come to pull the camouflage off the hidden guns. Everyone knew they could cause embarrassment to the faculty members being targeted. "I hope Dr. McNair and Dr. Reddick won't run," Grant said. He turned quickly to face Gray and Carter. "Do you feel I'm running out on you? Are you disappointed in me?" They assured him they had no such feelings, begged him to stay, and thanked him for all he had meant to them.

They visited the other faculty one by one. Dr. Reddick, a bachelor, and not a priest, thought the charges were hilarious. "Me? Well, I thank them for the compliment. I should be so lucky." He volunteered to go with them to see McNair.

Bob McNair was far more than a professor to Gray. McNair was his mentor all right, but he was also his close friend. Gray dreaded to face his trusted counselor with this debasing gossip, and probably that was why Reddick offered to go with them. To make it easier. Gray let Carter tell McNair the story of their visit with Edmond Orgill. At first McNair seemed stunned. He asked a few questions, then changed the subject.

"Do you want to sue the bastards?" Reddick asked, strutting around the room like a fighting game cock.

"No, Doctor Reddick," McNair said, with sarcastic weight on "Doctor." "I don't want to sue the bastards." He was not laughing and the others were trying not to. "It's a thought," Carter said.

McNair picked up a Bible from his desk and opened it. "Read the morning lesson for us, Mister Gray," the professor said, handing the book to Gray and pointing to a passage in Ephesians.

Duncan Gray read thoughtfully:

For we wrestle not against flesh and blood, but against principalities, against powers, against the rulers of the darkness of this world, against spiritual wickedness in high places.

"Here endeth the lesson," McNair interrupted, looking at first one and then another. His expression was exegetical but he added nothing verbally, just placed the Bible on the desk and opened the door.

As they walked down the corridor Carter said to Gray, "All I said was 'It's a thought.'"

"He's quite a man," Gray said.

They told the vice-chancellor about their conversation with Orgill, who, fearing that he might have told the students too much, had already called McCrady. "He told you that?" McCrady asked when Gray and Carter expressed their shock and surprise at hearing Orgill tell them of the strategy to get rid of the three faculty members.

"Yes sir. And he told us a number of other things we didn't know," Carter bluffed. He had been doing some of the talking, feeling it would be easier on Gray. Gray indicated his disappointment at how the matter was getting a lot nastier than he ever thought it could. There seemed a worry in the vice-chancellor's voice Gray had not heard before. But it was too late now to keep any secrets. *If* Orgill had told them any secrets.

Gray fought every brush fire that flared up. One rumor was that numerous seminarians, so mortified and disillusioned at the faculty's transgressions, were leaving the School of Theology, and in some cases abandoning their vocational commitment. Gray knew that was not true, knew every student who had transferred or dropped out and the true reasons. One man who was being quoted directly was Jim Buckner, a priest, who, like Tom Roberts, had been ordained after two years of seminary. Buckner seemed an impeccable source. Gray wrote Buckner, who was married to Gray's first cousin, a four-page letter, detailing the truth as he knew it and the manner in which Buckner's comments were being used against the faculty. Much of the rumoring could be dated from a visit to the campus by Bishop Frank Alexander Juhan, bishop of Florida, who had preceded Mitchell as chancellor of the university. Bishop Juhan's position opposing the faculty's advocacy of admitting Negroes to the seminary and their protest against the trustees had remained unchanged. It was rumored that he had his postulants spying on faculty and other students. This, too, presented a problem for Gray. Bishop Juhan had figured prominently at the elder Gray's consecration as bishop. Opposing him put Gray in the position of going against a close family friend. It was another painful choice he had to make. Still the issue was too clear for vacillation. In his letter to Buckner, Gray tackled every rumor with vigor and documentation.

The imbroglio continued into winter and spring. The Mountain reeked of controversy. The university was a small, isolated community, as the trustees had said in their decision not to admit Negroes. There was no larger community to absorb nor soften the friction. It just settled on the mountaintop and bubbled. A boiler room with all holes welded. Sides continued to be taken, words spoken in passion, editorials written in the national Church and secular press, letters to the editor in response. Most of the letters had to do with the faculty's response. Little with the issue as Duncan Gray continued to see it. He saw it as rejection of what had been affected in the person of Christ: the cadence of the Cross.

Ruthie and the children saw less and less of their spouse and father, though he tried to keep her informed on the day to day developments. His days were filled with classroom lectures. Nights found him in the library or in hours-long strategy meetings with the faculty or student body. Weekends were no different. Ruthie carried it as best she could. Yet she groaned at his burden, knew the estrangement he felt with his uncle, coupled with the humiliation he felt for Sewanee when he heard remarks made about it being a Jim Crow academy. He seemed especially low when he received hostile letters from Mississippi and throughout the South. Ruth reassured him when he questioned if he were just some upstart who didn't know what he was doing. She considered his health, but knew they were there to stay, that she would never hear him declare that they were packing it in and returning to the life of Westinghouse engineer. That was never mentioned. He had come to the Mountain to become a priest.

One night she decided to try a new approach. As nearly as I can reconstruct, this is how it went.

"Duncan, why don't you go and talk to your Uncle Ned?"

Gray didn't understand. He stood, paced the floor and was somewhat acerbic in his response as he explained that he talked to the vice-chancellor all the time. Sometimes two or three times a week. He told his wife that he didn't enjoy doing it but that he represented the students. When they had a grievance it was his responsibility to take it to the top man. But, he explained, it was always the same story. They didn't get anywhere. "So," he asked, "What do you mean, go talk to my Uncle Ned?"

Ruthie answered that she meant precisely that: talk to Uncle Ned. She explained that Gray didn't talk to his Uncle Ned, he talked to a man who was vice-chancellor and president of the University of the South. To an official. A position. For the student body. "Why don't you talk to your uncle? Edward McCrady. For yourself."

"I'll think about it," he said, still not quite understanding. "Maybe I'll see the secretary tomorrow. Try to set up another appointment for this week. I mean, if you want me to. If you think it might help." This would remain Gray's style throughout his life. Always reflective. Ever asking, "Is this the right, the appropriate way to handle this?" Always secure in using existing channels of authority, even when he was challenging; trying to clear the channel of obstruction. It was not his purpose to write his own system. Yet he was willing to listen to another's opinion.

Ruthie, ever ready to exert herself if the situation indicated, replied, with feeling, "Appointment! Appointment! Secretary! Secretary! Sure. Go through the proper channels. We must observe protocol at the great University of the South. We must be gentlemen." She had poured a small glass of wine and they were sharing it. She walked to the front door and opened it. Instead of walking into the yard as Gray thought she was going to, she closed the door, turned back and faced her husband directly and spoke again. "I'm talking about going over to his house. Like you used to do. You never had to make appointments. You just dropped in whenever you felt like visiting kinfolk. Just went over, had coffee, propped your feet up and talked."

Gray replied that it was easier to do that before all the controversy developed.

"He is vice-chancellor and president," Ruth drawled in a mockish Southern accent, throwing her hands in the air with feigned exasperation, almost spilling what was left of the wine. "But he's also your Uncle Ned." She came to him and placed her free hand on his shoulder. "That's all I'm saying." Gray could see her face reddening, a sure sign that her patience was waning. "A vice-chancellor can also be an uncle."

"You're talking about right now, aren't you?" Duncan said, starting to understand. "You're talking about tonight."

"And put your coat on," Ruthie said. "It's cold out there." She opened the door again as he was reaching for his cap. She kissed him lightly on the cheek as he passed her and added, but gingerly now, "And, by the way, friend. Good luck."

Gray walked the half-mile to Fulford Hall, the vice-chancellor's residence, a big, white mansion, built when the original Fulford had burned in the 1890s, and given to the university by an earlier dean who was married to an heiress of the Proctor and Gamble fortune. Mrs. McCrady invited him in, welcomed him cordially, and ushered him into the library where they were listening to classical music. McCrady turned the volume down, shook hands, and offered his nephew a chair. Mrs. McCrady said she would bring cookies and tea. At first Gray declined, then changed his mind. This was to be a social occasion. This wasn't the vice-chancellor's office and Aunt Edith wasn't the secretary extending courtesies to an official visitor to the university. "Just tea, please, ma'am," he said. Duncan waited until they were all seated to begin the little speech he had rehearsed on the way over.

"Uncle Ned, I have something I need to talk to you about." McCrady, assuming that it would be the usual, shifted uncomfortably in his chair and nodded for Gray to go on. Gray thought he was going to choke up and not get through it. But he continued. "Well, I guess it's no secret that we're on different sides on a very delicate issue. We have discussed and we have argued. And I'm sure we'll go on arguing and differing. But I just want to tell you that I love you and Aunt Edith and always will. I love you and I respect you." Gray thought he saw his aunt dabbing her eyes. He cleared his throat to gain his composure and continued. "We're family and nothing can ever change that. You're my mother's brother, I'm your blood nephew, and that's the way it will always be." McCrady continued to sit expressionless. Gray went on with what he had come there to say. "I know I have said things that offended you and I'm sure I will say things in the future that will offend you. I just hope you will understand why I have to do what I do and will go on loving me the way I will go on loving you." There was a long pause. Uncle Ned had spoken not a word. Gray had been careful not to ask forgiveness. He had thought of that coming over and decided against it. He was not there for absolution but for mending a torn garment. "Well, I suppose that's all I came over here to say," he concluded, standing up to leave.

Mrs. McCrady, a strong, sophisticated, independent woman from back East smiled approvingly, motioning with her head for Gray to sit back down. McCrady stood up and extended his hand, still holding the same determinate gaze. It was a long, solid handshake. Neither man rushed to loosen the grip. They stood with eyes fixed intently on each other, saying nothing. Resolute and imposing.

Finally Uncle Ned broke the silence. "I sincerely appreciate this, Dunc. I will cherish this visit. And I thank you, sir."

The nephew was twenty-six years old; the uncle considerably older. Perhaps Gray's speech was for the elder to have made instead of the younger. For whatever reasons, it didn't happen that way. Longevity is not a synonym for honor. In any case, it was a speech that should have been made. And it was.

As Gray walked down the icy gravel road toward the barracks of Woodland, by then the tarpaper covered with asbestos siding, the cold rocks crunched beneath his hurrying steps. He barely noticed the frozen puddles in the darkness, ignored the barking dogs that seemed to come at him from all sides. He heard the call of a nearby owl, remembered that the needle-claws sometimes mistook a fur cap for a hare; hurried along. He hummed, then softly chanted the *Nunc Dimittis* drawing on his two years of high school Latin. (He had studied Greek at Sewanee but not Latin.) *"Benedictus qui venit in nomine Domini"* ("Blessed is he that cometh in the name of the Lord"). He meant the canticle for his wife who had sent him on this mission, not himself and not the vice-chancellor.

As Gray approached the house he caught a glimpse of the half-moon, rose-flushed through snow clouds gathering from the west. He tapped lightly on the unlocked door instead of walking in.

"Who is it?" Ruthie called. With a mock kittenish inflection; knowing full well.

"Tu eres el mejor que yo vi!" he answered, opening the door, embracing his wife and laughing heartily. The Spanish for "You beat all I ever saw" had become a sort of pet saying with him. She had not seen her husband so light-hearted in a long time. A hallmark of his personality had been his joy. After all these years it still is. "I didn't mean to be unkind," he said.

He had never loved her more.

In the spirit of Duncan Montgomery Gray Jr. And in the spirit of his times.

Within the next few days Mrs. McCrady visited Ruthie and the children. Aunt Edith brought a pot of soup she had made. She stayed a long time, visiting and playing with the children. Neither one mentioned the problem on the Mountain.

"Things were better around our house after that," Ruthie says.

It would not, however, end the differences between her husband and the vice-chancellor. Gray would try to relate to Dr. McCrady as official and adversary. And try to relate to Uncle Ned on the level of kinsman. It was almost as if Edward McCrady were two different people. At both levels, however, there was never a loss of respect.

Aside from the decline of the Mountain from a sweet spirit of community to the garden of Proserpine, Gray was concerned that an academic drought would wilt the flowering fruits of St. Luke's Hall; that the pull of the South's unseemly past would leave little time for scholarship. Classrooms were engaging; chambers of *Didache, eschaton*, creeds of Nicea and Chalcedon, exciting lectures on Abailard and his lady friend Heloise, Tertullian of Carthage, Clement of Alexandia, or a frivolous snipe-hunt for some student's *paraclete* that got away last night.

Gray remembered the good times; classes as fun times. They laughed a lot. He feared the classrooms might become prosaic and remote; professors absorbed by things with which they were ill-prepared to deal, with little time for things they knew and loved. Maybe we laughed too soon, he thought.

Such fears did not become reality. At least not for long. Most seminarians worked even harder so as to reflect favorably on the faculty when the time came for canonical exams in their respective dioceses. They wanted to prove that the faculty members were the outstanding teachers the students knew them to be.

Gray also worried that the toll the strain was taking on individual faculty would lead to a distancing between them and the students. They had been relaxed, almost carefree. Each took a personal interest in the students, knew their problems, gave them extra help when it was needed, bonded with friendly banter. Fortunately, despite the new pressures on them, they did not withdraw. The adversity seemed to strengthen the bond that had existed already. This despite their uncertain futures of finding new teaching positions, uprooting their families and moving from the Mountain where most had intended to live out their careers and lives.

The tragic irony was that these men had not really comprehended the magnitude of what they were doing when they flung the gauntlet at the feet of the trustees and vice-chancellor. Though they were men of conscience, they were scholars, not social activists, zealots, or crusaders.

102

They were united in conviction that they had no choice but to do what they did; resign if the School of Theology remained exclusive. And when they did go, as a body, it was not so much to protest further. Their very presence had become the source of contention. Their witness had been usurped by the principalities. They cared enough for the seminary and students to remove themselves and let the trustees consider the issue on its merit; without excuse or hindrance. In effect, they had been put on the cutting edge of social change by forces they had not chosen. And when it was over they were not altogether sure how it had come about. Perhaps to be an unwitting tool in the hand of the Builder is the only authentic witness.

Gray was a scholar also, already giving thought to graduate studies and perhaps a career in teaching or serious biblical research. He had come to Sewanee with great expectations. Initially he had found them fulfilled. Now he feared a grand academy would be paralyzed by something he considered settled at Pentecost, when every race, nation, and tongue were all together, in one place, learning of the ways of God. *Integrated.* He dreaded the thought of seeing the message of Pentecost disabled by trivia and deception, gasping for survival, with only Caesar's statutes as defense—statutes doomed already by age and history and Gospel. The young candidate for Holy Orders saw it as the enshrinement of idolatry. First Commandment violation.

Gray, in addition to his academic accomplishments, was a man of fun as well. He liked to have a good time, and other students saw him as one who found humor in the most tense situations. Once a professor, who was seen by many of the students as taking himself far too seriously (he was sometimes privately referred to as "Buckethead"), stormed into Gray's classroom, threw open his academic gown, stuck his thumbs into his vest pockets and in Latin addressed the startled students for several minutes. Then he ceremoniously girded his loins with the imperious robe of academe, strode furiously to the door, turned back and barked, "In case you illiterates didn't understand me, I said that I am tired of casting pearls before swine." With that he slammed the door and they could hear him stomping down the corridor.

The classroom sat in silence. Until Gray stood up, gathered his books, and announced as he was leaving, "It's not the swine that bothers me so much as the pearls." The laughter that filled the room on that occasion was considered the better lecture of the day.

Gray, despite his small stature, was a good athlete. Before his father became bishop and moved the family to Jackson, Gray had lettered in football at Greenwood. At Jackson's Central High he was a starter. This was before the days of unlimited substitutions and the better players generally played defense as well as offense—for sixty minutes. Duncan ran from the old wingback position when the team was in the single wing; right halfback when they switched to T formation. Because he was nimble of mind as well as limb he was assigned to call signals. He was good enough to be honorable mention on the Big Eight Conference all star team that year.

The urgency of his duties during his final year at Sewanee left little time for sports, or any other diversion. Gray did, however, manage to stay on the "Theologs" softball team. He could hit, catch, and run. Davis Carter, deficient in all three, had the inevitable right field position. Gray was at second base.

There was a crucial game with the Kappa Alpha fraternity. The KAs, at the University of the South since 1883, were known to oppose the admission of Negroes. Sometimes it was expressed with teasing Old South rhetoric and sometimes with intensely serious words. Gray found neither to be funny. There had even been half-serious rumors of mayhem during this particular game. Gray was a fierce competitor, maybe accounting in part for his never giving up in the contest with the trustees and the vice-chancellor. As a matter of principle he did not want the Theologs to be defeated by the Kappa Alphas.

The closest thing to mayhem came when one of the fraternity's worst hitters sent a short fly toward shallow right field. The shortstop called, "Carter! Carter! Carter!" Just as the ball was about to drop, the shortstop, seeing that Carter wouldn't make the catch, yelled, "Gray!" who had dropped back to cover Carter. Neither man stopped running. When Carter awoke his head was resting on second base, Gray, his best friend, was standing over him asking if he was all right, and the fraternity brothers on the base line were jeering. The Theologs went on to what Gray saw as ignominious defeat. Though unhurt, Davis Carter's softball career was over.

By late winter what became known as the Pike affair added a fiery dimension to the controversy over the admission of Negroes. James A. Pike, then dean of the prestigious and well-known Cathedral of St. John the Divine, New York City, was scheduled to be the baccalaureate preacher for the class of '53 and was to receive an honorary degree.

An anticipated but highly displeasing development to the administration occurred when the Very Reverend Dr. Pike released a three-page letter he had written to his friend, Ned McCrady. The text of the letter that swept the entire nation informed the university that Pike would neither preach the baccalaureate sermon nor accept the degree. "I could not in conscience receive a doctorate in white divinity which Sewanee apparently is prepared to offer the Church hereafter. . . ." He described the action of the trustees as "apartheid policy" and said ". . . it is clear that the present faculty's stand is 'on the side of the angels' and I feel that I must stand with them."

Gray and his cadre felt that this development would enhance the chances of getting the trustees to reverse their position. Prior to that, most of the news of what was going on at Sewanee had only been in various church papers. Gray had feared the trustees' position would prevail, Sewanee would continue to be a segregated school, and the world would not know of any of it. Pike's letter made it national news. The administration was bombarded with telephone calls and frequent visits by secular journalists.

At the same time, however, it led to further polarization on the Mountain and in the wider church community.

Pike, formerly a prominent Washington lawyer, later a bishop of California who would leave the world in a swirl of controversy of his own, had already served as unofficial press agent for the faculty. He and Richard Wilmer Jr., chaplain of the university and a man of tremendous prestige and influence because his Sewanee lineage went back to the school's earliest beginnings (and thus one the university least wanted as adversary), were friends. Pike had ready access to the national media, as well as sway at the highest level of the church. Following the release of Pike's letter, that combination served the faculty well in keeping their case before the public. With a single telegram or phone call to Pike, the latest development could be in the *New York Times* and on the wire services, radio, and fledgling television networks in minutes. This was frustrating to the Sewanee administration, putting them constantly on the defensive; denying or clarifying news stories rather than initiating them.

Pike, writing as both priest and lawyer, further infuriated, humiliated, and insulted the trustees by presuming to enlighten them on both legal and moral grounds:

Whatever other considerations may be entitled to weight, the administration cannot hide behind the Tennessee law. The attempt to do so is dubious on both legal and ethical grounds. The Christian reaction to a law which prevents the exercise of serious ethical responsibilities should, I am sure, be as follows:

1. Challenge the constitutionality of the law
2. Seek the repeal of the law
3. Failing these two—where there is an important Christian principle at stake—disobey the law

The Church has never regarded the civil law as the final norm for the Christian conscience: "We must obey God rather than men" (Acts 5:29). The Church has often been healthiest when it was illegal; we got our start that way as a matter of fact. To follow the apostles and martyrs in this way would be very appropriate for a Church which makes much of apostolic succession. There is really very little danger that the administration and faculty would find itself in prison; but the picture of the theological faculty behind bars, instructing the students gathered on the lawn around the county jail, is one which could inspire us to realize that the Church is not meant to "conform to this world" and could attract many now indifferent people to a church which often all too easily blends with its surroundings.

Pike's letter fell as a bombshell, creating more crags and crevices on a mountain already in need of absolution. Few could deny that Pike's letter had the authentic ring of the early church. Yet many saw it as strident, hypocritical, arrogant, and self-righteous; a man who should be trying to calm the troubled waters contributing instead to negative publicity for a school that had offered him tribute.

Gray and the St. Luke's Society viewed it as the crossing of the Rubicon. Now the whole world was watching. On behalf of the School of Theology class of '53, Gray wired Pike immediately. "Congratulations on your defense of Christ's Church. . . . Faith can move Mountains." As a light touch, and to further emphasize their delight and approval of what Pike had done, they reworded the then popular Eisenhower campaign button to "I like Pike."

Pike wrote the class a letter of appreciation but it was mysteriously delivered to the president of the Order of Gownsmen, an undergraduate organization at the time, instead of to Duncan Gray for whom it was intended. The president of the Order of Gownsmen thereupon wrote Pike that most of the undergraduate students did not agree with him.

The celebrated Pike affair and Gray's role in it led to the first feedback from any of his close relatives. Gray had, of course, as was required by canon, kept in touch with his bishop, trying not to let his reports be complicated by the fact that his bishop was also his father and a trustee.

He never concealed his feelings and involvement from his father. So that Mrs. Gray would not be constantly worried by the friction between her son and her brother, the bishop asked Gray to send all communications to his office.

A letter that disturbed Gray greatly came from a close relative, a refined lady. After some stern words about family loyalty, couched in diplomatic subtleties, she demanded to know ". . . if it is true that you sent a telegram of congratulations to Dean Pike after his recent public denunciation of your Uncle Ned."

She repeated the same arguments that had been heard on the Mountain from the beginning:

> . . . You and I know this is not really a fight for the Negro. . . . You know as well as I that no one is more anxious to see the Negroes get fair treatment than your Uncle Ned. . . . It reminds me of the Civil War when the reform became corrupted, the true cause lost, and the result a battle for political and economic dominance. . . . No Negro has been turned down, because any of the other seminaries are equipped to take them. . . . At Sewanee there is no colored population to absorb the students if they came.

She reminded Gray that he was about to be ordained, faced a brilliant future, but ". . . never forget it is the Lord's work to which you have dedicated yourself." She warned that he might one day be on the receiving end of protest. (In that she was prophetic.) She granted that as student body president Gray had been on the spot, ". . . and for that reason we have all made allowances, but it is because of our loyalty to you that we have made these allowances. Now, what about your loyalty to your Uncle Ned?"

Gray was disturbed and concerned but not surprised by the letter from someone he cared about very much. But he went on.

Spring brought talk of graduation for the class of 1953. Both Gray and his friend Davis Carter had grade point averages to graduate *optime merens* (with highest merit). In addition to receiving high grades, an *optime merens* graduate was required to write a thesis. When the two men were discussing it one night over the first Scotch whisky they had shared in a long time, they agreed that they were not going to do the extra work just to graduate with highest honors from a place in which they were taking no special pride. Ruthie jumped quickly and vigorously into the discussion. "O, yes you will, Duncan Gray. And so will you, Davis Carter. Shame on both of you."

Both men gave all the arguments against it they could think of. Ruthie wasn't accepting any of them. She did not see it as a matter of concern for them alone. The wives had worked hard also. Mary was in San Antonio working as registrar for the diocesan summer camp and Ruthie was speaking for both wives. There were the children, the families, their futures to consider. "The way you feel today may not be the way you will feel tomorrow," she scolded. "There'll come a time."

"I just want to put out the fire, call the dogs, and head for home," Carter said.

Ruthie ignored him and said, "I'll make the academic hoods. Both of them. *Optime merens* you both shall be. I'll start the hoods tomorrow. (Later, the congregation of Grace Church, Canton, presented Duncan with a ready-made hood as a gift.)

Carter looked at Gray, shrugged and said, "Guess I'm licked, Amigo."

When Gray continued to resist, arguing that he would have more time with the children and more time to get ready to leave Sewanee if he didn't write the thesis, Ruthie gave him a stern but tender look, leaned back in her chair and said, "Please do it for me and for the faculty if not for yourself." Since Gray and Carter were the only two seniors who had qualified for *optime merens*, Ruthie felt their refusal to accept the honor might reflect poorly on the faculty.

"So what are you going to write on, Blotterbrain?" Carter asked, raising his glass in playful toast. Tom Roberts had started calling Gray "Blotterbrain" because of the uncanny way he had of hearing a lecture and remembering it all.

Gray's thesis would be, "The British West Indian in Cuba: A Problem and an Opportunity for the Episcopal Church." In exacting detail he described the history and plight of the Negroes in Cuba and the Caribbean, describing the cruelty of slavery, and the quasi-emancipation that followed with horrendous heights comparable to Harriet Beecher Stowe, comparing all of it to America's history and continuing colonial stance. America's role in the land ownership, market manipulation, and starvation wages in the one-crop sugar cane economy of Cuba were described as deeply troubling manifestations of economic greed and evil. America's foreign policy was presented as depraved imperialism and an extension of her notion of Manifest Destiny. The Spanish-American War, allegedly to gain Cuba's freedom, Gray summed up by quoting President McKinley: "While we are conducting the war and until its conclusion, we must keep all we get; when the war is over, we must keep what we want."

In essence Gray's thesis was a stinging indictment of America's failure to do justly with regard to the Cuban people, especially the black Cuban people. In its day, and in this day as well, the thesis could be described as a revolutionary document. One which, if heeded, might well have led to reforms that would have prevented the Cuban-American problems of the present.

Nor did he spare the Episcopal Church's complicity in the wrongs he described. While in his own mind the suggestions he made for the church's involvement were minor and would do little to cure the ills of this poverty-stricken island, most were seen as too drastic and few were taken seriously.

Because of the Anglican background of British West Indians, Gray saw the American Episcopal Church as being the only place they could look to for any degree of social reform. Gray called for some straight social work among the sick, undernourished, and uneducated, quoting both Scripture and Lambeth Conference Encyclicals as authority. "A hospitalization fund set up . . . could do a great deal of good."

He discussed the need for clothing and shelter and spoke of the many islanders he had seen picking up scrap and waste materials from the streets or building sites to put up pitifully inadequate hovels. "With just a little financial help, even in the form of a loan on very liberal terms, these people could purchase cheap materials and build habitable houses." (A variation of that idea would become a reality many years later in the form of the laudable Habitat for Humanity program, conceived not by an Episcopalian but by a Southern Baptist.)

Gray further suggested a social service center for British West Indians in Santiago and said that if their plight were sufficiently publicized, he thought there would be people to staff it. He stressed education for an area where illiteracy was the norm.

His most passionate plea was for the Episcopal Church to lead the way by the abolishment of every appearance of segregation within the church. That, he insisted, would be the most reasonable oblation the church could offer.

"Here we have," he concluded, "an opportunity to serve in a courageous and selfless way and thereby make partial retribution to a magnificent people for the many wrongs they have suffered at the hands of their 'big brother' to the north."

Not once did his thesis refer directly to the current misdeeds of the Mountain. But even a cursory reading of his paper would indicate that wrongs at home were much on his mind. It would also account for the fervor with which he was working for the integration of the institution whose name he would soon carry. *Optime merens.*

IF THE BATTLE OF SEVEN PINES IN WHICH THE UNIVERSITY Greys participated were fought today, giant airplanes with names like C141, C17, or C5, the modern mules of troop transport, would skirt the city lights of Richmond, set down one after another onto the runways of Byrd International Airport. There the soldiers would quickly deplane in full combat gear, make their way to Beulah Road and double-quick a few miles where they would engage an enemy strung along the Chickahominy River. Or maybe there would be no ground offensive at all. Maybe computer-aimed missiles from a thousand miles away would lay waste every living creature and the occupying soldiers would simply ride in and take over.

That was not the way it was for the University Greys on the last day of May in 1862. Instead they had come on foot the seventy-five or so miles from the mouth of the York River to a flooded area near Richmond they would call Seven Pines. Instead of the matter of minutes the cargo planes would take from take-off to touch-down, it took the Greys and Johnston's troops more than three weeks of meandering up the peninsula and edging toward Richmond. One day they marched thirty-five miles, a record they would not break.

Could they have imagined that a hundred years later the campus they left in defense of slavery would be turned into a battlefield because one descendant of slavery chose to enter? On this day the University Greys were not even thinking such a thing. Moreover, many of them would have denied that slavery was a factor in their being there, holding on to more laudable notions.

Arriving at the time of a spring freshet, the Confederates fought what was really an amphibious operation. In pursuit of the bluecoats they had to slosh through mud and hip-deep water. Canon shot falling around them threw walls of water like hurricane waves flooding the soldiers and their ammunition. Forward movement was useless, even if it had been possible. In the futile effort the Eleventh lost twenty-four percent of its troops, killed or wounded.

It was a bad day for the University Greys. Just when it seemed that their young captain was blossoming into a leader, there was a cruel intrusion of fate. As Lowry tried to edge his men out of the floodwaters of the Chickahominy, he was struck from the rear by a Minié ball. Interrupted in its intended trajectory, the bullet tore through his left ear, plowed a trench through the cheek, at the same time tearing away the bottom eyelid and destroying the projecting part of his nose.

The physical part of the wound was not life threatening. The wound to his psyche, however, would never heal. After some time in a hospital at Richmond, a furlough trip to Mississippi where several surgeons tried unsuccessfully to repair the cosmetic damage, Lowry returned to the Eleventh but not to his beloved Company A. Robbed of his command, his once proud and handsome face an ugly mask, the remainder of his life would be plagued with controversy. Moreover, the ball that had spoiled his comely features also brought to an end the spirit of community that had reigned among the Greys since late 1860 when they began planning what they thought would be a romantic detour in their journey to wealth and refinement.

A few minutes after Lowry was shot, General Joseph E. Johnston was also wounded. General Robert E. Lee was selected to lead the troops. He immediately named them the Army of Northern Virginia. It was an appointment that would forever alter the course of Southern mythology, if not history itself. As for the University Greys, they would steadfastly follow the general, though he would not gain legendary status until the war was over and his failing heart took him.

They went with him into four ghastly battles during the next three months. Gaines Mill. Malvern Hill. Second Manassas. Sharpsburg, or Antietam. All little known spots on the charts of military geography that would take their place in the annals of carnage. All places where an alliance of Mississippi's most promising would fight hard, suffer, die, their number whittled but no member abased, until finally at Gettysburg, in the shadow of an academy established to pass along the Gospel story, they would, one by one and in tandem, fall until the reckon reached one hundred percent and they were no more. In the while the University Greys would follow the man on a horse named Traveler.

A more detailed accounting of all that transpired during the years of 1952–1953 at Sewanee can be found in other places. The final outcome was that the faculty did resign as they had said they would.

They went from the Mountain with their students, bequeathing the books and chalk to other hands. Gray learned from them that there were still some in Christendom prepared to make personal sacrifices for principle. Certainly the academic aspect of his seminary years contributed greatly to his future as a preacher and scholar. But nothing would influence his life as a risk-taking priest, bishop, and human being so much as that act of honor and faithfulness to what the Church taught and, yes, believed in word but did not often in deed.

Even as the graduating students were making plans to take their exams and leave the Mountain, the trustees were preparing to reverse themselves and instruct the university to consider applicants to the School of Theology on the basis of merit alone. But it all came too late to stop the faculty from resigning. It was a small step, but at least it was a step. That was a buttressing for Gray of something that had begun for him in Santiago de Cuba: prayers are not reserved for faldstools of piety, but might be as well the screams of the oppressed. Also, that the Ordinary can be held to account by the minions, and the lance of justice seldom prevails without a hefty thrust from those outraged by inequity; that some things are just not right and that one's true freedom is found in liberation of the captives.

Gray was not alone with his burden as he marched in solemn assembly down the aisle of All Saint's Chapel on commencement day, June 7, 1953. The night before, Hodding Carter Jr. had addressed the alumni association. Carter, the progressive editor of a Greenville, Mississippi, newspaper, had written scathing editorials about the trustees' refusal to admit Negroes to the university. And, he mistakenly assumed that his good friend Ned McCrady, with whom he had grown up in Hammond, Louisiana, was heroically battling the board in the dark silo of bigotry, penned an article of praise for him in the *Saturday Evening Post.*

Ahead of Gray was the faculty, the intimacy of resignations weighing heavily beneath their florid cloaks of much learning. The chaos had vanished, at least for this hour of Latin rule.

Following the president of the Order of Gownsmen, who held aloft the mace, was Vice-Chancellor and President Edward McCrady. This was his first commencement as head of the University of the South. It had been a rough year. In the solemn procession, the mace, the symbol of authority, designed like the medieval war club used to crush armor, seemed to speak a language of its own. Part defiantly triumphant, part an announcement of comity, issue perhaps of the ark of the covenant that preceded Israel's journey in the wilderness, that in the conquest opened the Jordan River and brought down the walls of Jericho: "Arise, O Lord, and let thy enemies be scattered."

Had this commencement been a few years later there would have been a small Confederate flag on the mace and this inscription: "To the glory of God and the memory of General Nathan Bedford Forrest." That bequest would come later, ironically after the battle over racism was assumed settled. Just as well that it wasn't there for these harbingers of good news to follow behind. That might have been the straw that turned Gray back. For although General Forrest denounced the Ku Klux Klan after organizing it in a town about seventy-five miles from Sewanee, after he saw the spider's silk becoming a web of depravity, his name was still associated with the Klan in the minds of the black people Duncan Gray would continue to champion.

"Frankincense and myrrh," someone whispered as the mace was put in place and the ceremony was beginning.

There were four other Mississippians in the procession that day. They had all supported Gray as president of St. Luke's Society. Elmer Boykin was on his way to Belzoni and Lexington; one town in the Delta, the other on the edge of the Loess Bluffs. Hal Crisler, perhaps the most politically radical of the five at the time, had been assigned to Indianola and a mission in Inverness. There he would be physically attacked during the recessional one Sunday morning by a prominent planter and parishioner, angry over the morning sermon on race. The young priest, a former boxer, simply overpowered his attacker who was attempting to rip the vestments off the priest's body, continued to the church door, and took his place to greet the worshippers as they left. His liberalism later waned when he vehemently disagreed with Gray on the ordination of women as priests, saying one life could absorb only so many controversies. Peyton Splane went to Bolton and Bovina; Mike Engle to Grace Church, Canton, mother church of the Grays and McCradys. Engle would later break altogether with Gray, when he was bishop, over the revision of the *Prayer Book* and ordination of women.

Others scattered throughout the South, all to face the issue of race wherever they landed. Austin Ford, denied ordination by his canonical bishop who said his diocese had no room for insurrectionists, was salvaged by the death of the bishop and soon after graduation was accepted in Atlanta where to this day he works among the downtrodden. Davis Carter would go to Brady, Llano, and San Saba, Texas. Ed Coleman went first to Bunkie, Louisiana, later to Charleston, South Carolina, where he had as parishioners the fiery segregationist journalist Tom Waring and his liberal nephew, the heroic U.S. Judge J. Waties Waring, whose decisions on implementing *Brown* v. *Board* led to virtually total ostracism by his own people and at whose funeral there would be only a handful of whites and hundreds of blacks to mark and mourn his passing. That occasion, with the Reverend Edwin C. Coleman presiding, would be filmed for national television by Charles Kuralt.

Such was the class of 1953.

What happened that year had been a training ground for the ministry that lay in store for Duncan and Ruth Gray. And for them all. During the years to come they would see the same tactics, the same secret evasions of mind, diversions, equivocations, scapegoating, rationalizations, and sometimes outright lies used time and time again. All of it having to do with the church's and the nation's tardiness in confronting its untidy past. *Race.*

Gray drove down the Mountain in June 1953, heading back to Mississippi for good. Two months earlier, on April 8, he had been ordained deacon by his bishop and father, the Right Reverend Duncan Montgomery Gray Sr., in Grace Church, Canton. The ordination sermon was preached by his friend and mentor, Robert McNair, a choice met with palpable disapproval by many who had followed the saga of St. Luke's. Ironically, the first sermon ever preached in Grace Church, Canton, had been by "the fighting Bishop," Leonidas Polk.

Duncan was now a full-fledged clergyman in the Diocese of Mississippi, on his way to his first assignment: the Delta towns of Cleveland and Rosedale. He would soon receive an inquiry about joining the Episcopal chaplain's staff at Yale University. He did not pursue it. Gray was going home. Mississippi. Home for a radical integrationist. At a time when the subject of race would rage as it had not for a hundred years; rage that would make the conflict on the Mountain appear a modest intrusion on civility. But yes, Duncan Gray, a young intellectual with many other options, was going home.

As he edged the car pulling a rented trailer down the same steep slope that had brought them here almost three years earlier, he vowed that he would never, ever come back to this place. (That, too, would one day change. When it did, it would be Ruth Spivey Gray who would choreograph the dance.) Gray remembered the evening they had arrived at Woodland; the drenching entry to the world of theological tutelage. Perhaps an omen. Now the early morning fog had lifted and the sun made long wobbly shadows on killdeer spindlelegs as they skimmed along the moist, recently planted ridges, gaining uncertain altitude, searching for a nesting place. What did this scene portend?

As the car reached the bottom of the Mountain and gained highway speed on level ground, Ruthie busied herself getting the children settled in the back seat. Duncan Montgomery Gray Jr., B.D., UNIVERSITAS MERIDIANA, OPTIME MERENS, 1953, tried hard not to look back through the rear view mirror at the Mountain disappearing behind him. Not quite succeeding.

He was heavy of heart. Not over where he was going, for what that would yield he knew but little. Over what he was leaving. That he knew well. He felt that he had fought the good fight. He was, however, still troubled. Like a man provoked by an implausible dream. Perhaps the only word was anger. Young Dunc, as the family called him, taught from infancy to subdue such emotions, was angry. Not bitter, for bitterness was not of his temperament. But angry. And sad. He knew that he had been well-trained for a life as priest. Studying under so able a faculty, coupled with the soul-altering summer in Cuba, and finally front-line duty as student body president during this critical period in the University of the South's history had been training few candidates for Holy Orders would ever have. Still, the unpalatable past would not leave him. He remembered the faculty as the class of '53 presented each one with an engraved St. Luke's cross, to wear or secrete in bottom drawers of doleful memories; the destined passion of their eyes, looking of overloaded time, eyes wistfully pleading for tenured brotherhood. He recalled their somber benedictions; the deep saddening embraces as each professor bade him good-bye.

The eight faculty men were even then scattering, as the students were scattering, as if by some tasteless rite of separation. But not scattering in the South. From Chicago to New Haven to Great Britain. As it had done times before, the South was losing some of its finest. "A mountain trove rejected," Gray sighed to himself. Many of the remaining seminarians were transferring to other schools. The community spirit he and Ruthie had found when they arrived three years earlier was in shambles.

And yet, Duncan Gray was leaving with a degree of hope. There had been a rung of victory. Although the faculty he had known and loved was gone, the protests of faculty and students had not been in vain. The trustees had reversed their stand. There was something else to celebrate, he thought: grace abounds. He tried then to think only of the good things the three years had known. There were the friends he had made, those soon to be ordered priest as he would be, who would continue steadfast in the battles that lay ahead. Still, though he knew he must forgive, he could not find it in his heart to forget what the Mountain had done.

"I'll never come back."

He remembered the night he had sipped tea in Fulford Hall and told Uncle Ned that he trusted and loved him, and the feeling of renewal he felt on his walk back to the barracks of Woodland. Remembering helped him to banish negative thoughts. The inherent joy of life itself was welling anew. Suddenly the future looked brighter.

Forty-three years later I asked him directly to identify the bottom line, the one thing he would cite after all the incidentals and extraneous were dealt with, the lath and plaster wiped clean, what caused the upskuttle on the Mountain? What precisely was the issue? He answered without hesitation. "Race prejudice."

Then I said, "I must ask you now a difficult question. After all institutional responsibilities, job descriptions, allegiance and sense of place, duties of a presiding official have been dealt with, and all refinement, gentle manners and good breeding have been considered, where exactly did your uncle stand on the basic issue?"

He smiled, dropped his head, and I thought he wasn't going to answer. But he did. Distinctly and forthrightly. "Neither the vice-chancellor nor Uncle Ned wanted Negroes at the University of the South in 1953." He was still speaking as if Dr. Edward McCrady were two people.

I was uneasy pressing him further but went on. "Why?"

This time he laughed aloud, the way he would do when I asked a foolish question.

"They just didn't want it." He laughed again. Politely now. And I thought a bit sadly.

I started to thank him and say good-bye, but saw he wasn't through. "And sixteen years later neither the vice-chancellor nor Uncle Ned wanted women as students at the University of the South."

He followed as I started for my car. "But Doctor McCrady was a superb vice-chancellor and president of the University of the South." He was speaking hurriedly now, each word ringing with sincerity and seeming gratitude. "He accomplished a lot in his twenty years at the helm. When the decisions were made, he shook the Mountain to carry them out."

"I have heard that from many quarters," I answered.

"And my Uncle Ned was a good man. He was a dedicated churchman and outstanding scholar. A very fine man. I have learned at least one thing over the years. None of us is ever right about everything." By then Duncan Montgomery Gray Jr. was himself chancellor of the University of the South. And retired bishop of the Diocese of Mississippi. He seemed anxious to continue. He talked for a long time about his Uncle Ned, how, at Ruth's insistence, they had returned to the Mountain in the summer of 1960, visited the McCradys, and showed the Gray children the beautiful scenery and all the former haunts of their parents. After Gray became a bishop in 1974, and automatically a trustee, the family visited often and there were many happy visits with Dr. and Mrs. McCrady. Although retired, McCrady was still vigorous and active as he hiked with the Grays over property when they were searching for a place on the Mountain to build a house, pointing out the variety of trees, native flowers, and wild life. Gray talked also of relatives who had written him hostile letters, their subsequent reconciliation, his parents, and his children. And about Ruth. I had learned that when he spoke most reverentially and affectionately of his wife he said Ruth, instead of the more informal *Ruthie* that everyone else used. At first I had not understood why he did that. I had not perceived the depth and seriousness, truth and beauty with which he beheld her. He talked a lot now about Ruth. None of it related to the questions I had posed. Then he came back to my agenda.

"Yeah, Uncle Ned and I were all right. I visited his hospital room just before he died. And attended his funeral at Sewanee. After the service the relatives came to our house for dinner; a sad, yet joyful family celebration. Uncle Ned and I were all right." Now it was as if any reality of vice-chancellor and president of the University of the South had vanished forever from Gray's mind. It had become clear to me that in the 1950s these two men, one young, the other in mid-life, were so far apart in their thinking on race I was amazed that they were able to communicate at all on the subject. Perhaps that they could is a tribute to both. And maybe they could do so because Duncan Gray could see Uncle Ned as kinsman, and Dr. Edward McCrady as vice-chancellor and president of the University of the South. Whatever, now Edward McCrady was one person. The same person Young Dunc had come to know as a lad when the family gathered at Oxford when his grandfather, Edward McCrady the elder, was rector of St. Peter's Church and professor of philosophy at the University of Mississippi. The same person who, a few years later, took the teenage Duncan on his first spelunking outings in the caves underneath Morgan's Steep. The one of whom he spoke now was Uncle Ned.

There was another long pause, neither of us saying anything. Then, not a pause. A rare hesitation. A search. Like a painter studying a portrait for one needed, one last touch of the brush. A postscript. Finally, "We were related by blood. And by Faith."

Chapter Four

RENDER TO NO ONE
EVIL FOR EVIL

In Cleveland the Gray family moved into a new rectory. Until recently the rector had lived in Rosedale. It had been the larger of the two congregations. What was to become Duncan's signature benediction was not yet full grown but had been evolving since April 8, 1953, when he was ordained by his father as an Episcopal deacon in Grace Church, Canton, Mississippi. A few months later, on October 28, because the diocese was in need of clergy, he was ordained priest at St. Andrew's Church in Jackson.

By 1953, like so many river towns, Rosedale was declining and the inland town of Cleveland was attracting industry and growing; the rectory was located there. It was a modest but ample frame structure next to the church. There were two bedrooms, but with Duncan III four years old and Anne a year and a half, the dining room was converted into a third bedroom. Compared to the little Woodland apartment where they had lived for three years, the house in Cleveland was commodious.

The Delta was reminiscent of the Gershwin and Heyward *Porgy and Bess* folk opera. Summertime and the living was easy. Fish were jumping and the cotton was high. Gray knew nothing of cotton but loved to fish. Ruthie grew up in a small town and liked the atmosphere. The children enjoyed the unstinted attention from parishioners and neighbors.

Grace Church, Rosedale, was the oldest existing church of any denomination in Bolivar County, having been organized in 1879, more than forty years before there was an Episcopal Church in Cleveland.

Rosedale was the more colorful of the two towns historically. For many years it had been famous as a river town. Minstrel shows came year round. "Rabbit Foot," and "Silas Green" from New Orleans, bringing with them such people as Bessie Smith singing her Delta-flavored "Backwater Blues" and the legendary blues genius, Robert Johnson. Gamblers from riverboats, prostitutes, and a ready supply of illegal liquor made it a popular attraction for many.

A noted folk hero of the time was Perry Martin. He was remembered for years for killing five men at one time while protecting floating timbers and for the ensuing jurisdiction dispute between Arkansas and Mississippi when it could not be determined precisely which was the closest shore when the crime was committed. He chose to turn himself in on the Mississippi side, was tried, and went free. He was best known as one of the nation's most successful moonshiners during national prohibition and Mississippi's long dry era that followed. The P. M. whiskey label could be found from New Orleans to Chicago and New York. At Mississippi gubernatorial inaugurations he would be furnished state highway patrol escorts to deliver kegs of P. M. whiskey to inaugural balls, sometimes for governors who had run as staunch prohibitionists. When Martin died in 1968 at ninety-one, he had just run his last batch, the first run in a new still. The still was solid copper with silver welding. Martin was discreet in his dealings with the law and prudent in his craft. The only lead any man would suffer from his hand was from the barrel of his pistol, never from the barrels of his still. An occasional bottle with the P. M. label can yet be found in the cellars of connoisseurs and on the shelves of collectors.

Rosedale's reputation as an untamed town was not the reason it had a special place in Duncan Gray's heart. It was his father's first assignment. And four of the five McCrady sisters, including Gray's mother, had met their husbands there. His mother, Isabel McCrady, visiting sisters Mary and Martha, who were schoolteachers in Rosedale, had met Duncan Montgomery Gray Sr. there when he was a summer intern from seminary. Aunt Sabina, also visiting her sisters, met a successful construction contractor named Raymond Pierce, who had bid on a project in the Delta. The school-teaching sisters also found husbands and moved on. Such was the way things happened in those days. Such was Delta society.

Gray looked forward to being there. Though he had absorbed the age-old myths of Sewanee, loved the romps through ancient forests with buoyant colors of fall or frozen winter mist on mountain evergreens, he anticipated the flat sameness of Delta acreage as deliverance. It would be a short honeymoon, but nescience of the future is the greatest gift of the present.

Except for vacations and short visits, Duncan had not lived in Mississippi since leaving for Tulane University in 1944. Ruthie spent her university years in the state but left when they were married in early 1948. Now they were back, reliving old memories and looking forward to a relaxed life in a pastoral setting. Not far down Highway 61 was the Vicksburg church camp where fifteen-year old Duncan Montgomery Gray Jr. had met a quick-witted and resplendent young woman named Ruth Miller Spivey. Seven years later they were married in Grace Church, Canton, also not far away. Nor was Greenwood, where Gray spent his formative years and where he was living when he met the indelible Ruthie Spivey. Columbus, where Gray attended the first eight years of school and where he was confirmed, was on the far east side of the state, but a few hours on U.S. Highway 82 could get him there. Thoughts of Columbus provided a nostalgia feast for Gray. His teenage church camp director, the Reverend Cecil Jones, now his priestly colleague, was there. At camp, the courtship of Duncan Gray and Ruth Spivey grew to maturity under the watchful eyes of Cecil Jones. Gray had been introduced to the history and romance of the little city at an early age and he had fond memories of his years at the demonstration school of Mississippi State College for Women, the first state-supported institution of higher learning for women chartered in the nation. Local folklore insists that Decoration Day—the national holiday now known as Memorial Day— began in the Columbus Friendship Cemetery. That is questioned in some circles, but Gray grew up believing that in 1866 a small group of women, some of them recent war widows, met in a home called *Twelve Gables* to discuss a way to honor the Confederate dead. The decision was to take flowers from their gardens and place them on the graves. There was not a major battle nearby but Columbus was known as a hospital town. Both Confederates and Unionists were buried in Friendship Cemetery. While decorating Confederate graves, one of the gentle ladies said, "As long as we're here we might as well put flowers on the Union graves also." So they did. The story made the rounds to other cities and what they called *Decoration Day* emerged into the national Memorial Day. At first I thought the story apocryphal. Further research led me to accept it as fact, as Duncan Gray accepted it. And who's to say for sure.

Something that no one questions is that the Reverend Walter Dakin was priest of St. Paul's Church from 1905–1913 and while there lived in the same rectory that the elder Grays moved into when Duncan Jr. was three years old. Dakin's grandson, Thomas Lanier Williams, lived there also. By the time Duncan Gray Jr. moved to the Delta in 1953, Thomas Lanier Williams had become one of America's foremost playwrights, Tennessee Williams. All in all, whether stories were apocryphal or factual to a fault, Mississippi was a good place for the Grays to be in 1953. Or was until the dike that had held racial injustices in tow for centuries spilled over, and the anger and hurt of black Americans erupted in fierce determination to join the mainstream and claim their birthright, bringing with it immeasurable resistance from the status quo.

Gray had been known for his laughter since he was a small boy. Even during the feverish months at Sewanee, those who were with him remember that he laughed a lot. In the Delta, Duncan and Ruthie were able to laugh at things that were not funny at the time they happened. In late January of 1948, two weeks before they were to be married, the Spivey house was reduced to ashes, taking with it the trousseau of the soon-to-be bride. Two days after the wedding their car was burglarized in Birmingham and most of the clothes she had bought after the fire were taken. Not funny at all. Now they could laugh about it all, along with laughing again at the scorpions of Woodland. Ruthie reveled in her husband's joy.

It was as if their childhood ended when they reached the Delta. They were all grown up now. The old had passed away. The new had come. They began to feel they had never left Mississippi at all. Even the anger and hurt of the battles of the Mountain seemed to melt away. All that was past and had been part of the testing.

Throughout college and the three years with Westinghouse, Gray had tangled with the deep feeling that the priesthood was his true vocation. Although he was a deacon when they arrived in Cleveland, not yet entitled to administer Holy Communion, that would change in October when he became a full-fledged priest. Then he would stand where his father had stood, saying the words his father had said:

> The blood of our Lord Jesus Christ, which was shed for thee, preserve thy body and soul unto everlasting life,
>
> Drink this in remembrance that Christ's Blood was shed for thee, and be thankful.

In addition to his duties at the churches in Cleveland and Rosedale, he was also chaplain to Episcopal students at Delta State University in Cleveland.

Rabid segregationists among Episcopal clergy of the Mississippi Diocese were rare in 1954, although there were exceptions. Discretion when it came to harmony within the parish was a different matter. Although all of the priests had been nurtured by ethicists and theologians in college and seminary and were familiar with the moral ambiguities and contradictions of Old South ways, few were willing to risk disruption within the fellowship by openly challenging the status quo. "I'm a shepherd," said one. "Not a rodeo rider."

Not so the youthful engineer-turned-priest of Bolivar County. In June of 1954, three weeks after the U.S. Supreme Court ruled in *Brown* v. *Board* that public school segregation was unconstitutional, Gray was about to return to the ship of controversy. He had been out of seminary for just over one year. The issue would be the same as the one at the University of the South. The same as what had taken the University Greys from the University of Mississippi in 1861.

The Reverend Mr. Gray was one of four clergy and lay members that comprised the department of Christian social relations of the Episcopal Diocese of Mississippi. It was a little known department seldom heard from until then. That was about to change. The Reverend Duncan Hobart, rector of St. Paul's Church, Meridian, was chairman. Gray wrote Hobart and suggested that the diocese must take a stand on school desegregation. Both men had preached sermons in support of the court's decision the Sunday after what was already being called *Black Monday* in Mississippi. Meridian, a railroad town with more diversity and latitude for change at the time, gave tolerable acceptance to Hobart's views. Gray, in the heart of Delta country, saw immediately that he had poked a wasps' nest. To him it made no difference. A priest must poke the nest near at hand.

On June 4, 1954, Hobart sent a letter to the members of his department calling a meeting for June 30 at Camp Bratton-Green that by then had been moved to Rose Hill. In addition to Gray, the members were Mrs. Elizabeth Noble of Starkville, representing what was then called *the Women's Auxiliary*, and Mr. James L. Raspberry, a teacher of vocational arts at Okolona College, a small college for Negroes with close ties to the Episcopal Church. Raspberry, now deceased, was the father of the now distinguished columnist, William Raspberry. Mrs. Noble was the wife of "Dudy" Noble, then athletic director at Mississippi State University and the man for whom the baseball field was later named.

With dilated optimism Hobart stated in his convening letter that the one item on the agenda would be a discussion of what they could do "as we move toward complete compliance with the Supreme Court?" It would be eight years before there would be even a piddling beginning. And when that time came, the youngest member of their foursome would face the threat of death at the hands of a mob, all of whom claimed allegiance to the same God as he. Three years later, the school James Raspberry had served for more than fifty years would be closed, partly as a casualty of *Brown* v. *Board,* for among the effects of that decision was the rendering of such schools as inviable in what was beginning to be called a new day in the nation's higher education.

The first meeting at Rose Hill was little more than the sharing of ideas. Hobart felt that they should act quickly lest integration in the state's public schools soon be a *fait accompli* and the Church be in the embarrassed position of being once again last to speak.

The methodical and less quixotic mind of the former Westinghouse engineer had no such illusion. Still, it had been almost two months since the pronouncement of Caesar, and the church of Mississippi had said nothing. Gray's impatience focused on getting the current flowing from the turbine, ". . . as unto a light that shineth in a dark place."

Raspberry, the only Negro present, had experienced white talk of justice before. He participated in the discussion but was not overly sanguine about the immediate future. Possibly as a subtle and facetious challenge he reported that a fellow communicant at St. Bernard's Church, Okolona, upon hearing that Mr. Raspberry was on a committee to produce a document called "The Church Considers the Supreme Court Decision," had said, "The Church will consider it all right. And then table it." Tabling, however, was not on the agenda of any member of the department. Least of all, Duncan Gray.

Perhaps Mrs. Noble pondered the rampant exclusions of her sisters within the church, not segregated but relegated; assigned to humble rank. No matter their color. There would be no change in that for another twenty-two years for that was when the first woman was ordained priest. But for the while, Noble gave her best thoughts to the issue at hand, the implementation of a secular power's decree.

There was no question as to who would write the document. So on July 1, 1954, when the committee met again in Calvary Church, Cleveland, Gray had his document ready for their approval.

At twenty-eight he was the youngest cleric in the diocese. He had been a priest for eight months. Calvary Church had seventy-four communicants; Rosedale fewer than three dozen. One Baptist congregation alone in Cleveland had more than fifteen hundred members. United States

Senator James O. Eastland, the Goliath of segregationist politics, lived fifteen miles away. Daily, his fierce wild billows filled the U.S. Senate chambers with boasts that the Supreme Court decision was null and void and did not have to be obeyed. Walter Sillers, crafty white supremacist, prominent planter, attorney, and speaker of the Mississippi House of Representatives, was considered the most powerful figure of twentieth-century Mississippi politics. His home was Rosedale. The ghost of McCarthyism still stalked and intimidated, seeing communism ever lurking nearby, especially in matters of racial change. Preachers of every declension either remained silent or beat the drum of America as God's elect. Gray knew that he was operating from a base of neither political nor ecclesiastical power. Yet he knew the potential of the turbine; knew the promises. So like little David of biblical lore, he was not dissuaded. With no waving banners, hark nor hail to call attention to his stand, nor bushel to hide its light, he put pen to paper with words that would challenge and scorch the conscience of those who had ears to hear.

Only the exigencies of history would draw Gray back into the controversy of race so quickly. Although he had strong feelings about the sin of racial inequality, he had not chosen to be a crusader. While his theological growth had been heavily influenced by the neoorthodoxy of Reinhold Niebuhr and Howard Johnson, professor of theology at Sewanee, along with such existentialist writers as Kierkegaard, as well as Karl Barth and Emil Brunner, by temperament he would have been pleased to lean more toward the priestly than the prophetic role of ministry. And he never neglected the priestly, shepherding role, perhaps accounting for his vocational longevity and physical survival in a part of the nation that, throughout his tenure, seethed with hostility and racial brokenness. No one ever questioned that he was a good pastor to his flock and his community.

A mentor for Gray from within the Anglican tradition was William Temple, who in addition to being archbishop of Canterbury for a brief period was best known for his contribution to the ecumenical movement and his interest in social order. Across the broad spectrum of Christian theology, the Reverend Duncan Gray would see himself as conservative. But conservative in the sense that he understood Jesus as treating the social and spiritual needs of persons as one category. Not conservative in the sense of narrowness. In a just world he would have been content with administering the sacraments, ministering to the sheep as need indicated, pursuing his academic interests, leading the quiet life of a small-town scholarly parson. None of those things would be neglected. But that would never be the way his world viewed him. Not the height of the Mountain. Not the sea-level Delta.

The manner in which others might rate him on the theological scale was not Gray's concern that day when the group convened to respond to the historic decree of *Brown* v. *Board of Education*. The document he had prepared for their consideration had flowed from the depth of his being, with no thought of external influences.

Ruthie Gray, heavy with child, served the group a light lunch. Delta-grown sweet corn, green peas, fresh tomatoes, and fruit jello is her recollection. Perhaps a glass of beer, though she thinks it was iced tea. Despite what some saw as other excesses, particularly in pressing for social change, Gray was a moderate user of alcohol, although as the years went by his friends remember that he seldom declined a hefty Scotch when the work of the day was over. That, too, was always in the bounds of moderation. Moderation, though, was reserved for things of the body, not matters of the spirit.

For this meeting, the bishop (Gray's father), Duncan Montgomery Gray Sr., was present. He was fifty-six years old. A big man with an imposing presence and deep, gruff voice, the elder Gray came across to many as the quintessential Victorian father. Children were sometimes frightened by his brusque exterior and mask-like facial features. One of his priests affectionately said that when the bishop entered a room he reminded him of a big-mouth bass grinning from a glass tank. But, underneath the rough-hewn countenance, he was a soft-hearted, often humorous patrician who was known to tear over at the whimper of a child. On this occasion he was not opposed to what the four were about, but he knew that his firstborn child was about to embark on a perilous mission. He was not surprised by the zeal of his only son, now one of his priests. It was what he had taught him to be. He had seen his unwavering witness at Sewanee the year before when young Duncan went head to head with his blood kin over this same issue. Yet Sewanee, despite the befitting appellative, University of the South, with its halls of ivy, the residue of English Lords and Ladies, mountainous grounds that bespeak serenity, and its pride in being a seedbed of patrician values, was a long way from the raw, naked passion boiling over the hills and flatlands of Mississippi in mid–1954. Since May 17, when the court ruled as it did in the Brown case, sidewalk talk in Mississippi had been of little else. The bishop's journal for that day made no mention of that decision. He had been to Ocean Springs and Biloxi for a confirmation with the Reverend Edward A. DeMiller on Sunday. His entry for the next day, the May 17

126

that would be known in Mississippi for years as Black Monday, reads: "Met Mrs. DeMiller in Gulfport and she was my good companion to Jackson for a visit with her son, Edward A. DeMiller Jr."

The political and social unrest generated by the court's decision would almost match that of a hundred years earlier when the institution of slavery was being threatened. States' rights, interposition, nullification, massive resistance, amalgamation, and miscegenation became household words and topics of barbershop conversation. In a region where only a very small minority of those called *Negro* did not have one or more white forebears, as well as many whites who back there somewhere had dark-skinned cousinage, dread of miscegenation approximated the comical. Everyone knew that race mixing began with the slave trade and continued to that day. While everyone knew it, it was seldom a matter of discussion.

The bishop had cause to fear for the life and welfare of his only son. For the first time in his years as priest and prelate, the cross must have loomed as more than an icon.

During the morning session the bishop dropped personal and ecclesiastical caveats; befitting caution, demurrals couched in pragmatism. Perhaps they should hold a finger to the wind for, after all, the Episcopal Church consisted of less than one percent of the Mississippi citizenry. The bishop was not blind to the evil of Mississippi's racial system. But he also knew that inherent in his office was the survival of the institution and the keeping of relative peace within the household. His discretion, however, was not seen by the members of the department of Christian social relations as contention and they were not swayed by it, feeling that in his heart he was of them and with them.

During a long walk after lunch, alone, the bishop reflected on what was happening. And what could and might happen. To his beloved church. To his only son. He recalled the occasion of the lad's baptism that seemed so soon ago. No need for his *Book of Common Prayer* to recall the vows taken.

Dost thou, in the name of this child, renounce the devil and all his works, the vain pomp and glory of the world . . . ?

The answer came back to him, like an echo. Across crib, school days, chancel rails, altars, steeples, and the years:

I renounce them all; and by God's help, will endeavour not to follow, nor be led by them.

The bishop knew well the fanatic tenor and intrinsic perils of that answer. Knew precisely where such renunciation would take any man or woman in twentieth-century America who took it literally instead of as the perfunctory rite it had become. Baptism: a time for celebration and good times. Not a day of wailing and gnashing of teeth because kin and sponsors were vowing a life of rejection and tribulation for a little darling baby. Still . . .

I renounce them all.

The bishop knew further that the chicanery, the volcanic eruptions spewing from newspapers, pulpits, and politicians, the blatantly racist rhetoric blanketing Dixie like the waist-high cotton plants covering the alluvial acres through which he at that moment was walking were of satan's power. Of vain pomp and glory, he knew as well; knew that it was vainglory that fed the diatribes shouted from virtually every white quarter; knew that vainglory was the cardinal sin.

But it was daddy thoughts that troubled him now. Not musings of postulate, deacon, priest, nor bishop. Plain, calculated, idolatrous, daddy thoughts.

I am this boy's daddy. If he takes this bold stand he will be the most hated white man in the state. My boy is in danger. A bear feeling the magnet of his lair. Like watching the bus that pulls out of the station taking your child so young to war. Or the nagging pride the first time he rides his bike to school through incautious traffic.

He remembered, too, the words of confirmation, and the many times he had laid hands upon those who had been baptized, and come then to years of discretion. He felt again his heavy hands pressed down hard upon the heads of confirmands, as if to let every drop of grace within his own self drain into the being of those kneeling before him.

Do ye promise to follow Jesus Christ as your Lord and Saviour?

And the *Prayer Book* instructs that every one shall answer:

I do.

But this was not the rehearsed recitation of pubescent aspirants of first communion. This was big folk testing time; assaying of the bold promise to follow Jesus, the seditious criminal. As Lord. In all things. Wherever He led. First Commandment absurdity; the most radical of all the commandments. *Thou shalt have no other gods before me.*

128

This was not the platitudinous slogan, *Jesus Saves*, with which bumper stickers and highway billboards in Bible Belt Mississippi were rife. *Jesus Saves* exacts no sacrifice from the beneficiary. It is passive. The pledge "to follow Jesus Christ as Lord and Saviour" is active; a far more awesome matter. Lord denotes ownership. No "God is my co-pilot" melodrama. The confirmand is promising that Jesus Christ will be commander, head, master, and monarch. Who could possibly be serious in taking such a vow?

The fanatical demands of the question and the self-negating dimensions of the prescribed answer struck the bishop as perhaps never before. Could he ever in conscience ask it again? Certainly never again would it be mechanical. The covenant must be spelled out; the certain upshot perceived.

He knew that an unreserved commitment to that answer by every person in Mississippi marked with the sign of the cross would change the state's racial climate in a fortnight. He supposed that even the less than one percent of the populace under his numinous care could be a leavening agent that would alter the body politic forever. Such is the promise. Absolute commitment, unblemished discipleship is that revolutionary. It was not to be. Instead, the bishop's sheep were part of the lump to be leavened.

Making his way back to the rectory, hearing the hum of bees, seeing the constant flitting of leafhoppers, like the frenzy of the citizenry, feeling the air brushing his face like the soft touch of feathers, he pondered the fugacity of life's span, wondered why something so rudimentary as pigmentation could wrack the soul of creation with life so brief.

Taking a shortcut across a hay field freshly mowed, he noted the smell of death; molding grass stems left for the rain to turn to dust. The stubble crunched beneath his heavy steps, reminding him of warnings of Isaiah:

> It is He that sitteth upon the circle of the earth, and the inhabitants
> thereof are as grasshoppers . . . That bringeth the princes to nothing
> . . . He bloweth upon them and they wither, and the whirlwind
> taketh them away as stubble.

As he wondered if he recalled the passage aright he saw scores of black workers, some following mule-drawn equipment, some on front porches of tenant houses readying the long canvas sacks still used for picking cotton—the mechanized cotton pickers that would later displace them being few in 1954. Negro women hurried from big houses where they had cooked and cleaned to little houses where they would cook and clean again, this time for their own families. Their houses were owned by those who also owned the land. They were generally unpainted. Most had chinaberry trees that shed little nut-like berries good for nothing at all. There were the crepe myrtle bushes with their profuse red blossoms that would last until late fall. Laying hens, some with sorehead the locals thought was caused by pecking in watermelon rinds but was most likely from a diet deficiency, fluttering their mite-ridden feathers in beds of dust. Most front porches had barrel-shaped washing machines with roller wringers that had to be turned with a crank. And the inevitable porcelain or enameled night jars. Behind each cabin was a summer garden and a pen with several nearly grown hogs. Bishop Gray remembered the stories of how many slaves were allowed to raise vegetables and sometimes hogs and cattle that they sold, saving to buy their freedom or the freedom of their wives or children. He wondered if slavery would have eventually ended by those owned simply buying themselves and starting new lives. If that had happened there would have been no war and he would be back in his office in Jackson instead of in the heat of the Delta. No, it would never have happened that way. They were owned, there was a war, they are still virtually owned, and we have to do what we are doing.

All flesh is grass and we are all here dying together.

No matter the hue of exterior, and no matter the trophies on den walls or pennants of homage fluttering from flagpoles, death's shroud will cover us all with equalizing benediction. Still and yet, as they prophesied that day in Cleveland, Mississippi, there were white people, and there were black people. Not equal in benefits.

The bishop recalled that in 1860 Bishop William Mercer Green, a man separated from himself by only three in the succession of diocesan bishops, had confirmed twenty-seven black converts at St. Alban's Church, Bovina, Mississippi, at one time. And on Easter eve of 1861, twelve days before Fort Sumter was fired upon, fifty-four slaves from one plantation were confirmed, again at St. Alban's. As the department of Christian social relations deliberated on that July day in 1954, a young man who would follow Bishop Gray in the same numerical apostolic lineage as he had followed Bishop Green (three), was the paid sexton of St. Alban's. Bishop Alfred C. Marble was an eighteen-year-old lad preparing to go to the University of Mississippi. It could not be said that

130

the elder Gray's son was plowing new ground in his concern for black souls. He was in glorious company, going back more than a hundred years to Bishop Mercer Green. In 1854, at the now extinct parish of St. John's near what is presently Glen Allen, not more than fifty miles from where the four members of the department of Christian social relations were meeting, there were "more than 1200 colored persons" receiving religious instruction in preparation for confirmation. Twelve hundred. When, in the summer of 1954, these four pondered over another aspect of the long journey from slavery to equality of black human beings there were only 404 Negro Episcopalians in the entire diocese.

Where had they gone? Some of the balconies where slaves were seated after confirmation remained. No doubt, in part, the balconies led to the diaspora. The fact that in 1954 the three missions where all the Negro communicants attended had "c," for colored, following their names attests to their continued exclusion. Many followed the star to Chicago and Detroit City. Some, over the years, turned westward. Los Angeles, Portland, or Seattle.

On Wednesday, January 9, 1861, when Mississippi became the second state to secede from the union, Bishop Green heard the deafening applause from grave and dignified men, witnessed the wild tumult as an immense blue silk banner with a single white star was carried through the crowd outside the state house. He immediately wrote all of his priests that they were to change the wording in the *Prayer Book*, substituting "governor of the state" for "president of the United States," and in the prayer for Congress they were to say "this state" instead of "these United States."

A meeting convened in 1883 by the same bishop that had evangelized so fervently among Negroes a few decades earlier says much about the departure of black communicants. The national Church was petitioned by Bishop Green to establish a diocese for Negroes that would extend over all the states. The petition was denied by the general convention. Apparently for some, Christian charity and concern for souls came more easily with ownership than with freedom. Bishop Green, lamenting on the difficulty of ministering to the freed slaves, said, ". . . their imposed freedom has already reduced them to poverty and suffering," but added, "that many of them are beginning to find their best advisers and protectors in their former masters; and are also gradually returning to the altars of the Church." It was all part of the principalities and powers the young cleric Duncan M. Gray Jr. had to wrestle with in 1954. Sins of the fathers . . . sour grapes eaten . . . teeth set on edge.

The returning anticipated by Bishop Green did not happen. An explanation most often heard for the drastic reduction in Negro Episcopalians over the past century is the ritual and formality of the Anglican tradition: that a more spirited expression of the faith was a vestige of African ways. That is a weak argument. Those 1,200 under instruction at Lake Washington in 1854 were not recent immigrants holding onto religious folkways of the old country. Slavery had been in existence in America for more than two hundred years. Doubtless many slaves had deeper roots in American soil than their white owners. To be sure, there were remnants of various tribal religions remaining over the centuries. But the ancestors of a large number of slaves captured in West Africa had been Muslims, not as liturgical as Episcopalian but certainly not given to the vocal and bodily expression of Baptists and Methodists in the Great Awakening. It was no more likely that Negro Episcopalians would return to earlier religions than it was that Jefferson Davis would return to the Baptist fold he left in 1863 to become an Episcopalian.

Bishop Green himself was a first generation native, his father having migrated to eastern North Carolina from England. As the bishop prepared the slaves for confirmation it was the only religious training most of them had ever had, most, by then, native born, for the importation of African slaves had been stopped in 1807 by the Act to Prohibit the Importation of Slaves. Whatever tribal religions their ancestors might have brought from Africa might have been practiced during the period when slaves were not evangelized because it was thought that they did not have souls. Sometimes, no doubt, their religion was mixed with Christianity as slaves slipped deep into the swamps and forests to elude the slave patrols—the unsanctioned "Invisible Church" that often met all night. Food was provided by whole hogs roasting over hot coals that would send no telltale signal of flames to betray them; the antecedent of Southern barbeque. Slaves who were brought to the Cotton Kingdom of the new Southwest from Virginia and the Carolinas after the treaties of Doak's Stand in 1820 and Dancing Rabbit Creek in 1830 when vast tracts of land were made available had conceivably been exposed to bits and pieces of Christian teachings and biblical passages in those gatherings and elsewhere. Since 1701 when the Church of England sent forty missionaries to America, to be followed by a few hundred more, some slaves had been converted, though it was still generally frowned upon by the slavemasters. But most of those slaves Bishop Green was confirming were no more knowledgeable of doctrine and rituals of other religions than were other converts or confirmands.

So the question remains: Where did they go when manumission came and their numbers in the Episcopal Church began to dwindle? A more probable explanation for that rapid decline may be that there were no Duncan Grays around to proclaim to the former slavemasters that the vows taken in baptism and confirmation, and the Holy Communion of which they partook Sunday after Sunday, and sometimes daily, spoke far more loudly of the unity of all humanity, of the redemptive purpose and message of the one in whose name they ate the bread and drank the wine, and of the sin of segregation, than any court could ever decree, any priest the segregationists might want to silence would ever speak, as well as anything the signatories of Appomattox might have offered. That was the message spoken time and time again more than a hundred years later by the young Delta vicar. And that was the message the younger Gray proclaimed in his epistle to the flocks of Mississippi that hot summer day in Cleveland, Mississippi.

Whatever, in 1954, none of the Negroes Bishop Gray was seeing and greeting were Episcopalians.

The bishop continued to think as a daddy, but melding with it, blurring and challenging, the bishopric petition of confirmation crept in:

> Defend, O Lord, this thy child with thy heavenly grace; that he may continue thine for ever; and daily increase in thy Holy Spirit more and more, until he come unto thy everlasting kingdom. Amen.

"Continue thine." Perhaps in that moment the daddy let Dunc Jr. go as he had never done before. Perhaps in that moment his son was a man. Baptized. Confirmed. Ordained ". . . to use both public and private monitions and exhortations." Those were the words he had used when his young son had knelt before him in submission to God and the Ordinary. Then again, maybe the bishop prayed for the thornbush that had appeared when Abraham was about to offer his son Isaac on an altar of sacrifice in the faraway land of Moriah in obedience to the same God to whom his son had been dedicated in baptism, confirmation, and holy orders. If so, he prayed in vain. There was no thicket in the Delta that day. And no ram caught by the horns as surrogate for the bishop's son as with Abraham and Isaac. Instead, the altar of sacrifice beckoned as the bishop's son waited with words of monition to a people following a racist god.

The four members of the department of Christian social relations were in place when Gray's father, the daddy of one of them and the bishop of all, returned, awaiting his blessing of their admonitory counsel to their church of the impending danger at hand; a danger, in part, ushered in by the unfaithfulness of those who had taken the all-promising vows.

The bishop reopened the meeting: *The Lord be with you.*

Answer. *And with thy spirit.*

The discussion of Gray's document continued way past the quitting time of five. As the bishop turned his car and headed southeast the July sun, still hot, cast a wry, ambivalent shadow against the graying sanctuary wall. In his journal for July 1, 1954, there is this brief notation: "Edsel L. Keith took charge of Christ Church, Holly Springs, today. To Cleveland for departmental meeting. Lunch at the rectory." No mention of the nature of the meeting, the document, the ambiguous sign on the church house wall, nor what any of it portended. He would soon enough know.

Late that night Ruth Miller Spivey Gray gave birth to their third child, a little boy, and named him Lloyd Spivey Gray. For July 3 there was this entry in the bishop's journal: "Hastened to Cleveland to meet Lloyd Spivey Gray."

The document Duncan Gray Jr. had prepared, with the counsel of Duncan Hobart, Elizabeth Noble, and James Raspberry a few weeks after the *Brown* v. *Board* decision would be called, "The Church Considers the Supreme Court Decision." Since February 1, 1790, when Chief Justice John Jay convened the first session of the United States Supreme Court on the second floor of an arcade in New York City, where Broad and Waters Streets intersect, there had been just under twenty-three thousand other decisions when the court read these historic words in 1954:

> We conclude that in the field of public education the doctrine of "separate but equal" has no place. Separate educational facilities are inherently unequal.

After May 17, 1954, those words would constitute the "the Supreme Court decision." Few in Mississippi knew or cared about the other twenty-three thousand. When someone said "the Supreme Court decision," it was understood the subject of the conversation was going to be about black children going to school with white children. And steps to circumvent it.

It had not been glad tidings for that race-haunted clime called *The South.* Gray did not dwell on whether or not it was a welcomed decision. Instead, he opened his statement with a simple declarative summary:

On May 17, 1954, the Supreme Court of the United States handed down an historic decision in which segregation in the public schools in this land of ours was declared unconstitutional.

The announcement of the date alone, May 17, 1954, was enough to grab the attention of the most casual reader. Everyone knew what had happened on that date. Then to see the words Supreme Court cinched the eyes and emotions to what would follow.

Mr. Gray's document stressed the unanimous aspects of the court's decision. Unlike the first day of the Supreme Court's existence when Chief Justice Jay had no quorum present and had to adjourn, in *Brown* v. *Board of Education* the ". . . decision reached was unanimous. Not one voice of dissent was heard. . . ." Duncan Gray could state.

The next paragraph was a vigorous testimony of the importance and indispensability of the public school system as the basic premise of Christian democracy. The usage, "*Christian* democracy" was a tactical one. The paragraph ended with the bold assertion that "If we find ourselves resenting this, then we should examine our attitude toward democracy itself."

The bulk of the document was given to the biblical and theological dimensions of race as a human category in the first place. The biblical authority that kept running through Gray's mind, and that was inherent in the document he wrote, was from the apostle Paul who wrote to the church at Corinth that those of the new religion no longer regarded anyone by worldly standards, human categories. "Even though once we did," St. Paul wrote, "in our understanding of Christ, we do so now no longer." Gray appropriated those words, knew that they were addressed as much to the church in Mississippi as to the church at Corinth. Gray, like Paul, knew that race was a worldly standard, a human category. There was to be neither race nor nationality, bond nor free, male nor female in the household of Christ. Gray actually believed those words and understood them to be among the most revolutionary words ever written. To take them literally would reorder all geographic boundaries, and all of society's grouping, ranking, and sanctions would be of no account. All human beings would be equal in fact and free indeed. It was a radical notion the young priest was delving into that July morning in the middle of the Mississippi Delta. If those who read them had not grown accustomed to hearing Paul's words as something Holy, and thus, to them, innocuous, the anger that was soon to be directed at the writer of "The Church Considers the Supreme Court Decision" would have been far more fiery than it was. The strong inference was that the church was obligated to say more than the court had said. The court could only say, "Thus saith the Law." The church must say, "Thus saith the Lord"! To offend the law put one in minor trouble with the law. To offend the Lord, to violate the vows taken in baptism and confirmation, put one at far greater peril: the Judgment. Gray's words made it clear that the church should not ask the state to do that which was not the practice of the church. Segregated worship at the parish level was considered by most to be the norm. That, Gray declared, was unconscionable. Most importantly, the message throughout the document was the First Commandment, perhaps the one in the Decalogue most often broken. *Thou shalt have no other gods before me.*

Gray would go on from 1954 to have a long and fertile career within the household of faith. Much of it would continue to be controversial and out of step with the mainstream. Much of it would continue to concern the issue of race. All of it would be because of his commitment in ordination "to drive away from the church all erroneous and strange doctrines"; his refusal to bow down to other gods, whether gods of race, politics, ideology, or national allegiance. In that sense he was not a social activist; was not even a liberal, though that label was often used against him as reproach. Instead, it was that tenacious fidelity to the one true God that drove him. He was not a liberal in the classical sense of any ideological reference, seeing scientific progress as a remedy for human ills, or believing in the perfectibility of humankind.

He was a radical. Not a rabble-rouser. A radical. His total personality—personable, laughing, soft-spoken—was disarming. The term "radical" didn't seem to fit. Yet in the truest sense of the word that is what he was. Not a moderate. A radical. And what is that? Every now and then there comes upon the scene someone who goes against his culture and tradition. And, as with Jesus, that leads to rejection and persecution. Perhaps the greatest compliment to be paid Gray is that he never acknowledged that he was suffering and never internalized rejection. His wife put it best when asked the source of his courage in the face of a mob in Oxford eight years after the meeting in the Delta to approve "The Church Considers the Supreme Court Decision": "He didn't see it as courage," Ruthie said. "Duncan just didn't know any better. He was a priest, and that was what a priest did on that day. For him it was as much a part of his vocation as lifting the chalice in the Eucharist that morning."

So. That is what it means to be a Christian radical. *Thou shalt have no other gods before me.* Never, however, was that used as a shelter from the oft neglected addendum of Jesus: "And the second is like unto it, Thou shalt love thy neighbor as thyself." Love of God can be easily claimed and who's to say who does or does not love God? Love of neighbor exacts proof. That's the rub.

At the suggestion of the bishop, who was ready to move forward with the rest of them when the die was cast, it was decided to publish the document in the diocesan paper, *The Church News*, so that every Episcopalian in the state could see the entire text at the same time. Then step aside, in the words of Joseph Addison, and wait . . .

> . . . pleased the Almighty's orders to perform, rides in the whirlwind and directs the storm.

For a body as conservative, respectable, and generally noncontroversial as the Episcopal Church in Mississippi to accept and affirm such a decree as the one published as a diocesan treatise in 1954 was beyond thought.

The publication of "The Church Considers the Supreme Court Decision" was seen by many non-Episcopal white Christians of the region as blasphemous and heretical. Never quite sure of their Anglican neighbors anyway, the document by Mr. Gray raised further questions:

> Was not the Episcopal Church the national church of our Confederacy? Was not the great General Robert E. Lee of their persuasion? Their Jefferson Davis must be pleading anew at the throne of grace for deliverance of our Lost Cause. For what had Thomas Jonathan Jackson "stood like a stone wall" at Manassas and been mortally wounded at Chancellorsville? And what say they now to the spirit of General Leonidas Polk, so prominent in their diocesan history, founder of their revered Sewanee, dead at Pine Mountain? Maybe some fanatical fringe sect. Or the Church of Rome. Not even the Negro denominations of the state are applauding this pernicious dictum with such vigor. What has happened to this lovely child of the Church of England, accepted by us for so long even when we didn't understand them? What are we to make now of these honorable men and genteel ladies, as harmless, we thought, as the breath of evening?

The consternation from without was matched by the firestorm within. Many of those underneath the canopy of Canterbury were outraged and let it be known. While the department of Christian social relations of the Fourth Province, meeting in Atlanta the day following the May 17 ruling, had issued a statement approving the Supreme Court decision, no other diocese in the nation had taken such a noncompromising step as the Diocese of Mississippi essay. The voice of the province, consisting of fifteen dioceses, churches scattered from Louisiana to North Carolina, was weakened by miles and strangers. This was homefolk talking. Duncan Gray, Elizabeth Noble, James Raspberry, and Duncan Hobart were people they saw and knew.

A reprint from *The Church News* was then produced as a twelve page booklet. So in the August edition, three months after the court ruling, the Diocese of Mississippi was on record as believing that the decision was just and right, and that racial segregation was a sin against God. It would early be demonstrated, however, that there was not unanimity of agreement among the rank and file of Mississippi Episcopalians.

At first no printer in the state could be found that would print the booklet. Finally one man agreed to take the job but with the stipulation that he would not put his stamp of identification on it, fearing a boycott or personal harm. Such was the climate of fear in Mississippi in 1954.

Copies of the text were sent to all news media, every member of the state senate and house of representatives, the governor, and all elected officials. The response was immediate and caustic.

Cleveland was a small Delta town, yet one with a great deal of concentrated wealth and political power. Two of the earliest letters of contention came from just a few blocks away from Gray's church. The first one was from a prominent attorney and state senator. "I realize that you are utterly sincere in everything you say," he began. "However, I disagree with the conclusions reached in the pamphlet you mailed me. As a member of the state senate, I shall do everything humanly possible to insure permanent segregation in public schools of this state."

He stated that he had requested of his wife, ". . . in the event I passed away, to use a full one-half of my net estate, if necessary, to insure the fact that none of my grandchildren or nieces or nephews ever attends a non-segregated public school in this state." He added that he felt it would be utterly disloyal to his constituents if he did not fight to the last ditch to preserve segregation in the public schools. This despite the fact that his constituency in 1954 was more than two-thirds nonwhite with only a few residents registered to vote in the all-black town of Mound Bayou.

The letter continued:

I think there is ample scripture upon which to base a belief in segregation. I feel further that I am not under the slightest obligation to uphold this decree of the Supreme Court, which I personally intend to disregard completely. I do not think that the question has any religious aspects at all. I do not see how anyone could consider this decision of the court other than as one rendered by a stacked court at the behest of the N.A.A.C.P. and other allied organizations, most of which are treasonable and subversive.

In another long paragraph he stated that he intended to vote for a resolution to amend the Mississippi constitution so as to give the legislature the right to abolish the public school system. He said that he thought the churches had made "a drastic mistake in taking any stand in this matter which is primarily a political and economic matter and not a religious matter."

He concluded on the amicable note expected of every Southern gentleman, no matter the circumstance: "I know you are perfectly sincere and I respect you and have the deepest admiration for you. With kindest regards, I am, Cordially your friend."

It was what Governor Ross Barnett would say to James Meredith when turning him away from his court mandated entrance to the University of Mississippi almost a decade later. After several minutes of undiluted vitriol he said, "Therefore, I am denying your admission. And I do so politely."

On the same day as the senator's letter, another arrived from a state representative. It began with a curt,

> Dear Sir:
> I read the pamphlet which you forwarded to me stating the view of the Diocise [*sic*] of Mississippi with reference to segregation. I wonder just whose views these are that were expressed? Were they the views of the Bishop or all of the clergy or part of the clergy? I look at the matter of segregation from the practical angle and the idea of integration is out of the question as far as I am concerned and this applies to both schools and churches. Because of the wide gulf between the races in morals, background and culture, any attempts at integration would lead to the gravest kind of difficulties, particularly where the blacks outnumber the whites 2 to 1 as in Bolivar County. I feel that this is a time when the white people should stand together in Mississippi and by my observations that is pretty well the feeling of the people of Mississippi. I would hate to think that in this time of crisis the church took a different view from that of its people. My personal view is that the church should have its hands

full administering to the sick and needy in the community without doing anything to tear a congregation apart by taking such a stand on segregation. I would like to know who wrote this pamphlet which you forwarded to me if you would give me that information.

There was not the prescribed complimentary close of the gentry. The letter ended as abruptly as it began. Gray, of course, graciously responded that it was *he* who had authored the pamphlet.

The legislator was a parishioner. After the exchange of letters he did not return to services. With so few members, the parish was hurt financially when even one broke ranks. The budget was not a criteria for moral judgments with the young priest, so he was not deterred in his resolve to preach from conscience and not expediency.

Most members of the legislature responded. In his covering letter, Gray had urged them to do so. Sending the treatise to the state legislature was a spunky thing in the first place. That legislature had not yet ratified the thirteenth amendment to the U.S. Constitution freeing the slaves. That would not come for another forty-one years. Not until the spring of 1995 when a black senator, Hillman Frazier of Jackson, took the floor and anachronistically and with consummate seriousness moved the ratification of the thirteenth amendment to the United States Constitution. Not even the most vehement racist could find it politically expedient to speak against it by then. That would not have been the case in 1954. In the first place, there would have been no black senator to move the resolution in 1954. Some things have changed. The life and work of Duncan Montgomery Gray Jr. has contributed to the change.

Gray, in his letter, had assured the legislators that he was not speaking as an authority on constitutional law. "But," he said, "the church certainly does consider herself qualified to speak on moral and religious questions." His critics in the legislature would have much preferred for the church to profess legal authority. They had no difficulty handling them there. They were, after all, predominantly men of law. It was a moral neurosis that gripped them. Almost without exception they were active churchmen, deacons, elders, and stewards in their Baptist and Methodist churches. The morality of segregation was seldom questioned in their pulpits. For it to be challenged now, with the court of Caesar as buttress, was disquieting. As a consequence the greatest ire was directed at clerics who used Christian doctrine as their witness. The strategy was to silence them. When that was not immediately possible, the next step was to remove them. Neither tactic worked with Gray, though both were tried.

In churches with congregational polity, as with Baptists, the procedure was easy: simply ask for the resignation of the pastor and if he didn't submit it, vote him out. Even churches with a connectional system, as with the Methodists, became strangely infested with creeping congregationalism during those years. More than eight years after the Brown decision, when twenty-eight young Methodist ministers in Mississippi signed a mild statement regarding the University of Mississippi desegregation crisis, all of them were gone within the year. Other judicatories in the various denominations where the storm clouds of wrath had not gathered were often helpful in accepting displaced clergy. At times, those in religious authority seemed to find Mississippi a fertile field to recruit the finest priests and preachers. Methodist, later United Methodist, annual conferences, Presbyterian synods, and the Episcopal dioceses suffered the losses. Once Mr. Gray, writing to a friend in Texas, remarked that ". . . you must be seeing a lot of Mississippi expatriates because we have provided the Diocese of Texas with any number of priests in the last few years!" He sent personal greetings to six priests who had recently been caught in that shift of ecclesiastical demographics.

Gray himself was offered such an out when criticism and opposition were at their peak, both in the Delta and later. The National Council of the Protestant Episcopal Church, headquartered in New York, offered him a position that many in his situation would have found difficult to decline. Funds were appropriated to employ a staff person to work in the South in the general area of race relations. Dr. Almon Pepper, Dr. Moran Weston, and Mrs. Muriel Webb, all of the department of Christian social relations of the National Council, felt that Duncan Gray Jr. was the perfect choice. While the prospect of devoting his energies full time to lifting the shadows of racial bigotry was tempting, two factors mitigated against it. The first one was his strong feeling that social justice should not be some tangential appendage to the mission of the Church. Again, he was not a social activist. To him the very core of the Gospel bespoke justice. The preaching, the Eucharist, precept, and example of the priest were all of one cloth. His call, his holy vocation, would keep him in a quotidian little Delta town. And when the time should come to move on, the criteria would not be unpleasantness, pressure, or anything except the vows he had taken in baptism, confirmation, and ordination.

Since he was serving a mission church at the appointment of the bishop, his father, those who wanted him gone had little leverage. Only the bishop could remove him. Although his critics were passionate in their efforts to spread the word that there was an integrationist at large, the young priest was not an easy target. In the first place, his stance was not an adversarial one; he was not combative. He carried no doomsday placard, spoke through channels appropriate to his station, disrupted no one else's bailiwick. Ever the smiling, amicable Southern gentleman, it was difficult to convince anyone who knew him that he was a menace. His warm, soft voice was disarming.

Yet the message was clear and the detractors felt impelled to defuse it. Here was a respectable, intelligent, educated son of the South who believed that racial segregation was incompatible with Christianity, unacceptable in a democracy, and plain boorish in a genteel culture. Traditional white citizens had long seen Mississippi as unequivocally Christian, a bastion of Jacksonian democracy and a champion of gentility. This man was telling them that their time-honored traditions were idolatrous, their government imperialistic, and their culture churlish. He must be silenced. But how?

One route was to get the vestries of other parishes to dispute his words. In early fall the vestry of Trinity Church, Yazoo City, sent a letter to other vestries in the diocese. They enclosed a copy of "The Church Considers the Supreme Court Decision," and requested that each vestry convene ". . . a special meeting for the purpose of reading this publication in its entirety and discussing it fully." The letter stated that the vestry of Trinity Church had already met and held such a discussion and were in complete disagreement.

> We feel that the publication is not a representative expression of our diocese and that it should have been discussed with the membership of the entire diocese before publication.

That was a drastic statement. For a subject to be discussed with all members of all congregations would have been an unwieldy undertaking and inconsistent with Episcopal polity. Like the federal and state governments, the Protestant Episcopal Church in the United States of America is a republic. Decisions are made by elected representatives to the annual conventions consisting of both clergy and laity. The vestry of Trinity Church was certainly aware of that and was simply preparing for the annual convention that would meet in mid-January, 1955, at St. Andrew's Church, Jackson.

The letter concluded with these words:

Our vestry is most concerned over this publication coming from within our own diocese and would like an expression from you and your vestry after a complete examination of it.

Six weeks after that letter went out, another was mailed from the same vestry to all those that had not responded.

As you know, you have failed to answer [our] letter. This article denotes a definite trend in the thinking of some of our Church leaders which we believe to be contrary to the thinking of most of our Church members.

The letter stated that the publication of "The Church Considers the Supreme Court Decision" would be discussed at the annual diocesan meeting in January.

We feel that this matter is of such importance that we are asking the churches nearest to Yazoo City to meet with us to have a preliminary discussion.

A card was enclosed to list the names of those who would attend. The matter was addressed as of the utmost urgency. "We will expect the attendance of the representatives you name."

Both letters were signed by the junior warden.

It must be said that today the signer of the letter has moved far from the posture he took in 1954. The prophet Isaiah proclaimed it:

For as the rain cometh down, and the snow from heaven, and returneth not thither, but watereth the earth, and maketh it bring forth and bud, that it may give seed to the sower, and bread to the eater.

Their seeds bore fruit.

Only four vestries attended the meeting in Yazoo City. That, however, did not reflect a paucity of interest in the subject. The small number responding to the request for a special vestry meeting can be explained by the fact that it is generally the rector who convenes the vestry. Most of the priests were sympathetic to the position taken by the department of Christian social relations and did not wish to engage in the controversy.

All members of the department of Christian social relations of the Diocese of Mississippi, save one, have gone to their reward. But the saints can exult in the harvest and regret not the price they paid for the seeds they planted.

The issue was far from dead. News spread to all parishes and missions that it would be discussed at the diocesan convention scheduled for January 18–20 in Jackson. Sides were taken; battle lines drawn. The adamant contenders brought the matter to the floor of the diocesan convention as they had promised. Telephone calls had been made, letters written, and miles traveled in an effort to have the pamphlet produced by the department of Christian social relations rescinded. The detractors overplayed their hand. By continually lobbying the rank and file, they alerted some of a more moderate persuasion that they, too, should be prepared for a fight.

Judge Billy Neville of Meridian, a man not notorious for social radicalism but known as an ardent advocate of things in the Church being done decently and in order, began his own quiet campaign. A skilled parliamentarian, he coached the bishop on his options. Number one, the bishop was not required to give them an official place on the agenda. Bishop Gray felt that not to let them speak would lead to even more divisiveness, and would signal a feeling of weakness. The canny prelate proposed instead that the segregationist faction be allowed to read their statement, at the end of which he would thank them, then gavel on to the next item of routine business. It was a chancy compromise for both sides. The Neville forces, in effect, bluffed their way by letting the word go out that the rabid segregationists would lose in a floor fight. So they bought it, and the Gray document remained as an official statement of the diocese.

The fallout from the document of the department of Christian social relations was *deja vu* for Gray. All the arguments, all the rationalizations, threats, and compromises he had heard before when he led the protest at the University of the South. The battle at Sewanee had been a baptism of fire, an initial invasion, a landing on the beaches. Now the army was moving inland, deep within the belly of the beast. Trench warfare. Hand-to-hand combat. With no thought of surrender. The Reverend Duncan Montgomery Gray Jr. was ready. Sewanee had been a training ground that had prepared him for these days. He would not faint nor grow weary of the battle. He was a priest in the church of his people. And of his Lord.

NOW WHAT REMAINED OF THE GREYS WERE HUDDLED ON a ridge outside the little town of Gettysburg, Pennsylvania. Their ranks had been so decimated at Antietam in September 1862 that the regiment was sent to Goldsboro, North Carolina, for winter regrouping. They were returned to Lee's Army of Northern Virginia in time to go on the disastrous and tide-turning excursion into Pennsylvania.

Tommie McKie was crying. In the past, when he knew he was about to cry, he would find a place away from the others and stay there until he had cried enough. He was the youngest of the University Greys and one of the youngest in the entire Eleventh Mississippi Regiment. His crying was not from fear. He cried because he wanted to go home.

He really didn't care any longer if someone saw him cry. He had seen men a lot older and a lot bigger than he crying, even corporals, sergeants, and lieutenants. Before they came to Pennsylvania, a body servant from the Lamar Rifles saw him crying after the battle was over and told him he didn't have to worry about it, that it was all right to cry. "I seed de ole gen'ral jus' a squallin' foe we lef' ole Virginney. Ole Massa Lee hisself."

Must of been when General Jackson died, Tommie thought. He had heard the older soldiers talking about General Lee taking General Jackson's death pretty hard. "Anyways, you ain't nufin' but a puppy," the Negro said. "Jus' a lil' ol' boy. Oughta be home wif yo' mammy."

At the mention of his mother the young soldier started to cry again, then quickly controlled himself and said, "I'm older than you might think. I'm older than where I come from." He said it defiantly, annoyed that a slave had seen him like this, and that he would suggest that he was a child.

"Where you come fum, Sonny?" the Negro asked, not understanding what Tommie meant about being older than where he came from.

"I come from Mississippi," Tommie said, standing up and facing the slave directly. "And I'm not Sonny. I'm Thomas Fondren McKie. And the Fondrens and the McKies are some of the best people in Mississippi. In the whole hell damn world. And who the damn do you think you are asking me questions?" The Negro didn't answer, just continued to look at Tommie with a mixture of compassion and amusement. Tommie went on, "Best you get back to your master. He'll be looking for you. We're going to march again soon. That's what I heard anyhow."

The servant smiled at Tommie's profanity, thinking, "This boy ought to learn to cuss or give it up entirely." But he didn't say that. He felt sorry for Tommie and was trying to cheer him up. "What fo' you say you oldern where you comes fum?" he asked.

Tommie McKie started to walk away, turned back instead. "Cause Mississippi ain't but fifteen years old and I'm seventeen. That's why. And you think I'm a little boy but I ain't. I shoot and I march and I kill and I'm a hell damn good soldier of the University Greys. And if we was back in Mississippi my papa might own you. He owns thirty-something just like you. So don't trouble me none." The Negro smiled again at Tommie's poor swearing. "He mammy musta raised him right," he thought.

Tommie, of course, was wrong about Mississippi's age. In 1863 it had been a state for forty-six years, not fifteen. He started walking back to camp and the Negro walked along with him, not saying anything else.

Thomas Fondren McKie was not part of the original University Greys. In early 1862 the Confederate government was concerned that the various regiments were being depleted from casualties; killed and wounded. In addition many of those who had enlisted for one year were choosing to leave the ranks. To entice them to stay the soldiers were offered a furlough of sixty days and a month's pay if they would reenlist for an additional two years. Also, they would receive a tidy bounty for each new recruit they brought back.

The first week in January 1862, Thomas F. McKie was riding his horse to a store in nearby Springdale, Mississippi, a small town thirteen miles south of Oxford. His cousin, Joseph McKie, was riding with him. "Why don't you join up with me?" Joseph asked his cousin who was four years younger than he. "Didn't Joe Taylor talk to you? He said he talked to you." Joseph Lane Taylor was a junior second lieutenant who had joined the University Greys as a private when it was organized in 1861. He was a student at the University of Mississippi. His younger brother Joshua had also joined. While on furlough Joseph was determined to recruit twenty boys from the Taylor and Springdale communities. Among those he had already recruited were his brother Robert and Joseph Lufkin McKie. Now Joseph wanted Thomas, his cousin, to go also.

Thomas knew that Joseph was about to enlist but Tommie, as he was called, had just turned sixteen years old and had given no thought of going with his cousin. "I would go, sure, but Mother won't let me," he said forthrightly. "I just know she won't let me."

Joseph laughed, gave his horse a hefty kick and galloped far ahead of his cousin, who had humiliated himself with his innocence. After a minute or so he reined the sorrel mare he was riding to a halt and waited for Thomas. "Maybe you could take along a sugartit," the insensitive older cousin teased. Then he mimicked Tommie. "'I want to go to camp but my mommie won't let me. Mommie won't let me. Mommie won't let me.'" Joseph repeated the same words over and over in a sing-song fashion, laughing as he did. Tommie's face was beet red. Joseph tugged the reins to stop the mare from moving closer to his cousin. "Hell, boy, this is war," Joseph went on. "Don't you want to fight for your country? You want your papa to lose all his niggers? All his land?"

Thomas knew then that he would aggravate his mother until she agreed to let him go. For several days she tried hard to dissuade him, right up to the time he was going to the depot to leave. The boy soldier was thinking about that day as he hunkered in the shade waiting for orders to join the formation that would soon move toward a stone wall to try to kill other soldiers who, he imagined, were as miserable as he.

Almost from the first day he had regretted not listening to his mother. The drama of war and the romance of camp life did not exist as he had imagined it. Twice he had written to his mother begging her to write President Jefferson Davis and explain that Thomas was a minor, that he had joined against her wishes and he was needed at home and should be released from service immediately. He reminded his mother that they had walked into the garden the day he left and she had cried as she begged him to go down to the depot and tell them he wasn't going. He also wrote his sister urging her to write President Davis. The letters were anguished pleas of a sad little boy. "Somebody help me."

Another reason Tommie hadn't hidden to cry this time was that there was no place to hide.

The unhappy truth is the Protestant Episcopal Church in the United States of America did not have a firm position on race in 1954. Position as in *canon*. The Church had a position on, say, ordination. An irregular ordination of a priest could lead to a trial of the bishop or bishops who had ordained him. Even as late as 1974, when seven women were ordained as priests, the bishops who ordained them were charged and two priests who let the women administer the Eucharist were tried. No one was ever tried for heresy with the charge being the turning away from the altar of a black communicant. The reason was not that it hadn't been done. The reason was that there was no canon against it. So Gray's detractors had more going for them than they realized. If they had been more astute students of canon law and church history, they could have been an immense embarrassment to the entire Episcopal household by pointing out that if the Church saw racial segregation as such a grievous sin, why had it not been addressed by canon? A favorite invective hurled at those favoring integration was that their arguments were self-righteous rhetoric; that their own clubs, neighborhoods, schools, and, yes, churches were as rigidly segregated *de facto* as was the deep South *de jure*. In that, they were correct. The charge of Pharisaism, however, was no argument at all against the document Gray had written. His call was for racial segregation to be abolished in all arenas.

It was established early that Gray had written the publication and it was he who came in for the greater condemnation. He faced his accusers with neither malice nor an attitude of martyrdom. The more fierce the rhetoric the more gentle his response seemed to be. Still he gave no quarter. His demeanor was as if he had written the most ordinary and anticipated words on a subject of mutual agreement. Such a target is hard to hit.

There were no idle winds with regard to the issue of race in Mississippi in the 1950s. Not all the gales that blew were directed against Gray and his declaration. Most of his fellow priests and some among the laity saw it as appropriate, prudent and compatible with the basic tenets of the Faith. Numerous letters from within and outside the state poured in. An early one came from George Mitchell, the legendary director of the Southern Regional Council based in Atlanta. Mr. Mitchell seldom addressed a subject directly, choosing instead to tell a story to indicate his approval or dissent. Without mentioning the booklet Gray had authored, he wrote:

Here is a true tale of a young clergymen (married to Russell Bowie's daughter), who twenty years ago was Rector at Tuscaloosa. He had not been long in the parish when out one evening on his rural visits his car approaching the main road encountered a long line of Ku Klux autos. In one of the cars he saw a Negro woman. He quietly turned his car in at the end of the procession, and followed along, until the Klansmen came to a large field, entered, and parked so as to have their headlights make a lighted circle. Into the middle of the circle they took the Negro woman, and prepared to beat her, alleging immorality. The clergyman walked up to the group, took the woman by the arm, and said in a loud voice, "Let him among you who is without sin cast the first stone," and accompanied the woman back to his car, and drove her home.

Still without mentioning what Duncan Gray had done, George Mitchell signed the letter, "Appreciatively, for a noble act."

The Delta vicar would never have acknowledged that his action in any measure compared to the courage of the Tuscaloosa priest. Still he was nourished by the words of so illustrious a man as George Mitchell. The exchange led to a long and close relationship between Duncan Gray and the Southern Regional Council.

Almost immediately orders for bulk copies began coming in. Dr. Almon Pepper of the Episcopal headquarters in New York saw it as the best thing on the subject he had seen and wanted to distribute it throughout the country. Dr. Moran Weston, executive secretary of the Division of Christian Citizenship of the national Church, one of the few Negroes on the national staff, was exuberant in his praise and wrote, "What can we do to help? Do you need money? Do you need materials? Do you need additional manpower? If so, of what kind?" Gray, though never hostile to such offers, wanted only their prayers and understanding of the gravity of the problem. He knew that solutions must come from within.

One letter of praise that must have made the Mississippi cleric smile, but to which he responded with good will, came from a priest and headmaster of the prestigious Hoosac School, a college preparatory boarding school in New York state, located in a village setting almost on the Vermont border. The man had just returned from a high-level conference on desegregation. After effusively praising Gray for his valiant witness in Mississippi's racial crisis the headmaster added:

> We here do not have any great problem concerning negroes [sic] in our school. We do not have any at the present time but do not think there would be any difficulty in admitting negroes [sic] who would fit into the school's traditions and academic standards.

Traditions and standards? Precisely! The cultured pedagogue had bowed low to the two gods Gray had to combat daily. "If *they* were of *our* tradition. If *they* were up to *our* standards. Then . . ." Ah, the classes of idols that beset men's minds. Francis Bacon assigned them names: Idols of the Tribe, Idols of the Cave, Idols of the Market-Place, Idols of the Theater. Why could not the priest and headmaster have known what he was saying to the lowly vicar of the benighted Southland? Just to see lower case used twice for the word "Negro" must have brought a moment of dismay to one who had learned better at the table of his Mississippi mother.

The statement published by the department of Christian social relations was not long: twelve pages of approximately three thousand words. Each sentence, however, was packed with tough moral affirmations and unyielding challenges of ancient racial mores, all heavily laced with theological precepts and biblical undergirding. Even after more than four decades it stands as an exemplar of Christian ethics and leadership. Physically it exists today in archives, musty trunks and attics of retired or dead priests. But in its day it goaded the conscience of many a timorous mortal who knelt to receive the holy mysteries at altars where the god of white supremacy claimed ascendancy over all other gods. The fruit it bore is for others to tell. They alone can attest to the reshaping of their souls.

Through it all Gray's father kept in professional touch with his priest. And personal touch with his son. Each letter, no matter how weighty the subject, began with "Dear Dunc:" At the end there would be the typed formality, "Duncan M. Gray, Bishop." Above that, with the bishop's stylized script, there was always the intimate, "Pop." A bishop is Bishop. A daddy is Pop.

Almost immediately "Little Duncan" had been drawn into the highest circles of his denomination. The correspondence modulated from "How may we help you in Mississippi?" to "Will you help us as we seek to address the problem of race in America?"

Once again, the pain of the Southern priest was his understanding of the nature of tragedy. He could love, and not reject, his segregationist people because he knew that humankind was fallen. All of it. And because he knew the problem was a systemic one, not confined to the Mississippi Delta. But he was a Mississippian. And that was where he chose to wrestle with the principalities and powers diseasing the national body. The affliction of the headmaster of Hoosac School was that he didn't know what the powers and principalities were. And so wrestled not at all.

Letters and calls came from clergy of other denominations as well. One, especially encouraging, was from Bernard Munger, pastor of the First Presbyterian Church of Corinth, Mississippi. The Reverend Mr.

Munger had spoken on race at his synod gatherings and his views were well known. He, too, had been targeted by the strong segregationist forces: the Synod of Mississippi had declared that segregation was blessed of God. While in Jackson on church business, Mr. Munger had gone to St. Andrew's Church for prayer and found the issue of *The Church News* containing "The Church Considers the Supreme Court Decision." He said that he had the document in his brief case as he spoke on the synod floor against segregation. It was encouraging to have a minister of another declension in his lonely camp. Gray welcomed the letter from the Church at Corinth.

There were hundreds of letters, some polite and well-meaning demurrers. Far more were threats, insults, diatribes of vitriol and vituperation, all designed to frighten the Delta priest to a chancel of silence and retreat. It will not surprise the reader that Mr. Gray does not choose to strike back at his enemies by sharing those letters. They have been, perhaps conveniently, "misplaced."

Gray had not waited for the U.S. Supreme Court decision to violate the Delta social code. Traditionally, most priests take a day off each week. Gray decided early that he would not. Part of the reason for his seven day week was that no one could say he was sacrificing churchly time to do things unrelated to his priestly duties, though in his own mind the channels of communication he was unblocking and the friendships he was establishing across racial lines were ministry at its most vital level.

Getting acquainted as equals with Negroes was not easy in 1953. The shadow of slavery was still long and heavy in the Delta. And throughout the nation. Social stations were narrowly drawn and both whites and blacks were expected to remain "in their place." While constantly thrown together in the workplace, especially in the old plantation economy, there was a narrow proscription of fraternization. Duncan Gray did not honor the code.

Mound Bayou is an all-black town established after the Civil War by the sons of Benjamin Montgomery, a former slave of Joseph Davis, brother of Jefferson Davis. Montgomery and Davis knew each other as intellectual equals and Davis had made it possible for Montgomery to operate, and later own, Davis Bend, the family plantation. Montgomery's sons, Isaiah and Thornton, early visionaries who had witnessed the failure of various utopian ventures of the Freedmen's Bureau, established the town for Negroes which succeeded and still survives. Duncan Gray knew the history of the town; he soon visited and made friends with some of the residents.

At first there was suspicion on the part of Negro residents who had long resisted white encroachment in Mound Bayou. A comfortable opening came for Gray when he heard that one of the doctors on the staff of the noted Taborian Hospital in Mound Bayou was an Episcopalian. There had been a small Episcopal mission in Mound Bayou but by then it had services only a few times a year and was soon to be closed. Gray wanted to invite the Taborian doctor and his wife to Calvary Church, Cleveland. That was a brave thing to do in Mississippi in 1954. A manifest transgression of the code. Negroes and whites weren't supposed to go to church together. But Gray had come to the Delta to serve Episcopalians. He would do so.

Taborian Hospital served Negro patients in the area and for many years provided the clinical training for students of Meharry Medical College in Nashville when their students were not accepted in the white hospitals of the area. Gray wanted to get acquainted with their work. While visiting, he met Dr. T. R. M. Howard, the celebrated physician and business man who was superintendent of the hospital. Active in securing basic rights for Negroes, Dr. Howard was the dynamo of the Regional Council of Negro Leadership. He confirmed to Gray that the young staff doctor and his wife were in fact Episcopalians. Sensing that the young clergyman was not like the conventional white persons he usually dealt with, Dr. Howard invited Gray to attend the upcoming meeting of the Regional Council of Negro Leadership.

Ten thousand people crowded the bantam town of Mound Bayou. With the exception of a few reporters, Gray was the only white person present. Attorney Thurgood Marshall, then chief counsel for the NAACP Legal Defense and Education Fund was the featured speaker. Marshall had recently completed his arguments before the U.S. Supreme Court on the *Brown v. Topeka Board of Education* case challenging the constitutionality of segregated public education. All briefs had been filed and Negro Americans anxiously awaited the court's decision. At the meeting, the ten thousand people who crowded underneath the circus-size tent and onto the surrounding area sat and stood riveted, appropriating and appreciating Marshall's every word. He predicted the outcome correctly; the South must get ready to dismantle the dual system of education. Forthwith. Marshall had brought them hope. The hope he had brought them, however, would be mingled with gall more bitter than they could then imagine. Yet they would not have turned it down even if they could have envisioned the suffering that would accompany the deliverance of

152

which the eminent barrister spoke. Such is the zeal of a people in bondage. No price would be too great.

Gray sat with the ten thousand others, heartened, awed, wondering. He surveyed the sea of expectant black faces and marveled. What is happening here? What do these things mean? Here was a twenty-eight-year-old white man, nurtured by the carriage trade of the Old South, educated in all-white schools and universities, priest of a denomination not then known for social activism, standing as the only one of his race listening to words designed to turn his world upside down.

At the evening session Dr. Howard called on the only white man present and asked him to serve on a panel to discuss the future of deseg-regated public schools. Gray remembered the trials of the Mountain. His own experience there was not germane to what was happening here. Not yet. If educated, urbane Episcopalians, bellwethers of Southern society, responded so stubbornly to the relatively timid suggestion of a few black people in a graduate school of theology, what would the rank and file of Mississippi yeomanry do with the thought of their fair young damsels leaving for the prom with black escorts? The priest sensed the wrath to come. But his world had already been altered. Altered by the altar. He would not call retreat.

What was his role? What would he do? For now he would report to the vestry of Calvary Church, Bolivar County, Mississippi, that he had recruited two new worshippers. And they were black. It was to have been a beginning. The rector was soon to learn that there was a subject filled with more emotional intensity than race, at least for the moment in his tiny parish. He had organized a Men's Club at Calvary Church. This consisted of the vestry and any others who chose to participate. Gray made a practice of giving them some topics of substance to discuss so the meetings would be more than refreshments and talk of Ole Miss football. Meanwhile, the Chemical Worker's Union was in town attempting to organize Baxter Laboratories, one of Cleveland's leading industries that manufactured and bottled intravenous saline and glucose solutions for hospital use. Visiting organizers had asked the rector for permission to use the parish hall for meetings. Gray said he had no objection but thought the hall would be too small. Intending only to indicate to his parishioners that he was sympathetic to the labor movement, he reported the request to the monthly Men's Club meeting. The other subject he had given them for discussion that night was that he had invited a young Negro couple to attend services at Calvary Church. He was not prepared for the acrimonious debate that followed. The entire evening was given to the evils of labor unions and of how letting the chemical workers hold meetings on church premises would be a bad thing to do. When they turned finally to black worshippers, he sensed little opposition. As long as they were confirmed Episcopalians it would be all right. Although the priest had not intended it as devious strategy, the truth was that by the time the group got around to discussing what was most important of the two items (he knew already the parish hall was too small and would not be used) all the energy had been expended. The matter of integrating the church would not fare so well in the months ahead when it became clear that the young priest was in dead earnest about it. When the court ruled as it did, the entire state would become a battlefield of defiance. Unfortunately for the rector's plan, the court ruled on the Brown decision in two weeks; negative feelings about Negroes coming to white services escalated. In addition, the Taborian doctor moved away.

At the meeting in Mound Bayou, Gray had met two black men who would be friends and allies from that day forth, further involving him in the South's impending crisis. One was Amzie Moore. The other was Aaron Henry. Both were older than Gray. So he would address them as "Mr. Moore" and "Mr. Henry," another breach of Delta etiquette.

Mr. Moore was an employee of the post office in Cleveland. He also owned and operated a service station. The civil service job at the post office would serve as a buffer against the economic boycotts used by whites as a weapon to dissuade Negroes who became involved in civil rights activities. The service station had no such protection and suffered irreparable damage. Even so, Moore would prevail and would later be known as the spiritual father of the movement when hundreds of young black students flooded the Delta ten years later in what was called *the Mississippi Freedom Summer*.

Mr. Henry was a pharmacist and president of the then fledgling state NAACP. Though hard to believe today that so modest an organization would be seen as dangerous, in 1954 the average Mississippi white saw it as a subversive menace, out to destroy the Southern way of life. When the age-old barricades of suffrage came down, Henry would serve for many years in the state legislature. But that was far in the future when he and Duncan Gray shook hands underneath a tent at the Regional Council of Negro Leadership.

The meeting served as entree to large numbers of Delta blacks Gray had not known before. And plunged him into activities outside the parish. Following the May 17, 1954, Supreme Court decision, economic pressure began against anyone even suspected of favoring implementation of the decree. Negro sharecroppers were especially vulnerable, having no recourse if the landlord told them to vacate the land they worked. The National Sharecroppers Fund, a program attempting to salvage some degree of dignity and survival among destitute sharecroppers, was making small loans in the Delta. Although it was generally understood that the loans could never be repaid, a legal document was required. A representative of the National Sharecroppers Fund came to see Duncan Gray. He asked Gray to serve as emissary for the fund, to investigate hardship cases, and make recommendations for loans. Gray went first to Amzie Moore, knowing that he would be familiar with sharecroppers in the area who were being displaced. In addition to a list of cases, the service of a lawyer was needed. Moore told him Attorney Joe Feduccia was the one to see. Gray hesitated. The community leaders had learned that the National Sharecroppers Fund was assisting some of the Negroes targeted for reprisal and they considered them enemies. Feduccia was the law partner of someone Gray knew to be intensely hostile to him for authoring the document, "The Church Considers the Supreme Court Decision." Moore smiled. "I know. I know. But Attorney Feduccia is your man."

Following the Civil War and emancipation there was a movement in the Delta to replace black agricultural workers with Italian immigrants. Instead of becoming surrogate slaves, the ambitious Italian newcomers were soon landholders themselves. In two generations they had become Delta Americans. They were farmers, doctors, lawyers, merchants. Primarily Roman Catholic, many of them remembered the discrimination they had known when Catholics and foreigners were targets of an earlier Ku Klux Klan epidemic. Amzie Moore repeated, "Mr. Feduccia is your man."

Though still uneasy about walking into that law office on so delicate a mission, Gray went to see Joe Feduccia. "He never indicated that he had the faintest notion that he was doing anything except preparing the most routine promissory note," Gray recalls today. He does remember Feduccia making sure his partner was not hearing their conversation but never acknowledged that he was performing a service for an alien tribe. "Amzie Moore knew the Delta white people better than I did," Gray says.

Actually Gray was more sanguine about Mississippi's future following the Brown decision than most. "Maybe I was naive," he says. "But in those early days I thought things could be worked out without serious upheaval."

Mrs. Margaret Green, a prominent parishioner, progressive in her views on race and social issues, died one week after the Brown decision. Green, wife of a circuit court judge, was an active member of the Southern Regional Council (very unusual for white Delta ladies at the time) and had recruited Gray, her priest, as a member. Riding with three of the pallbearers from the church to the cemetery in Rosedale, Gray recalls that the school board chairman broached the subject of the Supreme Court's decision on desegregation. Knowing that Mrs. Green was receptive to social change he commented on the presence of Negro friends at the service. "This decision that has us all so upset, well, we can work it out," the man said. He said he knew it wouldn't be easy but, "We can work it out." Shortly after that a local optometrist, trying to be funny, said to the school board chairman, "You gonna have little darkies in the schools this fall?"

The chairman did not find the comment amusing and abruptly silenced the would-be merry-andrew by replying, "No, not this fall, but in a few years we will." Within months both the school board chairman and the optometrist were clamorous members of the White Citizens' Council, adding their own voices to the growing crowd of those screaming, "Never!"

Mr. Gray talks somberly of what happened.

> If we had had strong national leadership, if President Eisenhower and other leading political figures had commended the Supreme Court, had not dawdled at every rung, and if our own elected senators and congressmen had opposed the White Citizens' Councils instead of joining them, serving as their cheerleaders, well, yes, we could have worked it out.

Tragically, it didn't happen that way. Consequently, for the next thirty-five years Gray's energies would be drained by the fallout of what a small-town school board chairman saw as a minor bother that could be worked out.

Through Moore, Duncan met and became friends with Medgar Evers, the dynamic young field secretary of the Mississippi NAACP. The indefatigable Evers would challenge every aspect of the state's racial pattern. In 1963 he would be dead, assassinated by a lapsed Episcopalian who had gone to school in Greenwood with Gray and had been confirmed during Gray's father's tenure in Greenwood. In a long letter to Mrs. Evers in which he stated shock and sadness, Gray eulogized Evers as a man who had brought hope to the state and left a goodly heritage for his children. He ended with words few whites were expressing at the time:

> Medgar Evers is a hero among the Negro people of Mississippi; but I think you should know that there are many white Mississippians who regard him just as highly. It is a man like your husband who can make us proud once again to be Mississippians. He is one of the great persons our state has produced.

Within a short time Dr. T. R. M. Howard would be practicing medicine in Chicago, his Regional Council of Negro Leadership in shambles. He had fled Mound Bayou in fear of death. "I feel I can do more alive in the battle for Negro rights in the North than dead in a weed-grown grave in Dixie," Howard said. As numerous Negro leaders left the South, Duncan Gray remained at Calvary Church, Cleveland, and Grace Church, Rosedale, involving himself more and more in things his people saw as none of the church's business.

Cleveland police began following Gray when he drove into the Negro section of town. On one occasion an officer followed him to Amzie Moore's home, pulled to the front of the house and left his bright lights shining through the windows during the entire visit. Driving home Gray took a circuitous route, sometimes circling the same block. The police car stayed with him. When Gray stopped in front of his residence, he intended to approach the officer's car and ask if he might be of assistance. Instead, the policeman made a hasty retreat, leaving Gray standing in his yard. The next week he facetiously reported to his senior warden, a physician, that he appreciated the excellent protection he was getting from the local police. Apparently the doctor told the police chief that Calvary Church didn't need surveillance of their rector, for the harassment stopped. At least from the police.

His activities, however, were by then the source of much discussion in the Delta. The priest was seen as a threat to the status quo. As one of a team of ministers and educators at Religious Emphasis Week at Mississippi State University, Gray created a statewide furor the very first night on campus. Meeting with a Presbyterian student group he had been asked to speak on the "Social Implications of the Christian Gospel." In his speech he stated forthrightly that segregation was incompatible with Christianity. David Langford, now features editor for the Associated Press in New York, was on the staff of the campus student newspaper. Interested in stimulating such discussion himself, the student had tipped off a local stringer for the *Jackson Daily News* that the visiting priest was apt to throw a firecracker. The news that there was an integrationist speaking at Mississippi State University swirled over the state like prairie grass in a whirlwind. Leaders of the White Citizens' Council, legislators, alumni, and parents flooded the university switchboard with their protests. The university president, trying as best he could to walk the prescribed line of teaching the young without offending those at whose sufferance he served, quickly assembled the visiting team of speakers and asked that they promise not to mention the subject of race and integration in any of their sessions that week, explaining that the legislature was already threatening to close the colleges, universities, and even secondary and primary schools rather than obey the Supreme Court directive. He argued that education was the only hope out of Mississippi's affliction and with that gone there would be no hope at all. If the visitors could not make that promise it was clear that they should not remain. As John Compton, professor of philosophy at Vanderbilt University and a member of the team, remembers, "It was a request, but a request with a clear implication."

It seemed, certainly to the president, a reasonable request under the circumstances. One should not accept an invitation into a man's home and then complain about the decor. Some felt that perhaps they should comply with their host's directive.

A meeting of the team was scheduled for the afternoon. The agenda was a joint decision as to whether they would abide by the president's request or as a team leave the campus. One by one they took the floor to state their position. Some of it was nakedly pragmatic, at times couched in the finest Aristotelian logic. One well-known minister from nearby Corinth wept openly as he explained that to defy the edict would mean he would have to resign his position when he returned home; that he felt he was leading his people in the right direction, loved them, and could not let them down by making a hasty, glandular decision.

Gray, the perpetrator of their plight, was last to speak. He stood before them with no apparent emotion.

> Maybe I should apologize for attending the meeting, for I am not here to make up my mind. My bag is packed and in my car outside. I am sorry if I have caused anyone any trouble or inconvenience and I am not pleading with any of you to change any decision you might be inclined to make.

He explained that he could not withdraw something he had already said; would not if he could for that was what he believed. His words to his colleagues were sympathetic, courteous, understanding, and few. He concluded, "Of course, the president has left me, personally, with no option. I'm going back to the Delta." He asked no one to follow him. Most, however, after trying again to negotiate with the university administration, did. Including Professor Compton. It was a dramatic moment.

The news reached Bolivar County before Gray did. In a store where he often shopped, the owner approached him and with words inappropriate for the ears of a clergyman ordered the priest to leave "until you decide if you are black or white." At the next meeting of the Rotary Club no one would sit at the table with him. Eventually an aging Presbyterian minister, known as a segregationist, sidled over and sat beside him, attesting to the others that it was all right to associate with the transgressor in their midst. Later a local citizen, known to have killed two Negro men, claiming self-defense, put out the word that he would kill Gray if the vestry didn't get rid of him.

Major Fred Sullens, editor of the *Jackson Daily News*, entitled his editorial on the subject of Duncan Gray leading the walk-out at Mississippi State "Good Riddance Again." Sullens concluded his editorial with a call for only "home-grown" clergy to be invited to speak to Mississippi college students. He added,

> There is no time or place on a platform anywhere in Mississippi for men who want to blow off at the face in opposition to the Southern way of life, and who are so shallow-minded that they cannot see what integration, miscegnation [sic], mixed marriages and mongrelization of the white race would mean in the South—or anywhere else, for that matter.

Most ministers would have abandoned ship. Some would have reveled in their martyrdom at the next port. Instead Duncan Gray took it in stride, in what one friend called *amused toleration*. "His admirable sense of proportion and good humor carried the day," the friend reported. It was more than good humor that carried the day, however. It was his understanding of vocation; of who he was and his place in the world. Above all else Duncan Gray was a product of the radicalism of liturgy. He had been nourished, shaped, and tempered by the *Book of Common Prayer*. As a priest he was as much of a literalist as he was as an engineer, believing that when he stood in the pulpit or before the altar, the words of Holy Communion or Morning or Evening Prayer were to be taken with the same seriousness as Kirchhoff's Voltage Law in the field of electrical engineering. The words were as valid in the Mississippi Delta of 1954 as they were in Canterbury in 1549. And carried the same authority.

"Grant us grace fearlessly to contend against evil, and to make no peace with oppression . . ." meant, in context, the evil of segregation and the oppression of black sharecroppers, and laborers seeking to organize; all who were weary and heavy laden. To repeat, it was not sociological nor humanistic in origin. It was not from some vague liberal notion of the perfectibility of human nature, nor the romanticism of literature. "We have erred and strayed from thy ways like lost sheep. We have followed too much the devices and desires of our own hearts . . . offended against thy holy laws . . . no health in us . . . miserable offenders," was to acknowledge the existence of something called *sin*. And to Duncan Gray sin was the bedrock of America's racism. And the hemlock of the body politic. He was as conversant with the sociology and economics of it all as the best informed social scientist. But he did not see sociology and economics as the key to deliverance. Correction in those areas would follow the change of the human heart. "That we may hereafter live a godly, righteous, and sober life" meant there was hope of redemption; that things didn't have to be the way they were in human relationships. Not in Cuba. Not on the Mountain. Not in Mississippi. But: "He pardoneth and absolves all those who truly repent, and unfeignedly believe. . . ." *Truly* repent. Gray's call was not to build a kingdom on earth but to lead his people to repentance. Certainly he was concerned with the condition of the oppressed. No one could ever question that. But that concern flowed from his concern with the immortal souls of the dispossessor, and the teachings of his Church, no matter how far his parishioners—and he as well—might have digressed and deviated. That faithfulness to liturgy, hand in hand with deliverance from injustice, made him a prophet. In the lineage of Amos, who never proclaimed that the judgment of God would come to the Northern Kingdom because people were suffering. Rather God's judgment was to come because others of His children were causing them to suffer. It was the morality of the eighth century prophets clothed in the language of the sixteenth century; a remarkable blend for the moral confusion of the twentieth. Perhaps he intuited that morality without religion would not hold out against the day of perdition.

It was apt, however, that it was not a matter of intuition any more than his actions were a result of easygoing good humor. By the time of his graduation from Sewanee and ordination to the priesthood Gray was an astute theologian. He had grown up among ecclesiastics and even in his secular vocation his mind was never far from theological studies. At Sewanee he had been under some of America's finest teachers and his study of the various theological movements was meticulous and had continued.

Even before entering the School of Theology he had rejected nineteenth-century liberalism as being too shallow in accounting for the human propensity for unbending evil. He had come of age in a global holocaustic era and in a local system of racial wrongdoing. Theological liberalism, especially in the second generation of that movement, for example, the Social Gospel of Walter Rauchenbusch, was appealing to him because it espoused that for which he stood: a just society. But he early rejected the Social Gospel Movement as being more the deification of man than the incarnation of Christ. He came to believe that the theological aspect of the racism with which he was wrestling daily had its roots in the shift from incarnation to deification in Christian belief; the shift in emphasis from *God become human* to *human become God*. Again, *Prayer Book* Christianity was his base. F. O. Matthiessen had earlier pointed out this inversion in his treatment of the American renaissance when he wrote, "Anyone concerned with orthodoxy holds that the spiritual decadence of the nineteenth century can be measured according to the alteration in the object of its belief from God-Man to Man-God" (*American Renaissance*, Oxford University Press, 1941, p. 446). Matthiessen understood this as a shift from belief in the salvation of humans through the mercy and grace of a sovereign God, to belief in the potential divinity in every human. In no country was this theological development more rapid than in Protestant, democratic America. The preaching of the early church concerned a God who had become human, a Christ whose birth was unique and whose nature was divine; who was crucified and who died back into eternal life. Gray stood with the early church. Theological liberalism, particularly second-generation liberalism within Protestantism, interpreted Jesus as a rebel prophet who was murdered by a society that was unable to abide the horror of truth. Accordingly, man *became* God. Thus God was no longer incarnate in the person of Christ. He did not become human by being "in Christ"; rather, the human Jesus became God (*American Renaissance*, Oxford University

Press, 1941, p. 446). In this formulation, Christ did not descend from the right hand of God to be born of a virgin, to suffer under Pontius Pilate, to be crucified for us and for our salvation, as Gray had recited in the creeds since childhood. In fact, the liberal position did not really acknowledge the incarnation. Jesus was thrust by humans to the right hand of God as a reward for the life he had lived and the deeds he had performed. This was, in short, deification.

It is evident that the meaning of the crucifixion and death of Christ was completely changed by that theology. Gray saw as one of its most serious consequences the rejection of the doctrine of the absolute sovereignty of God, and that rejection had far-reaching implications in the whole field of Christian social relations with which Gray seemed to his critics to be preoccupied. They saw Gray as a liberal when in fact he was more conservative in his theology, certainly more orthodox, than they. As the racists concerned themselves with human as subject, the basis of their segregationist arguments, they were rejecting incarnation and accepting, at best, the deification of Jesus; the celebration of man's triumph, whereas "God in Christ" (incarnation) had to do with the sovereignty of God. A God who, in the words of the *Book of Common Prayer* and Holy Scripture, had made humans, all humans, in His image. Thus, to call some of God's creation unclean or inferior was to violate the Second Commandment: "Thou shalt not take the name of the Lord thy God in vain; for the Lord will not hold him guiltless, that taketh his name in vain." Gray's preaching had to do with what the sovereign God had done. He did not tackle the problem of racial injustice from the vantage point of human-centered (humanitarian) individual rights. Rather with God's rights and commandments. Again, incarnation, not deification. With God as sovereign (subject), the basis for human oneness was, as Matthiessen suggested, ". . . in man's common aspiration and fallibility, in their humility before God" (*American Renaissance*, Oxford University Press, 1941, p. 72). With humans rather than God as subject, the motivation for sister and brotherhood was lodged firmly in humanitarianism; to "go about doing good" in order that the spark of divinity in every one might shine forth. The typical do-gooder was likely to badger people into loving one another, to tell them that all humans are good and worthy, and, accordingly, there should be no discrimination among them. The segregationist was apt to counter with facts and figures about some humans who, by his standards of goodness and worthiness, were due only a second-class citizenship. Gray did not question their facts for they were of no account in the white heat of what God in Christ had done.

It should be noted that the myriad detractors of Gray never assailed him on theological grounds. He was too orthodox for them to win on those grounds. If his had been a message of law and order, human dignity, an appeal to the nation's courts and their interpretation of the Constitution alone, or to the then in vogue shibboleth "brotherhood of man and Fatherhood of God," his critics might have scored winning points. It is true that the important document he authored concerned itself with a decision of a human court. But his argument was not predicated on the notion that because a human tribunal had issued a decree, it was therefore of divine origin. Rather his argument was that the court had now said what the Scriptures and liturgy of his church had said all along. His concern was not that his people would be held in contempt of court. Dean Pike had said to the trustees of Sewanee, and Gray had concurred, that in certain situations defiance of human law was in keeping with Godly vocation. Gray's concern was that his people not be in contempt of the Holy. His point of departure was the absolute sovereignty of God; his footing was incarnation; his authority was scriptural as presented and celebrated in the services, prayers, and hymns of the ancient church.

He really believed that something momentous, efficacious, and triumphant happened in the person of Christ, His life and passion. And that it spoke to every relationship between persons, races, and nations. To the here and now in race-obsessed Mississippi. What some saw in him as social activism, or humanistic behavior, were in him thanksgiving. The words of the General Thanksgiving ". . . that our hearts may be unfeignedly thankful; and that we show forth thy praise, not only with our lips but in our lives, by giving up our selves to thy service . . ." spoke as with a thunderclap directly and vigorously to his Delta vocation. Whether his words and works were marked or not, when in the service of Holy Communion, on those occasions when the Exhortations were used, the call for racial reconciliation, and the warning of deception were clear:

> For as the benefit is great, if with a true penitent heart and lively faith we receive that holy Sacrament; so is the danger great, if we receive the same unworthily. Judge therefore yourselves, brethren, that ye be not judged of the Lord; repent you truly for your sins past; have a lively and stedfast faith in Christ our Saviour; amend your lives, and be in perfect charity with all men; so shall ye be meet partakers of those holy mysteries.

This was not maudlin symbolism to the Delta priest. This was harsh reality. Though he barred no one from the Communion rail, leaving that to God and the conscience of the communicant, the words about the great danger in receiving the elements of Communion unworthily were in reality an enhancement of the words of the priest inviting sinners to the altar:

> Ye who do truly and earnestly repent you of your sins, and are in love and charity with your neighbours, and intend to lead a new life, following the commandments of God, and walking from henceforth in his holy ways. . . .

The great danger of which the *Prayer Book* spoke was that if they were not in fact truly and earnestly repenting, did not intend to lead a new life, were not in love and charity with their neighbors, it would be best if they not make their Communion at all. Gray was painfully aware of some earlier words of St. Paul, preaching to a little flock somewhat like Gray's own flock:

> Wherefore whosoever shall eat this bread, and drink this cup of the Lord, unworthily, shall be guilty of the body and blood of the Lord. For he that eateth this and drinketh unworthily, eateth and drinketh damnation to himself, not discerning the Lord's body. For this cause many are weak and sickly among you, and many sleep. (1 Cor. 11: 27, 29–30)

The warning of the Rubric and the Scripture was a frightening consideration for the young priest and cast a heavy shadow over each celebration. Were he and those who knelt before him actually eating and drinking to their own damnation? Would they be better off not being there at all? Were they, by being there eating the bread and drinking the wine guilty of shedding the blood and bruising the body of Christ? "For this cause . . . many sleep." Already spiritually dead? Those were the words he read and the reading weighed heavily upon him. What if this is literally true, precisely the case? he found himself wondering. Should he then simply drive them from the altar as Jesus had driven the money changers from the temple? That he could not, would not do, knowing that he, too, was a sinner.

His point of reference was God as subject. Humans, the object.

> It is he [God] that sitteth upon the circle of the earth, and the inhabitants thereof are as grasshoppers; . . . That bringeth the princes to nothing; he maketh the judges of the earth as vanity. . . . their stock

shall take no root upon the earth: and he shall blow upon them and they wither, and the whirlwind shall take them away as stubble.

Those were words he had heard his father read many times, the same words that had run through his father's mind that July day when "The Church Considers the Supreme Court Decision" was being approved. When the generally composed and dignified rector recited those words of Isaiah, opening a clenched hand and blowing across the palm as if scattering ashes to the wind, there was no doubt of what he was saying: The folly of racial division was as a quarrel between the Locustidae and Acridiidae families of grasshoppers that inhabited the Delta fields of summer.

It was to be true to the vow he had taken in ordination: "Will you be ready, with all faithful diligence, to banish and drive away from the Church all erroneous and strange doctrines contrary to God's Word; and to use both public and private monitions and exhortations . . . ?" He had answered, "I will, the Lord being my helper." It was his intent to be faithful to that response.

Assured by the words of the canticle that followed:

Drive far away our ghostly foe,
And thine abiding peace bestow;
If thou be our preventing Guide,
No evil can our steps betide.

With that assurance, he would carry on. Sometimes with fear and trembling. Not fear of those who threatened him with death for he knew there was something more awesome than death that could befall him. And it was not something as simple as the admirable sense of proportion and good humor of which his friend spoke that brought and kept him here, saying, doing the things he was. It was the radicalism of liturgy again; his belief that the words of Scripture and the *Book of Common Prayer* were to be taken with the same seriousness as Kirchhoff's Law of Voltage.

Chapter Five

STRENGTHEN
THE FAINTHEARTED
SUPPORT THE WEAK
HELP THE AFFLICTED

The gentle reverend seemed to have been a lightening rod for the days of trouble. Some of his friends began referring to him as Joe Btfsk, the little man of Lil' Abner fame who always had a dark cloud of adversity hovering over him, following wherever he went. It was during Gray's stay at the University of the South School of Theology that the school went through the most severe crisis in its history. Then he arrived in the Delta on the eve of the Supreme Court's decision outlawing segregation in public schools. With the Delta being the home of the White Citizens' Council, Senator Eastland, and Speaker of the House Walter Sillers, it was where the first seeds of defiance were planted. By the time he arrived at St. Peter's Church, Oxford, the fire had spread eastward, crossing the Loess Bluffs, through the Red Clay Hills, and into the Flatwoods region.

Then while in Oxford, Gray would be caught in the most violent upheaval the town and the University of Mississippi campus had seen since the Civil War. By the time he arrived at St. Paul's Church, Meridian, in 1965, the scroll of fury had unrolled from the coastal pine meadows on the Gulf Coast to the Tombigbee prairies and the northeast hills, leaving in its wake charred houses of worship, dynamited dwellings, and dead bodies, with most of the populace intimidated into silence.

Gray and his wife, Ruthie, were glad to be in Meridian. For many years it had been seen as the most progressive town in the state. It had been a town where the Southern Railroad and the Gulf, Mobile, and Ohio intersected, bringing traffic and commerce from south to north and east to west. As a railroad town it had attracted a medley of views, religions, and cultures from various parts of the country. There had existed an inter-faith sensibility not known in the rest of the state. From the beginning of its history Jewish citizens had been an integral part of the community. In business, government and clubs, Jews, Christians, and non-affiliated worked, played, and contributed together. When St. Paul's Church house was being built the congregation met in the synagogue and there was reciprocation when the synagogue was being rebuilt after a fire destroyed the old one.

Citizens with names like Elliott, Poindexter, LeLaurin, Meyer, Ward, Neville, Rosenbaum, Carmichael, Davidson, Rea, and Price greeted them. They were Jews, Episcopalians, and Christians of other declensions. Meridian had been proud of its reputation as being different from the rest of the state with regard to race relations. The Grays arrived when that was changing. Despite Meridian's standing as the most broad-minded of the state's cities it was becoming the center of the most untamed Klan activity. A year earlier there had been the most heinous of all the crimes committed in the civil rights era. Three young men, James Chaney, Michael Schwerner, and Andrew Goodman, volunteers in a program of voter registration headquartered in Meridian, were murdered in nearby Neshoba County. That brought federal officials from the highest level in a fashion not known since Reconstruction, further inflaming the passions of local racists. The climax came when the three bodies were found buried in the embankment of a farm pond and it was determined that Neshoba County lawmen were involved in the killings. It was ironic that the Ku Klux Klan would be in the Meridian area since not even the rela-tively more moderate White Citizens' Council had been as strong in Meridian and Lauderdale County as it had been in other areas. On the other hand, perhaps the fiery rhetoric of the Citizens' Council served as an escape valve for the hotheads who otherwise would have resorted to violence. Whatever, trouble had once more tracked Duncan Gray.

In researching Gray's years in Meridian, I spoke with Mrs. Jo VanDevender, a Meridian woman in her seventies, who answered readily regarding Gray. "I think Mr. Hobart sort of paved the way for Duncan Gray at St. Paul's Church." With her at one interview were her two sons, Karl, a graduate of the University of the South and prominent Nashville physician, and Michael of Bay St. Louis, Mississippi. All had been parish-ioners of Gray when he was rector of St. Paul's Church, Meridian.

It was a Sunday morning in my cabin. Dr. VanDevender excused himself to make a house call on a hundred-year-old patient in a neigh-boring county while the other two visited with me. During our talk, the life and ministry of Gray at St. Paul's Church flowed easily. His presence seemed much with us.

"Duncan Hobart was at St. Paul's?" I asked. I had known he was in Meridian before moving to St. James, Jackson, and of course on the department of Christian social relations, but didn't remember that he had been at St. Paul's, Meridian's oldest Episcopal church.

"Yes, yes," Mrs. VanDevender answered. "For nineteen years. Mr. Gray was not Mr. Hobart's immediate successor but those two were on the same wave length where important issues were concerned."

"You say he paved the way? Sort of Duncan Gray's John the Baptist?"

"Yes, yes. That's it. Duncan as Duncan's John the Baptist," she laughed. "Ah, our two dear Duncans. Hobart and Gray. Marvelous leaders. Both of them. Good men."

"Interesting," I said, trying to remember something about Mr. Hobart. "They seemed so different."

"Not really," Mrs. VanDevender said. "Actually they were a lot alike."

I was afraid I had offended her. It was obvious she had a high regard for both men and I learned early that she was not given to great flattery of the human species. So I knew she was sincere in her assessment of the two. "Well, I mean. You know," I stammered, not wanting to offend more. "Well, what I meant was, Gray was indigenous to those red hills. But wasn't Duncan Hobart a New Yorker?"

"Upstate," Michael answered quickly, smiling, as if explaining Hobart further. Even excusing him for not being a native Mississippian.

Mrs. VanDevender added, "Mr. Hobart came to us from Atlanta. Bishop Gray, Duncan's father, brought him to Mississippi." Neither mother nor son felt any reason to apologize for Hobart. He had been their priest, preacher, pastor, and friend. And they were beholden to him.

We went back to Hobart being the trailblazer for Gray. "Mr. Hobart came to us in nineteen forty-three. Things were not so tense then," Mrs. VanDevender explained. "The war was on. The whole country was united in that, you remember. Even then, though, his sermons had to do with social justice. Race relations included. Oh, some folk didn't like it but there was no threat at the time. I suppose we thought segregation would last forever. Later on, after the Supreme Court ruled that public school segregation was unconstitutional, things did heat up. Politicians fanned the fires. Even then, it seemed far away. He didn't beat us over the head with it but there was never a question as to where he stood."

"How about in nineteen sixty-four?" I inquired. "When Duncan Gray arrived?" "Sixty-five," Mrs. VanDevender corrected. "Mr. Gray came in sixty-five." Hearing a priest referred to as *Mister* always seemed strange to me. When I was growing up in Baptist Mississippi, the minister was called *Brother*. My granddaddy called him *Pastor*. Like the Lutherans do. Some referred to him as *Preacher*. If we saw someone with a clerical collar we knew we were supposed to call him *Father*. But like his daddy before him, Duncan Gray Jr. preferred to be called *Mister*. Or, if one knew him well, *Duncan*. Mrs. VanDevender seemed to sense my difficulty. "He never liked high church titles. Or high church anything. 'Smoke and bells are not for me,' he used to say."

She moved back to my question. "It was different by then. In sixty-five. Race had become a volatile issue. Lines were drawn. Everyone had to be on one side or the other."

I had heard that Mrs. VanDevender was considered liberal on the issue of race during the period of the civil rights movement. "You were a parishioner. What was your position?" But she only smiled and changed the subject.

"Some people thought she was a communist," Michael teased. "Go on, Mom. Tell him." But Jo VanDevender is a modest woman and doesn't like to talk about her own deeds.

Instead she said, "I supported Mr. Hobart and Mr. Gray in all their efforts because they were right."

"*Right?*" Michael laughed. "I thought it was *left*."

Jo VanDevender wasn't in a teasing mode. The matter was much too serious. "I supported integration because I knew it was inevitable. And because the direction in which our rectors were leading us enhanced our spiritual growth." She cast a mildly chastising look at her son. "It was the right thing." Still looking at Michael she said, "I supported Mr. Gray's efforts to get the community to assume responsibility for itself, for its own integration." Turning to me she added, "My sons have a way of embroidering the truth. I was no hero." We let it go.

"I was a teenager during Duncan Gray's watch," Michael says. "Part of it anyway." I asked him to tell what he remembered. "I wasn't thinking much about civil rights and all that. Just a kid. I do remember our daddy didn't think like Mom on those issues." Mrs. VanDevender chuckled and nodded concurrence. "Of course, that was the big issue. I had attended segregated schools and, I suppose, I thought a lot like the kids I ran with." He said he remembered well weekly conversations he had with the rector when he was working on his Boy Scout God and Country award. "We talked about things like that. I remember how he would never hit me over the head with his own opinions. At the same time, though, you knew where he stood." Michael said Mr. Gray made you feel that you had a responsibility to think things through but didn't make you feel evil if you didn't agree with him. "But you had better think it through before you made up your mind permanently. When you left his office you knew you had a responsibility, a duty, to make a decision."

His mother prompted that Gray has also prepared him for confirmation. "Oh, yes. Sure. I remember that well. Even in that he didn't patronize, didn't talk down to us." He faced me and winked. "Of course, a twelve-year-old boy sometimes had other things on his mind. There's only so much catechism a boy that age can take in one sitting."

Mrs. VanDevender named the boys who had gone on to become priests while Gray was at St. Paul's: David Elliott III, now rector of Holy Trinity Church, Vicksburg; Tom Ward, Rhodes scholar, now chaplain of the University of the South; and Gray's son, Duncan III, rector of St. Peter's, Oxford—where his father had been before moving to Meridian and where his great-grandfather McCrady had served 1928–1939.

Mrs. VanDevender wanted to remind me of Gray's advocacy of women in the church. "No woman had been on the vestry before Mr. Gray. He encouraged it. Mary Elliott, David's mother, was the first." Mary Elliott, sister of writer James Street, in addition to being a pioneer woman in the Episcopal Church, was also the state's premier woman Democrat.

Michael added that his mother was the second woman on the vestry. She smiled, shook her head and sighed, "Ah, my boys."

Recovering quickly from her modesty she became uncharacteristically excited. "You know what else," she beamed. "The very first female to register at the University of the South was from St. Paul's. How could I forget that?" She delighted in telling the story. Judy Ward of Meridian, Tom Ward's sister, was in the first class to admit women. So that she would be sure of being the first female to register, she took her station in the registration line and remained there all night. It was clear Mrs. VanDevender was leading up to a dramatic cap for the story. Smiling, almost laughing, she went on. "And, she has just been elected chair of the board of regents of the University of the South."

"Chalk up another first, Mom, for Mr. Gray and St. Paul's," Michael bantered.

"Mrs. Judith Ward Linebach. That's her name now. The very first female to register. The very first woman to head the board of regents." It was evident that Jo VanDevender was proud of her Meridian sister. And proud of her church and former rector.

"But that's not the most important part of your story," she said, almost apologetically, regaining her posture of interviewee.

"What is?" I asked.

"His compassion. Duncan Gray was, is, a compassionate man. As a priest and as a bishop."

I asked for examples. "He visited, came into our homes." She explained that it didn't matter if one belonged to St. Paul's Church or to no church at all. It could be the most notorious rogue or the most saintly parishioner. Rich or poor. Black or white. If he knew a family had trouble, he was there. "Not many ministers do that anymore," she said.

"He ate with publicans and sinners, eh," I said. "I believe that was one of the charges against Jesus."

"Don't ever let Mr. Gray hear you say that," Mrs. VanDevender said. "He wouldn't tolerate being compared to Jesus." We discussed whether that trait was innate humility or some deep-seated feeling of inadequacy. At the peak of success and accomplishment he never seemed to know he had done anything special. We agreed that it was a commendable quality but wished that he might know something of his worth. We all fell silent.

Dr. Karl had returned and we were winding down. His mother nodded for him to have the last word. "Compassion is the right word I think. He always made you feel like you were somebody." The doctor hesitated, like there was something he wanted to add but wasn't sure he should. "Well, Mother remembers. I had a certain vocational uncertainty." His mother smiled as if to tell him it was all right, patted him approvingly on the knee. "I considered becoming a priest, went off to England for two years after college to study philosophy and theology, came back, thought I wanted to be a farmer, went back to school, tried farming, thought about being a lawyer and wound up going to medical school. Duncan Gray went through all that with me and never once made me feel ashamed. That has to be compassion."

There seemed nothing else to say. "I'm glad you wound up going to medical school," I said.

"Why do you say that?" Mrs. VanDevender asked. She didn't know her son was *my* physician.

"Because I probably wouldn't be alive if he hadn't," I said. The doctor said it was time to go eat.

Duncan and Ruthie Gray arrived in Meridian at a crucial time for their growing family. Catherine was three, Lloyd eleven, Anne thirteen, and Duncan III was almost sixteen years old. All except Catherine would attend public schools at a time when desegregation was just beginning. Although at the time Gray's salary was meager compared to that of other professions with comparable training, it would have been possible for them to arrange for their children to attend private boarding schools. That was never an item on the family agenda. Duncan and Ruthie Gray had too much class and too much accountableness to principle to work so diligently for integrated public education and then consider anything but public schools for their own children. Even one's children can become idols, as the biblical story of Abraham and Isaac had taught them. They did not, of course, feel that they were sacrificing their children by keeping them in public schools. Meridian had one of the most progressive school systems in the state. With good teachers and administrators dedicated to nurturing young minds. But that was not what mattered. Integrity mattered.

It was also a climacteric time for the city of Meridian and Lauderdale County. The winds of change were blowing but the crosscurrents of resistance were fierce and continuous. It was, after all, the sixties. When nothing slept.

As a priest of the Episcopal Church, Gray did not choose to be out front in what was becoming faddish in professional church circles—the Ecumenical Movement. In a rare moment of cynicism he once chuckled in agreement when, in an interdenominational meeting, someone said that to merge every mortuary in town would not produce a house of the living. Only a big house of the dead. That is not to say he did not cooperate, and lead, in ecumenical efforts. He was always there, side by side with other clergy, be they Pentecostal, Roman Catholic, Jew, or Baptist. He saw the best ecumenism exhibited in clergy working together on community issues. From their own terminal. "If we do the same things together long enough, some day we might find that not much separates us," he said. Meanwhile, he saw service to humanity as paramount. Where his various colleagues were on Sunday morning, Friday night, or Saturday didn't bother him.

When the bombings and burning of Negro churches occurred, Gray was active in the formation of the Committee of Conscience, an ad hoc organization to raise funds to rebuild them. Sensitive to tactics, he insisted that the Reverend Harold O'Chester, pastor of the largely blue collar Poplar Springs Baptist Church, be chairman. Brother O'Chester was a conservative Southern Baptist, and a segregationist, but it had been he who led the Lauderdale County Baptist Pastors Association in the first condemnation of the ". . . burnings, bombings, shootings, which have plagued our community in recent weeks."

The Committee of Conscience was interdenominational, interfaith, and interracial. Rabbi Milton Schlager, a target of bigotry for no reason except his religious heritage, was a prominent participant and gave the committee its name. Several members of his Beth Israel synagogue served on the committee and contributed generously. Southern Baptists and National Baptists, the latter a predominantly Negro denomination, were the most numerous on the committee, which included Dr. Beverly Tinnin, pastor of the large and prestigious First Baptist Church, and the Reverend C. O. Inge, pastor of New Hope Baptist. John Speed and S. S. Barnett were among the Methodists. Titus Bender was a Mennonite pastor and Father John Scanlon represented the Catholic Church. David Shepperson was a Presbyterian and Charles Johnson was pastor of the Fitkin Memorial Church of the Nazarene. It was ecumenism at its finest. People working together for good. And the kind of interracial activity Duncan Gray exulted in. Organizations represented were the Chamber of Commerce, the League of Women Voters, and the Lauderdale County Republican Party. "Anyone involved in interracial activities in those days were dubbed communists," Dr. Tinnin says today. But, "our makeup made it hard for them to call us communists."

As was the case fourteen years earlier when Gray wrote the Episcopal document, "The Church Considers the Supreme Court Decision," he also directed the writing of the statement of purpose for the fund-raising group. Ever the strategist, he did not choose as epigram one of many appropriate New Testament texts. Instead he paraphrased a passage from Deuteronomy, a portion of the Bible both Jews and Christians held title to: "Thou shalt not see thy brother's church or House of worship destroyed, and hide thyself from them. Thou shalt restore it to him."

The text of the statement was succinct:

> The Committee of Conscience wishes to make it possible for men, women and children of goodwill to respond to violence, hatred, and destruction with concern, compassion and construction. So, we are initiating a community effort for concrete and personal action in response to the physical losses and personal injustices and indignities suffered by congregations whose buildings have been set afire by arsonists.

The statement explained that such attacks were attacks on all houses of worship, on religion itself, and upon the constitutional guarantee to assemble and worship.

> Contributions from individuals, churches, synagogues and businesses are urgently needed to carry out the work of the Committee. Contributions and inquiries should be addressed to the Committee of Conscience, P.O. Box 707, Meridian, Mississippi 39301.

To list individual names, addresses, and telephone numbers would have been foolhardy. So they didn't do it. A post office box number would have to suffice. The Committee of Conscience raised $750,000 to help rebuild the destroyed Negro churches. When there were dedications of the restored buildings, Gray was there. In normal times the Committee of Conscience would have been so tame and innocent a thing as to offend no one. Not so in Mississippi at the time. The most innocuous utterance, any minor act of kindness could be interpreted as soft on white supremacy and bring acts of retribution from the decanter of foul play hoisted by the White Knights of the Ku Klux Klan.

Even so, Duncan Gray did not hide his affiliation with the Committee of Conscience. Known as a priest who did not base his ministry on ideology, he was sometimes sought out by Klansmen and former members. Delmar Dennis, a member of the White Knights of the KKK and a minister in a sect known as the Southern Methodist Church, came to Gray for counseling. Because Gray related to him as a priest, he will not discuss the sessions regarding Dennis's Klan activities. On another occasion Dennis heard one of Gray's sermons denouncing the bombing of black churches on radio and called to express his admiration for any preacher who would speak his mind on so controversial an issue and asked if they might again get together. During the conversation Dennis said that he had a personal problem and would the priest intervene on his behalf. His wife had left him, feeling that he had violated his Klan oath when he testified in the trial of Klansmen involved in the murders of the civil rights workers based in Meridian. She was back in Scott County with some of her relatives who were notorious racists and active Klansmen. He asked Gray to drive over to Scott County and talk with the estranged wife and see if a reconciliation might be possible. Again, the priest said that he would. A more cautious radical would have suspected a trap, for Scott County is a rural and remote bit of geography. Duncan had to make several stops for directions on the back roads. He admits to feeling something bordering on apprehension when leaving an isolated country store he noted that the men on the porch were paying particular attention to his car as he drove away. Suddenly he remembered there was a Support the Committee of Conscience sticker making its frank announcement from the rear bumper of his car. Also an Episcopal Clergy decal. The clergy decal got him parking privileges at the hospitals but he reckoned it was not designed for such missions as this. He made it back safely but does not remember if his Klan friend's wife came home. When Dennis left the Klan, Gray became his counselor and confidant.

Nineteen sixty-four, Gray's last year at Oxford, had been the capstone year of civil rights activities in Mississippi and with it had gone the most barbarous resistance by white vigilantes. Since 1954 the White Citizens' Councils had been the wellspring of opposition to implementation of the court's decision outlawing segregation in public schools. People like Gray had found the councils' methods of economic pressures and political machinations morally reprehensible. The State Sovereignty Commission, little more than the legal arm of the White Citizens' Council, had affected what amounted to a police state with Gestapo-like tactics. Because of his straightforward racial views and what they saw as liberal political leanings, Gray had been a target of both groups. Their *modus operandi* was to gather or manufacture information, spread rumors, gossip, and hearsay—plant the seeds of suspicion that would undermine any effort to break down the walls of segregation. The object was to influence neighbors, friends, or employers to bring pressure and affect silence. It was highly effective on all except the most resolute. They found Gray to be in that category. What they considered a threat to the status quo was to Gray his doctrine of the church, his understanding of sin, his unwavering commitment to the liturgy he recited daily. If his detractors had understood the reality of the promises made in baptism, confirmation, ordination, and Holy Communion as Gray understood them, he would have been a threat far beyond their toleration. But what Gray saw as the most radical and earthshaking words ever written, they sometimes heard as harmless Sunday School drivel, pious rhetoric. It was when he put those things into action, as he always did, that led to controversy. And those to whom he related directly knew that his words meant response.

Gray read to them from Second Corinthians:

With us therefore worldly standards have ceased to count in our estimate of any man; even if once they counted in our understanding of

Christ they do so now no longer. When anyone is united to Christ, there is a new world; the old order has gone, and a new order has already begun. . . . (2 Cor. 5:16–17 NEB)

He knew precisely what the Scripture was saying to Mississippi of the 1960s. It was saying race was not a category for those baptized; that it was a worldly standard that had once mattered but for those united to Christ it mattered no longer. It meant the old order of segregation and discrimination had passed away and a new order of justice, harmony, and oneness (integration) had begun.

And when he recited from the *Magnificat* at Evening Prayer:

He hath showed strength with his arm; he hath scattered the proud in the imagination of their hearts. He hath put down the mighty from their seat, and hath exalted the humble and meek. He hath filled the hungry with good things; and the rich he hath sent empty away.

He was speaking to those who alleged themselves the powerful but who in reality awaited death's shroud with the deemed weak. The rulers would soon sleep with their fathers, and others would reign in their stead. The Reverend Duncan Gray knew it was an awesome consideration and his sermons quickened the potency of liturgy for those slow of discernment.

His sermons generally addressed a current event. Never bombastic, never designed to increase the membership rolls nor fill the collection plate, he related one of the lessons appointed by the *Prayer Book* for Morning Prayer or Holy Communion to what was going on in Meridian, Mississippi. Simply and forthrightly.

Dr. Martin Luther King Jr. was assassinated three days before Palm Sunday in 1968. Though the birth of Dr. King is now celebrated as a national holiday, it is curious that in 1968 the vast majority of mainline white Southern ministers made no mention of his death from their pulpits. Indeed, some that did related it to God's judgment on a wicked man, often using as a text, "Whatsoever a man soweth, that shall he also reap." Such was the pall of fear that covered the land.

Duncan Gray gave his entire sermon to the man, his life, his work and cause. The parallel to what had happened two thousand years earlier was manifest in every sentence. Acknowledging early that Dr. King was not a popular figure in their environs, and in fact hated by many, he added unequivocally:

> . . . there is nothing more certain in the long run of human events than that your children, your grandchildren, and your great-grand-children will read about this man and regard him as one of the truly great prophets and saints of the 20th century.

Gray discussed Dr. King's dream, and stated that cynics don't think much of dreams. But Gray had been too much of a dreamer of justice and oneness of all people himself to question the dream of another. And too much of an optimist to doubt that good would come of the death of the dreamer. His was not simply a meditation on the life of one man. The majority of the sermon was given to what those sitting and kneeling at St. Paul's Church could personally do to advance the dream and have it come true. It was hard sayings for a congregation in Lauderdale County, Mississippi, in 1968. But by then none present were surprised by what their rector said. Even the hymns were chosen with care to speak to the affairs of the day. Of his own singing Gray says the Psalms tell us to make a joyful noise. It doesn't say we have to be a virtuoso. So he sang the hymns with gusto, generally off meter and often in a different key, sometimes drowning out the choir. Daughter Anne, who insists she did not inherit the more melodious musical genes from her mother as the other children did, loved to hear him sing. "Most Episcopalians are timid about singing," she says. "If we aren't professional we hang back. Not Dad. He sings like a Baptist. Singing for him is a wonderful expression of joy." Liturgy, Gray says, is not a spectator sport. The priest and choir are not there to put on a show. It is of the people.

Mrs. Gray talks freely of some of the hymns that have been so much a part of her husband, quoting lines that exude his very life: "To hear him sing 'O Master let me walk with thee, In lowly paths of service free,' is to realize his closeness to his God. 'Help me the slow of heart to move, By some clear winning word of love' is to overhear his private prayer as he approaches the altar. His desire and prayer was to be an instrument, an earthen vessel, radiating the love of God which he saw as the only power of healing and redemption. It was never a matter of, 'Lord, I'm mounting that pulpit to straighten out these folks for you.'" His wife, sitting before a roaring fire in my writing cabin, calls out the hymns by numbers as she recalls his songs in times of crisis. As she calls I check the hymnal she has brought with her, and we recall an occasion when each was sung.

It was the morning of the Oxford riots that he sang these lyrics:

God of grace and God of glory,
On thy people pour thy power;
Crown thine ancient Church's story;
Bring her bud to glorious flower.
Grant us wisdom, grant us courage,
For the facing of this hour.

Lo! the hosts of evil round us
Scorn thy Christ, assail his ways!
From the fears that long have bound us
Free our hearts to faith and praise:
Grant us wisdom, grant us courage,
For the living of these days.

"Number four-ninety-four," she calls. He sang of his brothers and sisters in Cuba. And the bitter fruit of the Industrial Revolution. Written by another courageous Southern priest, and a mentor, Walter Russell Bowie.

Hark, how from men whose lives are held
More cheap than merchandise;
From women struggling sore for bread,
From little children's cries,
There swells the sobbing human plaint
That bids thy walls arise!
O shame to us who rest content
While lust and greed for gain
In streets and shop and tenement
Wring gold from human pain,
And bitter lips in blind despair
Cry, "Christ hath died in vain!"

On many Sundays when the week had seen racial strife the song was this:

O brother man, fold to thy heart thy brother:
Where pity dwells, the peace of God is there;
To worship rightly is to love each other,
Each smile a hymn, each kindly deed a prayer.

"Once to Every Man and Nation," "In Christ There Is No East Nor West," "Where Cross the Crowded Ways of Life," and then words written by a former dweller on the Mountain, William Alexander Percy.

Suddenly Ruth Spivey Gray begins to sing. Unlike her husband, she is a fine vocalist. I join her, though my own timing is worse than that of the off-metered reverend:

Lead on, O King eternal,
Till sin's fierce war shall cease,
And holiness shall whisper
The sweet Amen of peace;
For not with swords loud clashing,
Nor roll of stirring drums,
But deeds of love and mercy,
Thy heavenly kingdom come.

And we understand without commentary. Then, from nowhere in particular, she says, "You know, Duncan often ponders and reflects on the wonder, mystery, and majesty of God. But he does not act out of fear of God's vengeance but out of thanksgiving. That which shapes him and compels him to be involved in social causes is primarily his understanding of human sin and his profound gratitude for God's gift of redemption and His many other blessings. This gratitude and the desire to be faithful make him what he is. They have also enabled him to overcome fear for his personal safety."

We sit in silence as I considered her words. Then, as I poke the dying embers before us she says, "Look at page six in the *Prayer Book*." I turn to it. It is the General Confession. I read it silently, almost as if I am reading it for the first time.

. . . We have erred and strayed from thy ways like lost sheep. . . . And there is no health in us. But thou, O Lord, have mercy upon us, miserable offenders. Spare thou those, O God, who confess their faults. . . .

"Some find the words routine, repetitive, and boring," Mrs. Gray says. "Duncan is almost ecstatic every time he recites them. Not at the recitation of offenses against the Deity but ecstatic at the assurance of pardon that follows." Again I realize it is the radicalism of liturgy that has shaped Gray to be the thing he is.

It was almost exactly two months after Dr. King was slain that Temple Beth Israel, the Meridian synagogue, was bombed. Though there were exceptions, most white preachers, as well as most of the press and elected officials, had been strangely silent when it was only Negro homes and houses of worship being bombed and desecrated. Not so Duncan Gray. He had condemned all of it and had worked tirelessly in the Committee of Conscience to rebuild them. He surely would not let the bombing of a non-Christian edifice go unchallenged.

Rabbi Milton Schlager, now living in Sumter, South Carolina, relates the events of the night of the bombing in the fashion of ancient rabbinic storytelling. It was past midnight and Rabbi and Mrs. Schlager were preparing for bed. Their three small children and Mrs. Schlager's mother were asleep. A thunderous explosion filled the night, like the violent summer storms that sometimes raked the central hills of east Mississippi with little warning. It shook china in kitchen cabinets, and sent birds scampering from their roosts, their distress signals adding to the panic inside. The temple was three miles away but the rabbi knew. He had been expecting Temple Beth Israel to be bombed, and had warned his congregation. But because the Jewish families dated back to Meridian's beginning, they were as indigenous to the area as Methodists and Baptists. There had never been the kind of anti-Semitism that existed in Jackson and other places, they felt secure. "No, no, Rabbi. Not in Meridian." The synagogue in Jackson had been dynamited earlier, as well as the home of Rabbi and Mrs. Perry Nussbaum. Rabbi Nussbaum had been active in the Mississippi Council on Human Relations with Mr. Gray, and Duncan had driven to Jackson to visit the Nussbaums after each bombing.

Even before Rabbi Schlager and his wife could finish dressing there was a knock on the door. "It was Duncan Gray standing there, the street light casting a looming shadow inside the dimly lighted room, making the silent figure seem twenty feet tall," Rabbi Schlager says today. "And to us he *was* twenty feet tall. My friend appeared to try to speak but words did not come. Only a protrusion of tears. I had never seen tears flow in a rushing stream like that before. Certainly not from a grown man." After all these years the rabbi has difficulty completing the story. "The three of us stood there in a deep embrace. No one spoke a word. Until the police came the three of us just stood together. Sobbing." The rabbi knew his Christian brother was not crying over the damage done to the synagogue. That could be replaced. "His heart was truly broken," Rabbi Schlager says. "His tears spoke so much more than mere words could have. I will never forget that expression of authentic love of a Christian for his Jewish neighbors."

Gray went with the Schlagers so they would not be alone when they viewed the remains of their house of worship that had been completed just four years earlier. Gray remembers the drama of seeing a memorial given to the Temple by a group of Meridian Christians the year before, and in which he had played a part: six perpetually burning gas lights in memory of those who died in the Holocaust, the stone tablet reading: "Am I My Brother's Keeper?"

Rabbi Schlager quotes from an Hassidic story that says the world is upheld by thirty-six righteous men. "I don't know the other thirty-five," he says behind laughter. "But I knew one of them in Meridian, Mississippi, during some hectic years." Finally the rabbi adds, "We have a word for such as he. *Mensch*."

The Sunday following the bombing of the Temple was Pentecost Sunday on the Christian calendar. It was also the day St. Paul's Church would honor the graduating high school seniors. Some must have wondered how their priest would tie those three things together. For him it was patent.

> As we gather together for worship this Sunday morning in St. Paul's Church, three things are on our mind: the graduating seniors whom we honor at our eleven o'clock service, the crisis in our community pointed up once again so vividly and so tragically by the bombing of Temple Beth Israel, and the feast of Pentecost, or Whitsunday which we observe in our churches today. As we reflect on these things, I believe we can find a meaningful relationship among the three, and I want to think with you about these this morning.

From that his message to the young was. "Get involved. Get involved. Get involved, and stay involved." We are one people, he explained, quoting some classic lines from John Donne. "Never send to know for whom the bell tolls. It tolls for thee." He talked of Pentecost when every tribe and tongue were all together, in one place. Each is responsible for the other. And to whom much is given, much is expected. "We are privileged, we of St. Paul's. There are few barriers in our way. Racially, religiously, economically or socially. Excuses cannot be tolerated."

For the adults he gave no quarter. "The bombing is our fault for we have not stood against it," he admonished. "In the first place, the perpetrators of such crimes [eight black churches attacked by arsonists and bombers before the Temple, all in the past two months] assume that they have at least some measure of community sanction. They assume a certain amount of support from many in the community who would not set the fires or place the bombs but would not be especially disturbed."

Gray was not reluctant to call names. J. B. Stoner, the notorious racist and anti-Semitic head of the National States' Rights Party, had recently been in Meridian for an organizing drive and had said it was the ideal base for his organization. Gray saw Stoner's choice of Meridian as the most gross insult any community could receive. The preaching priest listed what Stoner saw as enemies of his effort—the chief of police, the city council, and the Chamber of Commerce and said they should be singularly complimented for making that list. "Sadly enough," Gray added, "the churches were not included as enemies of this anti-Semitic, anti-Negro hate group." He begged the pardon of his congregation that his laughter for once was sardonic.

So that none might hear the sayings of the rector that day as humanistic and sociological analysis, with no place in the niceness of a Christian edifice, the sermon concluded with a return to the Day of Pentecost:

> Whitsunday reminds us of the conditions which must exist before we can know the power of the Holy Spirit in all its fullness. 'They were all with one accord in one place,' the Book of Acts tells us. It was the corporate desire, the corporate hope, and the corporate will of that apostolic band that brought the Spirit upon them in all its power. When you and I and all the decent people of this community really decide that those burnings and bombings are going to stop, they will stop. When we decide that the time for neutrality and fence-straddling is past; when we decide that we are no longer going to stand back in the shadows; when we really want this kind of violence to cease badly enough to stand up and be counted and to commit ourselves—our time, our energy, and our resources— fully and irrevocably, regardless of the possible consequences; then it will stop.

One of the final lines of Duncan Gray's customary benediction, "Rejoicing in the power of the Spirit," must have struck an ambiguous chord that day. Many were fearful of invoking so powerful an ally as the third member of the Trinity in what they still considered a matter of states' rights.

The other members of the Gray family would become as involved in community activities as the rector. Mrs. Gray taught in a Head Start Program in a black church. She remembers with much sorrow driving to school one morning and seeing the building in smoldering ruins, and the tired, confused, sad eyes of the little children.

Lloyd, Gray's third born, was in the tenth grade when his class was transferred from the formerly all-white Meridian High to the black Harris High at midterm. The Meridian desegregation plan was for the eleventh and twelfth grades of the formerly all-black Harris High to be transferred to formerly white Meridian High while the tenth grade of Meridian High would be sent to Harris High. Dire predictions had been made as to the outcome. Threats of violence from the more rabid segregationists, and talk of mutiny among many of the students were rampant. As president of the tenth grade class Lloyd wrote a letter to his classmates. With prose that might have been a portent of the successful journalist he would become, he wrote with neat subtleties of flattery and realistic expectations. Without denying that there would be problems and adjustments to face as they left familiar surroundings and moved into a strange, new, and at times perplexing situation, he challenged his fellow teenagers to maturity; to rise above old ways and attitudes and ". . . show our elders and the world that we are able to rise to this challenge and meet our responsibilities in a constructive manner. It is our opinion that we are indeed equal to the task." Signed "With hope for the future," the letter also carried the signatures of three student council representatives.

Since the exchanges would be made in the middle of a school year there would be two class presidents. Lloyd had a black friend who had been one of the few to transfer to Meridian High under the freedom of choice plan that had been instituted to discourage mass desegregation while at the same time satisfying the courts. It did neither and thus the unitary system developed in which all of some classes would be in one school, all of other classes in the other school. Lloyd's friend, a charming young intellectual named Obie Clayton, was a devout member of the Church of Christ, a denomination vastly different from the Episcopal Church in polity, theology, and form of worship. No matter for the two young boys. They became fast friends. Together they worked on plans for a smooth transition to Harris High where Obie knew everyone and Lloyd knew very few. Later, his friendship with Obie Clayton was helpful when trouble developed at Harris High and there was a walkout by most black students and biracial negotiation was needed. After graduating, both young men would attend Millsaps College in Jackson, Mississippi, an institution of academic excellence. Obie is now Dr. Clayton, director of the Morehouse College Research Institute in Atlanta. After graduate studies he taught at the University of Massachusetts and the University of Nebraska. He is now an active Episcopalian.

Lloyd had previously written a poem for an English assignment called "All Men Brothers?" in which the influence of his parents was apparent. His teachers were not surprised by his purpose and attitude. They were pleased that his interest in race relations was more than academic.

More and more Duncan Gray was drawn into activities some considered to be beyond his responsibilities as priest. But he was never content to generalize on the plight of the poor. He did not keep his concern within the confines of the steeple, nor hide behind the rhetoric of Old Testament prophets. His faith and *Prayer Book* liturgy thrust him into the arena of their needs. As president of the Mississippi Council on Human Relations, the only interracial organization in the state committed to integration, he was in the forefront of the battle for civil rights. He also served on the board of the Southern Regional Council, the parent organization of the Mississippi Council. As a vehicle for St. Francis Homes, an organization concerned directly with housing for the poor started under Gray's leadership, he was a constant advocate. When Mississippi Action for Progress (MAP) was organized, he became involved immediately. MAP was a statewide effort to draw together white and black Mississippians to address the racial and economic ills of the state, primarily by sponsoring Head Start Programs in many parts of the state. Working with such people as Charles Young, prominent and prosperous black Meridian businessman; Hodding Carter III, then publisher of the progressive Greenville *Democrat-Times*; Oscar Carr, the Delta planter who had helped Duncan in his budget crisis in Oxford; and Claude Ramsey, head of the Mississippi AFL-CIO; Gray served as chairman of the Lauderdale County Head Start Program for four years.

Gray was vice-chairman of the Lauderdale Economic Assistance Program, a community action arm of the War on Poverty. He was also on the advisory committee that allocated Title I funds, primarily to minorities. He had been a part of what became known as the War on Poverty from the beginning. In 1964 St. Peter's Church had the Reverend Daisuke Kitagawa for a preaching mission. Dai, as he was affectionately known, had a long history in the area of conflict resolution going back to World War II when he was in a Japanese internment camp (America's rendition of concentration camps). Already a priest, he continued in his ministerial role with his fellow inmates. Following the war he had worked with the World Council of Churches in Africa in various areas of strife. When Gray invited him to Oxford in 1964, Kitagawa was on the national Church staff.

The two men drove around the state talking informally in parish churches about race relations. One Saturday evening at Clarksdale was especially memorable. A meeting was arranged at St. George's Church. Things were especially tense in Coahoma County on the racial front in 1964 and there was not a lot of enthusiasm among white citizens to talk about it with a Japanese cleric and a native priest whose position was well known. With deference to their rector, the Reverend Charles Chambers Jr., a number of parishioners agreed to come for a short while. Saturday night was party night in the Delta and most showed up in evening clothes, intending to remain a polite few minutes and be on their way to the dance. They had not reckoned with the charisma of Dai Kitagawa, Gray remembers. The meeting lasted until eleven o'clock, with people revealing hidden misgivings about the status quo they had never discussed before.

The next summer Gray invited Mr. Kitagawa for another preaching mission, intending to stir the Delta waters once more. He said he would come but would not go back to Clarksdale unless he could talk with Negro citizens. He wasn't going back to Mr. Aaron Henry's hometown and talk only with a group of white people. (Aaron Henry was president of the Mississippi NAACP and close friend and colleague of Gray.) Mr. Chambers said to come on. This time a well-integrated group gathered and the session progressed from talking about how bad things were to what might be done to make things better. It was the beginning of the Community Action Program in Coahoma County, with a prominent Episcopal layman serving as chairman. Mild perhaps by today's standards but in 1965 it was a bold step for the Mississippi Delta.

Gray was not one to preside at meetings and go home. The East Mississippi State Hospital, a facility that had been established largely through the efforts of Gray's grandfather as editor of the Meridian *Star*, was nearby. As president of the Lauderdale County Mental Health Association, Duncan could often be seen on the grounds, walking with patients or visiting in their wards. Many, he discovered, had little or no dementia at all. They were simply old, infirm, and unwanted by their families. The hospital was part of his larger parish.

Still he insisted that he was a non-joiner. And he really didn't join anything that was not locally based, feeling that anything that was not local did not exist. Of course, anything Mississippi based was local to him. A national society was formed to attack the social ills of society, with particular emphasis on civil rights. Called the *Episcopal Society for Cultural and Racial Unity* (ESCRU), the membership engaged in demonstrations, sit-ins,

186

and the like. They were good people: conscientious, courageous, and dedicated to the task. But like so much that happened in those days their activities were generally strikes of short duration. Gray, while not disapproving of their motives, saw little value in a visiting Boston priest marching in the streets of a Mississippi town, perhaps spending one night in a Southern jail and then returning to Boston or Schenectady. Again, he did not object nor try to hinder them. It simply was not his vocation; not his style. He had enlisted for the duration. From Little Theater to Little League baseball coach; Kiwanis Club to Federal Credit Union; Symphony Society to Tuberculosis and Respiratory Association; from high visibility in civil rights activities to the most tame and uncelebrated activity in town— Duncan Gray was in the world.

On June 28, 1968, three weeks after his Pentecost sermon addressing the bombing of Temple Beth Israel, Gray planned a quiet evening at home with his wife and children. But before he left his office at St. Paul's Church, he received a phone call from Ken Dean, executive director of the Mississippi Council on Human Relations of which Gray was president. Gray had been on the board of directors of the council since shortly after graduating from seminary. He was supportive of his executive director but did not interfere in the day-to-day operation of the council. It was not unusual to be called by Dean at any hour. This time, however, Gray sensed an unusual urgency in Dean's voice. He said the two needed to talk and he and Mary, his wife of a brief time, were leaving Jackson immediately to drive to Meridian.

Dean was a young, unflagging, and bright Baptist preacher, a graduate of Colgate-Rochester Divinity School. From a poor family in East Tennessee, he had worked for a time at the Oak Ridge nuclear plant until he realized what was happening there—research on further development of nuclear weapons—and walked away. He worked his way through Carson-Newman College playing football and operating the Coca-Cola vending machines on campus for a commission of the profits. Some saw him as brash, with an exaggerated flair for the dramatic. Gray, however, always took him seriously and had never known Dean to be wrong in reading the signs of the times. Gray said he would be waiting.

The story Ken Dean told Gray was so bizarre as to strain credulity. But Gray was a listener and heard Dean out. Dean reported that he had reliable information that money had been raised, partly with help from the Anti-Defamation League of B'nai B'rith, to pay two Klan informers to arrange a bombing attempt on a Meridian Jewish residence in which two suspected terrorists, Danny Joe Hawkins and Thomas Tarrants, would be killed when they tried to carry out the bombing. Tarrants and Hawkins were suspected by the FBI to be the ones responsible for acts of violence on black and Jewish citizens. The FBI, however, had not been able to get enough evidence to arrest and charge them. Both Tarrants and Hawkins were young. Hawkins was twenty-five; Tarrants, a native of Mobile, twenty-one.

Jewish citizens, after bombings of their houses of worship, the home of a rabbi, and numerous threats, were understandably outraged and decided to fight fire with fire. Ken Dean, who gave no quarter when it came to advocacy of civil rights for everyone, saw this *"extra-legal"* plan as a threat to the constitutional rights of everyone. This was, to him, a clear case of entrapment and he had come to Meridian to stop it if he could. His Christian faith led him to abhor violence. But as an inflexible civil libertarian he opposed methods that were patently illegal; judge, jury, and executioner. At the same time he understood the fear and rage of the Jewish community at the violence directed at them. There were survivors of the Holocaust in Meridian and that genocidal intrusion in human history weighed heavily. Still, Dean could not accept entrapment and assassination as the antidote for moral lunacy.

Today Dean describes that visit with Gray as pastoral. "He did not criticize and he didn't tell me I was suffering from nervous exhaustion and was in need of rest and rehabilitation as has been reported." Instead, Gray asked Dean what they could do. They sat at a table in the rectory and discussed the situation and all it portended. They agreed that they could not call federal or local law officials because they were said to be party to the entrapment. At that point Dean did not know either of the Klansmen or he would have alerted them personally. He had tried to locate Hawkins before leaving Jackson but failed.

Nor did Dean know the identity of the intended target of the bombing. Gray knew most of the Jewish families and he and Dean made a list of names and addresses of those known to oppose the reign of terror Meridian was experiencing.

With a map the two men drove slowly, methodically and inquiringly around town, back and forth by houses of Jewish families. They gave particular focus to the home of Meyer Davidson, president of the Southern Pipe Company, one of the South's largest distributors of plumbing supplies. Because of his outspokenness and openness in denouncing the bombing and burning of black churches and homes, as well as the personal violence, he was apt to be singled out, Gray reasoned. If not the Davidson residence then Duncan thought a likely target would be the home of Alfred and Lucile Rosenbaum. Mr. Rosenbaum, prominent insurance executive, and his wife were both outspoken supporters of public schools. It was Friday night and they also made several passes by the home of Rabbi Schlager and the synagogue that had been dynamited about a month earlier. Gray's St. Paul's Church had offered the use of their facilities, as had been done years before when a fire destroyed the old synagogue, but the congregation decided to continue to worship in the damaged building.

As Dean and Gray toured the area, the utter obscenity of it all was alarming to Gray. The Davidson and Rosenbaum families, Rabbi Schlager, and most of the families at whom threats of violence had been directed were Gray's friends. He had worked closely with the rabbi and Davidson on the Committee of Conscience.

Ken Dean was certain that his information was correct and that Friday night, June 28, 1968, was the date that had been set for the well-planned ambush on the two Klansmen who had been set up by Klan informers. Finally, after all the cruising, and finding nothing that seemed at all suspicious, he began to feel that possibly he had been given bad information. Or, conceivably, he really was exhausted from the strain of a civil rights job in Mississippi in what amounted to warfare, and needed a rest. Throughout the drive Gray remained supportive and cooperative. When at last Dean said that he and Mary would drive to Maryville, Tennessee, to visit his mother, Gray, his friend and organizational president, said he thought that was a good idea and that they would stay in touch. Then Gray invited the Deans to spend the night in his home and leave early Saturday morning. If anything did happen later that night both men would be on the scene.

The two men missed the predicted violent eruption by twenty-four hours. On Sunday, Ken Dean, returning from Maryville, considered going through Meridian to photograph previously bombed and burned sites of Negro churches, businesses, and homes. Instead, he returned to Jackson and was shocked to hear on the 10:30 P.M. news that his worst fears were confirmed. There had indeed been a stake-out by FBI agents and Meridian police. There was in fact an effort to bomb the home of Meyer Davidson and his wife. And in the planned effort to kill two Klansmen, one person was dead, three others—a police officer, a Klansman, and an uninvolved navy man—were critically injured. Thomas Tarrants, the Klansman critically wounded, was not expected to live. The person riding with him, however, was not Danny Hawkins, the other Klansman marked for death by the entrapment. It was a woman,

Kathy Ainsworth, a twenty-six-year-old Jackson schoolteacher. By day she was a highly regarded pedagogue. By night she was a terrorist engaged in various Klan activities against Jews, Negroes, and alleged communists. When Mary Dean heard the news account of Ainsworth's death in Meridian, she exclaimed that Kathryn Madlyn Capomacchia had been Mary's sister's roommate at Mississippi College before Kathryn married Ralph Ainsworth. The death trap had come closer to home than either Ken or Mary Dean had imagined.

Dean went back to Meridian so he and Gray could put the pieces of the story together. Both men were deeply troubled at what they found, some of which they had good reason to believe was scheduled to happen and had tried to intercept—but had the wrong night.

Ken Dean had been told by A. I. (Bee) Botnick, the staff person of the Anti-Defamation League, that brothers Raymond and Alton Wayne Roberts were the informants who would set the trap. Both were known members of the White Knights and close to Danny Hawkins and to Sam Bowers, Imperial Wizard of the KKK, who would have to approve the plan. Alton Wayne Roberts was free on an appeal bond following his conviction in a federal trial involving the murders of Chaney, Goodman, and Schwerner, the three civil rights workers killed in Neshoba County and buried in a farm pond dam. It was generally believed that it had been Alton Wayne Roberts who had fired the fatal shots. It was also believed they had bombed the Meridian synagogue. Thus it was thought they would be the most apt candidates for a bribe. They could make some money and at the same time have some of the heat taken off them by being informers. By a combination of intimidation, money, bargaining, and two weeks of late-night intrigue of spine tingling magnitude, the Roberts brothers were convinced that they had no choice but to cooperate with the police and FBI or be killed themselves. It was a difficult choice for the brothers. If they became informers and were found out, they would certainly be killed by the Klan. If they refused to cooperate they feared they would be killed by lawmen in a set-up in which they would be the objective. Apparently the sight of a briefcase filled with stacks of money tipped the scale in favor of betraying their Klan comrades.

The Roberts brothers said they knew the names of the two who had dynamited the Beth Israel synagogue in Meridian and could arrange for those same two to attempt a bombing in Meridian. They understood that the plan was one of assassination of their fellow Klansmen. The Klansmen would not be taken alive. The brothers were too involved now to turn back.

Danny Joe Hawkins was a shrewd and cautious operative who generally made his own plans. This time he was convinced by Raymond Roberts that a bombing in Meridian, on an occasion when the Roberts brothers would have a perfect alibi, would take some of the pressure off him and his brother who were suspected of the synagogue bombing and the burning of black churches in the area. Hawkins agreed. During the next two weeks Raymond Roberts made several visits to Jackson so that he would have flawless information on when and where the attempted bombing would be. The final plan was funnelled to the Meridian police and FBI agents.

All that, of course, was not immediately known to Dean and Gray as they sought to get the story. What they were able to establish, however, was what had happened when the shooting began at the residence of Meyer Davidson at the corner of Twenty-ninth Avenue and Thirty-sixth Street.

As Thomas Tarrants eased the green Buick Electra within fifty feet of the Davidson house, with Kathy Ainsworth on the passenger side, the moonless summer night was ghostly still. It was later learned that Ainsworth had just told Tarrants, "This one is going to be easier than the last two." It was past midnight. It had been decided at almost the last minute that Ainsworth would accompany Tarrants instead of Hawkins. Her husband, who knew of his young wife's segregationist and anti-Semitic views but was not sympathetic with her Klan activities, was away doing his summer National Guard training. Kathy was to travel to Miami to visit her mother and Tarrants would drive her there after the bombing. In addition, Hawkins was kept under almost constant surveillance; because of his reputation, his being on the mission would pose a security risk. Although Tarrants had participated in a number of bombings he was not then as well known as Hawkins.

The Davidson couple had been taken to a local motel for the night. Because there had been a similar stake-out two nights earlier but nothing happened, Meyer Davidson had not wanted to go, agreeing, finally, on condition that his favorite chair would be taken in which he could sit to pay the month's bills.

Inside the residence across from the Davidson house were two FBI agents. Scattered around the area, in ditches, behind trees and clumps of shrubs were more than a score of agents and officers, all thoroughly briefed, all prepared to do what they were there to do. "Drop'em!" was the terse directive. The last bit of intelligence had come from Roberts only minutes earlier. To acquaint them with the area, he had driven Tarrants and Ainsworth past the Davidson house when they arrived from Jackson. Then they had taken Roberts to a bar where he and his brother would have witnesses to their whereabouts when the shooting began. From there Raymond Roberts had telephoned one of the agents and given him an exact description of the car. Inside the vehicle, he told the agent, were two machine guns, a .45 caliber pistol, approximately twenty sticks of dynamite in a Clorox box and a smaller box containing a timing device. Actually Roberts had underreported the deadly munition the car contained. He had also told the agent that a woman he did not know was with Tarrants, not Danny Joe Hawkins.

As soon as Tarrants stepped from the car, the dynamite in one hand, an automatic pistol in another, there was a yell to halt, followed by gunfire from the vastly outmanned Tarrants, the FBI agents, and Meridian police. A description of the barrage that filled the night at that point would be impossible to itemize. Everyone was firing as one, almost miraculously missing each other and not detonating the box of dynamite that would almost certainly have killed most of the agents and officers in the area if it had exploded. Tarrants, hit immediately in the upper part of his right leg, dropped the gun and dynamite as he struggled to get back in the car. Kathy Ainsworth was hit in the shoulder by two loads of buckshot before a rifle bullet tore through her spine, killing her instantly.

With superhuman strength Tarrants, though wounded, broke the cordon and sped away in the already riddled Buick. Firing continued in a chase that ended fifteen blocks away when he was subdued, still firing a machine gun, by numerous blasts from shotguns, rifles, and pistols. Before finally going down he had critically injured a police officer. A navy man visiting the neighborhood from the nearby base was severely injured in the crossfire. When at last the mangled Tarrants crumpled to the ground, felled in the end by an electrically charged fence he was trying to scale, he already had enough wounds to be dead. Both legs had been shot and his right arm almost severed. Shotgun blasts had exploded as they tore into his abdomen and other areas of his body, blowing away entire sections of bone in one arm, destroying big areas of tissue in their indiscriminate explosions. A shotgun aimed at his head from a few feet away would have finished him off but had no shell left in the magazine. As alarmed residents began to gather and witness what was happening the shooting stopped, leaving Tarrants at that moment with barely enough life to contend with death. When the shooting stopped Thomas Tarrants was supposed to be dead. But he wasn't.

Duncan Gray was incredulous as the story unfolded. But it was not incredulity his executive director, Kenneth Dean, was feeling. He was morally and constitutionally outraged. He saw the entrapment and shoot-out as a grievous miscarriage of justice and referred to it as a federal lynching. He was unwaveringly opposed to violence against blacks, Jews, or anyone at all. He understood the visceral determination to stop it. But there had been no arrest, charge, arraignment, jury trial, conviction, nor sentencing. He did not see the erosion of the American system as the way to preserve that system. In the years to come he would devote a great deal of energy to conveying the dangers inherent in any extra-legal maneuver to quell violence with violence.

Gray was deeply disturbed by the irony. The burning and bombing of black houses of worship and the violence against black citizens had been met with little attention by the FBI and local police. Often the destruction of a church would not even be reported by the press. Violence directed against whites had elicited this response. Yet he would continue on his path of grace. Law would have to be left to Law.

The shoot-out had occurred on the first breath of the Fourth Sunday after Trinity on the church calendar. The Collect in the *Book of Common Prayer* for Fourth Sunday after Trinity was:

O God, the protector of all that trust in thee, without whom nothing is strong, nothing is holy; Increase and multiply upon us thy mercy; that, thou being our ruler and guide, we may pass through things temporal, that we finally not lose the things eternal. . . .

His heavy inflection was on "things temporal" and "things eternal." The Gospel was from St. Luke:

Be ye therefore merciful, as your Father also is merciful. Judge not, and ye shall not be judged: condemn not, and ye shall not be condemned: forgive and ye shall be forgiven: give and it shall be given unto you; good measure, pressed down, and shaken together, and running over, shall men give into your bosom. For with the same measure that ye mete shall it be measured to you again. And he spake a parable unto them, Can the blind lead the blind? shall they not both fall into the ditch? The disciple is not above his master: but every one that is perfect shall be as his master. And why beholdest thou the mote that is in thy brother's eye, but perceiveth not the beam that is in thine own eye? Either how canst thou say to thy brother, Brother, let me pull out the mote that is in thine eye, when thou thyself beholdest not the beam that is in thine own eye? Thou hypocrite, cast out first the beam out of thine own eye, and then shalt thou see clearly to pull out the mote that is in thy brother's eye.

To the Reverend Duncan Gray, the Collect and Gospel reading appointed for that day spoke directly and forthrightly to what had happened in their city just hours before. And of the relevant radicalism of the Word of God when brought from the printed word to the reality of the present. His sermon was brief but exacting: *The wind blowest where it listeth.*

There is an addendum to the story of Thomas Tarrants, the man known as mad-dog killer. With the help of a Jewish lawyer who raised money to have Tarrants killed, one of the FBI agents who participated in the entrapment, and Kenneth Dean who would not give up on the soul of even a mad-dog killer, Tarrants was given early release following what all saw as a genuine religious experience in prison. He had served six years of a thirty-year sentence. He attended the University of Mississippi and made almost perfect marks, majoring in philosophy and religious studies. Today he teaches in a theological school that trains people to work in urban areas where dwell those he once despised and sought to eliminate. He is dedicated to fighting extremism, particularly the kind that singles out Jews as the scapegoat for the world's problems. A quiet family man, no one who knows him doubts his utter sincerity and assiduous dedication to his vocation of breaking the chains of darkness. Duncan Gray lays claim to no part in that miracle. But who's to say?

Although Gray understands the powers and principalities with which we wrestle, and readily agrees that the institutional church is subject to those powers, he has chosen to remain a part of those structures. Some have seen the choice as a weakness and contradiction of principle; a serving of what his faith would seem to oppose; a futile effort to renew the unrenewable. In an essay he wrote for a small magazine, *Journal of the Committee of Southern Churches*, not long after the Meridian shoot-out, he explained his position well. He was still in Meridian at the time, 1969—a year of the country's most violent upheavals. If there was ever a time to despair of old ways, structures, and institutions, it was then. His activist friends knew Gray to be in sympathetic league with them. Still he continued to operate from a base they saw as a dark, persistent smudge of hopelessness; an archaic relic of past oppression—the Episcopal

Church. And residing in the belly of what had become the asylum of KKK dementia. Meridian, Mississippi. *"Why doesn't Duncan join us in the streets? Where the action is?"*

But Gray knew where the action was. At least for himself. He penned an essay, "In Defense of the Steeple." He began by acknowledging the criticism of the parish church and accepting most of it as valid. Nowhere was the failure of the church more obvious than in race relations, he wrote. He agreed that the institutional church is not a very effective agent of social change, that it is conservative, slow to change, and abides more in apostasy than in faithfulness. Then, admitting that he was a social activist, he questioned the long-term effectiveness of manning the barricades, marching in the streets, or sitting in at the Congress. As proper and necessary as those things may be, he saw them as falling far short of the radical nature of the Gospel. In effect he was telling the crusaders just how reactionary they were when it came to solving the problem of race. They were not radical, as they believed themselves to be, because they saw the solution to the nation's ills as political and legislative in nature. He wrote,

> We have enough laws, court decisions, and executive orders in effect already to bring about reconciliation between white and black, if such could be accomplished by these alone. And yet the degree of separation and alienation seems to be greater than ever before. As important as legal action may be, it still does not get to the heart of the matter: the human heart.

When the essay appeared, some considered the Mississippi priest in strange company. Also appearing in the same issue were James Bevel, then a leader in the generally unpopular (in white circles) Student Non-Violent Coordinating Committee; Julius Lester, a young black intellectual and activist; Jacques Ellul, the French barrister, professor, and prominent theologian; Daniel and Phillip Berrigan, repeatedly jailed anti-war protesters; and Raymond Cranford, a well-known leader of the North Carolina Ku Klux Klan who wrote a letter to Richard Nixon called "Quaker to Quaker." (Ironically both President Nixon and the klansman were reared Quakers.)

Many saw the rector's words as quaint, a baroque ornament of retreat: a cop-out. The quarter century since he wrote those words, however, has verified his position. Law has not solved our problems. Politics, legislation, and court decisions have hardened more hearts than they have thawed, often exacerbated problems more than corrected, and even the decisions and bills designed to promote justice have often been appropriated by the forces of darkness to inflict more injustice upon the poor and minorities.

Referring to what the church can authentically offer, Gray challenged the Western movie syndrome of good guys and bad guys as he continued. "When we deal with real people, caught up in the common perplexities, joys, and sorrows of this life, the distinctions begin to blur, and we tend to see different degrees of need, rather than different degrees of evil." It was his way of saying there is none righteous. For those honestly seeking societal redemption, he said that he had seen many diehard racists in his day but, "I know of none whose basic affliction could not be cured by the same things that I require for my own soul's health: love and acceptance, mercy and forgiveness, compassion and grace." Finally he appealed to the church itself, to be a fellowship living by the real "Good News" that God loves us all, accepts, forgives all, where we are and as we are. And He does that for everyone equally, Gray insisted. Not just the good guys in their zeal—for often they saw no need of forgiveness—but also for the bad guys in their intransigence as well.

Far from being a weak apologia of the parish church it was a hard-nosed credo, a challenge to those who claim allegiance to Jesus to be what they are; reconciled to all creation. No exceptions. No color code, no status, no power. All humanity is one. His appeal to the larger society was that the parish church was where they would find the people, and if anyone truly desired to work for a better society they should go to where the people are to be found. To him, being a parish priest meant more than minding altar fires and attending tea parties. And, as for him, he was content to labor in a small venue some saw as contributing little to the cause of *The Movement*.

The success of most Protestant pastors is measured more in terms of new members, budget increases, and building campaigns than the intangible spiritual growth of the congregation. Gray paid scant attention to the first three and worked unrelentingly on the latter. I found no member of St. Paul's Church who doubted that their understanding of and commitment to the cause of Christ was enhanced by Gray's presence amongst them. During his almost decade at St. Paul's the membership grew by less than one percent. However, unlike Oxford where members expressed their displeasure with the rector's activities by withholding their offerings, the revenue at St. Paul's more than doubled. The increase was used in service to the community and the world at large.

One year after going to Meridian, Gray's father, and his bishop, retired. The day the bishop's retirement became effective, his wife died. Three weeks later The Right Reverend Duncan Montgomery Gray Sr. followed his wife in death. Losing both parents, whom Gray loved very much, as well as his bishop, to whom he looked for support no matter how severe the controversy, left a serious void in Gray. But he would carry on. He would be what his father had baptized and ordained him to be: a Christian. More he never promised nor aspired to.

In 1973 Bishop John Allin, who had succeeded Gray's father as bishop, was elected to be presiding bishop of the national Church, to become effective in 1974. A council was soon to be convened to elect a new diocesan bishop. Gray, as priest of St. Paul's, Meridian, would be expected to attend the council, dutifully cast his ballot with the rest and return home. But before the council meeting a totally unexpected development occurred. Judge Billy Neville tarried at the church door on Sunday following Morning Prayer. When they were alone he said, "Duncan, Tom Ward and I have been talking. We want to ask your permission to nominate you for the office of bishop." The astonished rector tried to parry the request with a hearty laugh. In the first place, he had given such a thing no thought at all. More than that, Gray was not unaware that he remained a controversial figure with many in the Diocese of Mississippi. The document, "The Church Considers the Supreme Court Decision," he had written as a young priest in the Delta had marked him as an enemy of the Southern way of life where racial segregation was concerned (to many a more sacred trust than the vows of confirmation and ordination). His role in the University of Mississippi crisis had further alienated him from the mainstream. His continuing activities as president of the Mississippi Council on Human Relations and his opposition to the White Citizens' Council, the State Sovereignty Commission, and the gothic politics of the era had not endeared him to many who would be casting ballots for the Ordinary.

When Gray realized that his friend, parishioner, and vestryman was serious, he explained his position. He thought it would be a futile gesture but appreciated the thought. He had never aspired to so lofty an office in the Episcopal Church. He knew he would not accept the office in any other diocese. However, if elected to serve the Church in Mississippi he would accede to the will of the council. It would be composed of people who knew him well, what he stood for, and where he would try to lead them. He would not run for the office. Nor would he run from it. To do either would have been a gross violation of his doctrine of the Holy Spirit.

The response of the rector was enough for Judge Neville and Mr. Ward. They would play the hand they were dealt.

AT GETTYSBURG, THE UNIVERSITY GREYS WERE WAITING for battle with thousands of others from General Robert E. Lee's Army of Northern Virginia. In their immediate area was what had been Major General Henry Heth's division, now commanded by Brigadier General J. J. Pettigrew, a scholarly North Carolinian who had replaced General Heth when he was wounded the day before.

Already moving into position on the right of Pettigrew's division was the division commanded by the flamboyant, cocky, romantic Major General George Pickett. Behind him were fifteen regiments, all Virginians. The place where they were gathering was a few hundred yards from a theological seminary. Tommie McKie had heard one of the officers say it was a Lutheran school. He was a Presbyterian and had never met a Lutheran that he knew of.

Gettysburg Seminary was established in 1825 by German Lutherans. The original faculty had consisted of one man, a Southern pastor named Samuel Simon Schmucker, then pastor of the Lutheran Church in New Market, Virginia. There had been an extensive search for a place in a serene environment, a spot where young men preparing to be Lutheran pastors would not be disturbed by the activity of the outside world. For nearly four decades the spot they chose had served that purpose well. But the events of the day of which Private Thomas F. McKie and the University Greys were a part, July 3, 1863, would change that forever.

In ways Pastor Schmucker, president of this Lutheran school, was similar to Dr. F. A. P. Barnard, president of the University of Mississippi when the University Greys organized as Company A, Eleventh Mississippi Infantry Regiment, CSA. Both men were ardent opponents of secession. Both were ministers. Pastor Schmucker had also been active in the Underground Railroad movement. With contacts in the upper South he had assisted fugitive slaves in their flight to freedom. A house occupied by one he had benefitted was in the middle of the battlefield and Private McKie could see it from where he sat. The black family named Bryan had fled the Gettysburg area, along with Pastor Schmucker, at the news the Confederates were approaching. Pastor Schmucker would be a likely target because of his abolitionist activities and the Bryans would be subject to capture and re-enslavement. Although the Bryans were legally manumitted no Negroes found in Northern territory by Confederates could be presumed safe. Ironically, the Bryan house and barn would figure prominently in the drama that was unfolding.

The University Greys, of course, knew none of that. They knew only that they were exhausted from the long march, hungry, and some were sick with diarrhea from eating unripened fruit they found along the way. Many could not remember when they had last bathed. The hair and beards of most were heavily infested with lice. Their clothes, too tattered and dirty to qualify as uniforms any longer, hung on them like scarecrows. Those with shoes at all were the exception. McKie had shoes but they were little more than worn soles held on his feet with what had once been the laces. One reason, it was believed, for the excursion into the town of Gettysburg in the first place was to forage for shoes. Since the Federals had been first in the town there were no shoes left. None of this, however, was as painful to young McKie as the awful homesickness. That was more disabling than anything physical.

Young Tommie McKie was not alone in what he was feeling. The town of Gettysburg reminded the university men of the town of Oxford they had left two years earlier. When they marched through the Gettysburg Seminary campus, the main building looking somewhat like the Lyceum Building of their own campus, they were plagued with nostalgia. Gettysburg and its seminary was a close cousin of Sewanee and its School of Theology, though the University of the South was still mostly a dream in July 1863. The Sewanee dreamers were fighting this war that Gettysburg's Pastor Schmucker abhorred. George Fairbanks, Josiah Gorgas, Charles Quintard, Francis A. Shoup, Joseph Johnston, Leonidas Polk. All important in the early history of Sewanee. All Confederates in 1863.

An open field separated the Greys from the Federal forces they would soon move out to fight. The University Greys, along with the rest of the Eleventh Mississippi, were waiting in a grove of trees on what was already called *Seminary Ridge*. Generally, in camp, soldiers would be in small groups, playing cards, talking, often singing to the accompaniment of fiddles, banjoes, or guitars. Sometimes a doleful harmonica or the tinny sound of a homemade timbrel. They were too exhausted for any of that now. And hungry. A foraging body servant of the Taylor brothers had caught an aging rooster during the march from Cashtown where the Eleventh Regiment had been left to guard the wagon train. "If'n he's too old to fly, he be too tough to fry," the slave told them. So he had been boiling the old rooster since shortly after daybreak. Some of the hungry soldiers were milling around the fire, watching the Negro drop gobs of moistened flour into the pot, the dough tinged with red from the bloody water he had dipped from a small gulch before dawn. By the time the University Greys reached Gettysburg only thirty-one of their company remained. Even so, one tough rooster and a few blood-tinged dumplings were meagre rations for that many famished soldiers.

McKie would eat none of it. As he looked across the field toward what the artillery men referred to as Cemetery Ridge and Big and Little Round Top, the sight would have killed his appetite even if his spirits had not been so low. Although the field was not the area of the most fierce fighting the day before, there were many corpses scattered; men and horses that had been driven or stumbled onto the open field where they died. One body stood out like the monuments that would one day garnish the entire area. From where the Greys were milling around it could not be determined if that particular corpse was a bluecoat or butternut. It didn't matter now. The soldier was lying on his back, his right arm forming a right angle above the body as if protecting his face from further harm; a rigor-mortised farewell. Multifloras swallowtail butterflies fluttered from one corpse to another, sometimes stopping to feed on the few milkweed pods still standing. The bloated bodies of horses, many piled three and four together, looked like breastworks erected for the next battle.

"We have a new general," McKie heard someone say. "You mean President Davis's prissy nephew?" another soldier asked. Brigadier General Joseph Davis, nephew of Jefferson Davis and controversial as an officer partly for that reason, was commanding the Fourth Brigade of the Heth Division.

"No, I don't mean him. I mean him," the first soldier said, motioning to where General Pettigrew was standing. Tommie had been trying to write a letter for almost an hour. Twice he had asked a sergeant where they were.

"You don't know where you are, Junior?" the sergeant asked.

"I know we're in Pennsylvania," McKie said, not flinching like he used to when someone called him *Junior*. "And that's all I know. What difference does it make anyhow?" "Gettysburg," the sergeant said. "Start your letter, 'Gettysburg, Pennsylvania, July 3, 1863.'"

"I already know what day it is," McKie said assertively. "It's two days after my mother's birthday." The sergeant didn't answer. "And she's forty years old now. I didn't even know where I was on Mother's birthday," the boyish Confederate added.

"You were at Cashtown," the sergeant said. "And on your way here."

"I wonder if I'll ever be forty years old," McKie mumbled to himself as the sergeant moved closer. He stood beside McKie for a moment, looking down at the crumpled sheet of paper he had placed on a medium-sized Bible. There were just a few words on it. He turned the Bible sideways, as if trying to keep the sergeant from reading what he had written. The sergeant had given McKie special attention because he was so young and because he was chronically dispirited from homesickness.

"You want to go to church?" someone asked. McKie shook his head. His mother had told him to attend services regularly and for a time he did. Not any longer.

Nearby, Dr. Thomas D. Witherspoon was conducting a worship service in an old barn on the back edge of Seminary Ridge. He was chaplain to the Second Mississippi Regiment but served the entire Fourth Brigade. The barn also served as a field hospital. While the surgeons busied themselves, scattering hay in the stalls for beds, making an operating table by stacking fence rails and topping them with old boards, designating an area to throw arms and legs they would have to remove (an area they hoped would be out of sight of their patients), and filling containers with fresh water, sometimes the only treatment they could offer a dying soldier, Dr. Witherspoon was preaching and praying for God's blessing in the impending battle. Witherspoon, a Presbyterian who had two degrees from the University of Mississippi, had argued the issue of secession publically with Dr. F. A. P. Barnard of St. Peter's Church, the same church where Duncan Gray preached a hundred years later.

Most of the University Greys found Calvin's doctrine of election of individual souls in sharp conflict with God's preference for the Confederacy. Would there not be individual Yankees God had chosen prior to the national schism? And would He not be aiming their muskets as surely as He pointed the rebels'?

Less than a mile away another chaplain, Father William Corby, chaplain of the famed Irish Brigade of New York, was praying for God to do just that. He had given absolution to his troops and, according to some witnesses, warned them that any soldier who turned and ran would pay in hell for the sin. There is no doubt that Father Corby was as rigid in his admonitions as the Reverend Dr. Witherspoon. Each was certain he was following the scepter of the Almighty.

Both chaplains would be important educators after the war. Dr. Witherspoon, in addition to pastoring some of the South's largest Presbyterian churches, also became a professor at the Louisville Theological Seminary. Father Corby became president of the University of Notre Dame and is still a campus legend. A life-sized statue of him stands on the Gettysburg battlefield where the Irish Brigade fought the Greys. A replica is on the Notre Dame campus. Standing erect, his right hand extended straight up in blessing fashion, playful Notre Dame students refer to the statue as "fair catch Corby." All of that lay far in the future as the Calvinists of the Eleventh Mississippi and the Catholics of the Irish Brigade sought the favor of the same God when the order came for each to try to kill the other.

Chapter Six

HONOR ALL PERSONS
LOVE AND
SERVE THE LORD

On January 12, 1974, Duncan Montgomery Gray Jr. stood about the same chance of becoming the next bishop of the Diocese of Mississippi as the Minnesota Vikings had of winning the Super Bowl against the Miami Dolphins the following day. A chance, but the spread was wide. Fran Tarkenton, the Vikings' quarterback, was ailing. He was expected to start the game but his team was not predicted to win.

Gray would also be a starter when the special council to elect a bishop began at 9:15 A.M. at St. Andrew's Cathedral, Jackson. Like Tarkenton, he was not expected to prevail. Unlike the spectacular quarterback, Gray was in perfect physical condition. His only handicap was the long memory of many of those gathered. They remembered Sewanee, Cleveland, Oxford, and Meridian. In their collective mind they conceded that he was a good man, very intelligent, and was by disposition, training, and experience eminently qualified to lead. He was, after all, the only son of their revered Duncan Montgomery Gray Sr. who had served as bishop from 1943 until 1966. But the bishop's son was seen by many as too far to the left to be captain of the ship. What his detractors failed to realize was that he was too conservative to suit them, not too liberal. Conservative in the sense that he held firmly to the doctrines of the *Book of Common Prayer*. His was a fierce commitment to the creeds and the Scriptures from whence they came. Any test given to him on the General Confession, the Apostles and Nicene Creeds, or anything else contained in Evening and Morning Prayer or Holy Communion would find him nowhere on the left or right.

I believe in God the Father Almighty, Maker of heaven and earth: And in Jesus Christ His only Son our Lord: Who was conceived by the Holy Ghost, Born of the Virgin Mary: Suffered under Pontius Pilate, Was crucified, dead, and buried: He descended into hell; The third day he rose again from the dead: He ascended into heaven, And sitteth on the right hand of God the Father Almighty: From thence he shall come to judge the quick and the dead.

I believe in the Holy Ghost: The Holy Catholic Church; The Communion of Saints: The Forgiveness of sins: The Resurrection of the body: And the Life everlasting. Amen.

Line by line there would not have been a single demurral. But that was not the test. The uneasiness did not have to do with what he believed about the unity of the Godhead but on whether or not he believed in a hierarchy of human beings God had created. Thus they, not he, were the humanists standing outside the parameter of doctrine.

They had not forgotten that it was he who had authored the document they had not yet in their heart accepted. "The Church Considers the Supreme Court Decision" stood well within the guidelines of the Apostolic Faith. It denied nothing of orthodoxy. They were the words of a conservative Christian, espousing ancient teachings. Nothing modernist there. They had lost on this very floor in their effort to defeat that treatise as an official document of the diocese. And they remembered.

They looked back twelve years to the days Gray had stood in the pulpits of St. Peter's Church, Oxford, and Holy Innocents, Como, and castigated them for their moral delinquency in not speaking out against the evil empire that almost destroyed the University of Mississippi. They saw him again, clinging to the side of the Confederate Monument trying to quell a riot of which—in their heart of hearts—they had approved. At least they had done nothing to prevent it, and he had told them so.

They remembered his unfaltering opposition to their governor and legislature. He had been a leader in the Mississippi Council on Human Relations which, they supposed, had been responsible for what they saw as compromise. They had not forgotten. And they had come to see that he was not rewarded now for his sabotage of Southern mores on race. He had done them sufficient mischief already and they would have no more.

But the "they" presented above were not the entire story. Far from it. Duncan Gray had the confidence and support of most clergymen in the diocese as well as a sizable number of the laity who had allowed themselves to know him up close. In addition, much had happened in the past decade. The ice on the frozen pond of racial segregation had been cracked, and for economic reasons if nothing else, many of Gray's critics had permitted, even helped with, the cracking. Now, though, they were remembering. The floating fragments were thawing too rapidly for their continuing resistive bent. Black people were voting as they had not since Reconstruction. The Public Accommodations Law of 1964 had opened restaurants, hotels, theaters, and parks. Schools were desegregated and the private academies their children attended to avoid schooling with their croppers' children were expensive. Even interracial marriage was no longer against the law. Now the periscope of prejudice, though its lens was fogging, scanned the pond surface for hard-line survivors. The focus was on the election of a church prelate. The church: shamefully the last parapet of racial exclusion. They were not as brazen as they had been when the young Delta vicar took them on twenty years earlier, but still they remembered that it was he who had troubled the waters all those years.

Others were equally determined to say them nay. Of those who had come to support the rector of St. Paul's for bishop, some had earlier opposed him on the issue of race but now had either forgiven him for being, in their minds, wrong, or had accepted the changes he had espoused as being inevitable in the body politic or indeed, just, right, and necessary in the kingdom. In any case, there were those who had come with the same determination to elect Duncan Gray Jr. as their next bishop as those who had come to make sure he was defeated.

It was a cold day in Mississippi as the delegates gathered on that Saturday morning. Light snow was falling in places with the temperature hovering near freezing. As Mississippi Episcopalians began arriving in Jackson to elect their seventh diocesan bishop, the nation concerned itself with the impending impeachment or resignation of its thirty-seventh president. The shuttle diplomacy of Secretary of State Henry Kissinger had him in Aswan, Egypt, that day on his third peace mission since the Arab-Israeli war the previous October. On the state level, the Penitentiary Board was considering ousting its chairman for misappropriation of penitentiary funds. At the Jackson airport that morning a Delta Airline 727 had slipped off the runway during inclement weather.

From Olive Branch on the Tennessee border to Ocean Springs on the Gulf of Mexico; from Vicksburg on the west side (that but for an impromptu bend in the Mississippi River would have been in Louisiana) to Columbus on the eastern border (that might as well have been in Alabama), they had come.

Episcopalians are remarkably, and sometimes deceptively convivial. And that quality had not been neglected the night before as friends rendezvoused at the old Walthall Hotel, the Heidelberg, or the Jackson Country Club to talk of Ole Miss football, tell church camp stories, fight past wars, argue politics, and all the things grown-up Anglican chums talk about at toddy time.

When they began entering the narthex of St. Andrew's Church before nine o'clock Saturday morning, the mood was uncharacteristicly subdued. This was serious business. They were doctors, lawyers, planters, and successful businessmen. None of them was poor; few were black. To the more devout it was a time to seek the guidance of the Holy Spirit on a matter of grave import. To some it was an occasion for balancing some old accounts. With a few of the diehards, it was a matter of an archenemy getting his comeuppance.

The meeting began with the celebration of the Holy Eucharist with Bishop John Allin presiding. He was assisted by the Very Reverend Robert Oliver, dean of the Cathedral; the Reverend Canon Fred Bush, canon to the Ordinary; and the Reverend James Horton of the cathedral staff. There were approximately 375 persons present, not all of them delegates; some there for reasons of their own.

Bishop Allin had been coadjutor under Gray's father for five years before becoming diocesan in 1966. Bishop Allin had been recently elected presiding bishop of the Episcopal Church and would be moving to New York to assume that office on June 1, 1974. Although the council was convened to elect a bishop coadjutor—one who is elevated to bishop automatically—those present knew that they were electing, not a second in command (except for a very brief period), but a bishop of the diocese.

The delegates, alternates, and visitors sat attentively as even the most perfunctory business was conducted. Mr. Reynolds Chaney, chancellor of the diocese, read the adopted procedures for an election. Confidentiality would be assured by several measures. The voting would be by secret ballot. There would be three ballot boxes. One for clergy. Another was for lay delegates in cities *A to J*. A third for those from cities from *K to Z*, though the alphabetical listing ended with Yazoo City. No nominations were to be made from the floor and no speeches on behalf of any candidate would be permitted at any time. There would be separate colors for the two Orders. At each box there would be an alphabetical listing of those qualified to cast a ballot in that box. Each box was under the supervision of one clergyman and one lay delegate appointed for that purpose. As each clergyman presented himself to ballot, his name was checked from the eligible list before he was allowed to vote. Lay delegates were told to state their name, church, and city to the tellers and await verification before the delegate was allowed to cast a ballot. One might have thought he was in a disputed Cook County precinct meeting. All procedures were repeated for emphasis. It was manifest this was going to be an honest election.

The election committee consisted of ten men. Three priests and seven laymen, representing every part of the state; big congregations and small. Mr. Harold Miller Jr. of Jackson was chairman.

The first ballot was for nominations. The more sanguine thought three or four might be nominated and they could be on their way by noon. Instead, when the tellers returned, there were thirty-seven nominees. They were from Virginia, North Carolina, New York, South Carolina, Alabama, Florida, Texas, Illinois, Kentucky, Tennessee, Mississippi, and Zomba, Malawi. "Surely you jest," a down-state delegate was heard to mumble when Malawi was announced. Actually the nominee was Jack Biggers, a highly respected young priest, native of Corinth and graduate of Ole Miss. Even so. A bishop from Africa? For Mississippi?

Five of those nominated asked that their names be withdrawn. That still left thirty-two. Those names were then listed on a large board in alphabetical order, with no indication as to how many times a person had been nominated. When the first ballot was reported, the votes were so scattered that hope for an early adjournment melted like the snow that had fallen on Capital Street before dawn. Only three men received more than five clergy votes. Only five received more than ten lay votes. Seven men nominated received not a single vote from either order on the first ballot. Apparently one of two things had happened. Either they had nominated themselves so it could be said they had once stood for bishop in the diocese, or some vote trading had already begun.

Duncan Gray received twenty-nine clergy votes and thirty-five laity, short in both Orders. Thirty clergy and seventy-three lay votes were required for election. Gray's early showing was a surprising development. Precouncil talk had been that the clergy were united behind him, the laymen solidly against him. Instead he had made a respectable early start among the non-priests. Next to him in lay ballots was the Reverend Clifton McInnis of Vicksburg. On social issues the views of the two men were not far apart. But McInnis did not have the activist reputation Gray had garnered over the years and many believed the Vicksburg priest would be seen as a violable compromise by the die-hard segregationists. On the first ballot that did not seem to be the case. McInnis had received only twenty-three lay votes. That would change quickly.

During the lunch hour, after the second ballot, apparently some politicking took place. McInnis's votes almost doubled in both orders. But Gray was also stronger. Neither man was personally involved in the maneuvering. By the fifth ballot something of a pattern had emerged. McInnis received seventy-three lay votes. Exactly the number needed. But although he had gained more clergy votes as other nominees were eliminated, he was still sixteen short. He never lost the momentum among the laymen for the rest of the day.

It was clear that the election for the seventh bishop of the Diocese of Mississippi had become a horse race between McInnis and Gray. Only one other priest remained in it at all. The Reverend Alex Dickson Jr. was headmaster and rector of All Saints' School in Vicksburg. Under his leadership the school had become coeducational. He had also recruited and admitted black students. That alone, despite his high standing throughout the diocese, had made him as suspect in some quarters as was Gray. Still he made a strong beginning and his name remained until the day ended. Since the second ballot, Gray had had enough clergy votes to be certified the winner. His support among the laymen also climbed in two ballotings, but then a downward spiral developed. McInnis continued to have more than enough of the laity, not enough priests.

After the seventh ballot Chancellor Chaney moved that if there be no election after the next round of voting the bishop be asked to set another date for the council to reconvene. After brief but heated debate the motion was defeated. The anti-Gray faction was smelling victory. Their preference was to let the voting continue. McInnis had eighty lay votes, seven more than were needed, and if nine clergy switched to him the election would be over.

An eighth ballot showed little change, except Gray had lost five more lay delegates. Someone moved for a recess until 7:00 P.M. The motion was never seconded.

As the ninth ballot was being tallied, the foyer and washrooms were lively with conversation. Trying to break the tension someone called out, "Ambrose for bishop! Ambrose for bishop!" motioning at the same time at the governor's mansion directly across the street. Ambrose was a civil official in fourth century Milan who was unexpectedly elected bishop of Milan when there was a deadlock. There was a minor problem. Ambrose had not been baptized. Institutions, sacred and profane, then as now, have a way of skirting barriers when it is for institutional succor. So Ambrose was hastily baptized. Then, during the six days that followed he was ordained to the various priestly orders and consecrated bishop.

When Chairman Miller reported that there was yet not an election, Duncan Hobart, Gray's friend of many years, with him when "The Church Considers the Supreme Court Decision" was released twenty years earlier, moved that the special council be adjourned. A hearty but tired voice vote adopted the motion. It was after five o'clock, an important hour for many Mississippi Episcopalians in 1974. The bishop would bring them together at a later time.

Fran Tarkenton and the Minnesota Vikings did not win the Super Bowl. Don Shula's Miami Dolphins carried the day. The score was Miami 27, Minnesota 7. Those who supported Duncan Gray Jr. for bishop had not won either. The score was 103 for McInnis, 94 for Gray. But bishopric elections are not scored like football. There was no winner.

Gray went back to Meridian and continued his priestly duties, undaunted by what many would have interpreted as rejection by his people. His laughter had become as much a trademark as his benedictory blessing to conclude a service. So he laughed now. But it was not a laugh of derision. It was instead, as always, a doxology.

A second special council was called for March 9. Again it would be in St. Andrew's Cathedral Church. The same rules as before were followed.

During the interim, a number of things had happened. Bishop Allin had asked the Standing Committee of the diocese to produce a profile of just what sort of person the diocese wanted for its next bishop. They were also to interview the major candidates and bring to the council a profile on each one.

Also, from January 12 until March 9 some of the council delegates had not been idle. Apparently those determined to defeat the nomination of Gray felt that they would not be able to elect McInnis. A delegate approached both Gray and McInnis and said that if they would withdraw their names from nomination, the task of finally electing a bishop would be much easier. Neither man could look with favor on such an obvious ploy.

Some of the Delta contingent visited Duncan Hobart, then rector of St. John's Church, Leland, and told him they knew he was supporting Gray but that they could not. One of them asked directly, "If Duncan Gray were not in the picture, who would be your candidate?"

Hobart was an honorable man, not given to devious means. When asked a question he would answer. Still one must wonder what was in his mind when he replied, "I would support Moultrie Moore, suffragan bishop of North Carolina." It was a strange response. Bishop Moore had been nominated at the January 12 council meeting but had received one vote on the first ballot, one on the second, and his name did not appear again until the ninth ballot when he got one clergy and one lay vote. Of all those who had been nominated in January, he was the least known in the diocese. Surely Hobart knew the Tar Heel suffragan stood no chance against a well-known and local priest.

Hobart had answered honestly for he was a friend and admirer of Moultrie Moore and he truly would have been Hobart's second choice. Still he knew Moore stood no chance of being elected. If he answered as a matter of strategy, it worked. The first special council had been a contest between Duncan Gray and Clifton McInnis. Because of Hobart's statement, the second contest was between Gray and Moore. After four ballots Gray still did not have enough lay delegates. Finally, on the fifth ballot, with barely half of the laity for him, he had five more than the number necessary to elect. The election was over.

Saturday, March 9, was an Ember Day, when the Church generally prays for human needs. A befitting day for Duncan Gray to become a bishop, for human needs had been the substance of his entire ministry. It is also the time when postulants and candidates for holy orders communicate with their bishops.

We don't know much about the hereafter, or at least I don't. But surely there must have been some spiritual bandying as the Bishop Gray Sr. in eternity looked down upon his son, new bishop on earth, as the final ballots were being counted. Bishop Allin, when the totals were announced, was led to say, "My faith in this life and the life to come enables me to speculate on one real comment—the comment that must have been made in these last few minutes of eternity by the Fifth Bishop of Mississippi. I would love to have heard what Bishop Gray Sr. had to say. It would be priceless and quotable." No doubt the son was at one with his father in that moment.

Gray was pleased and accepted graciously and humbly. He would be about the new task. Ruthie would notify the children. Duncan III had finished two years at Virginia Theological Seminary and was working for Senator Mark Hatfield for a year as an intern. Anne was married and living in Laurel, Maryland. Lloyd was a student at Millsaps College. Catherine was the only one still in the nest.

Duncan Gray Jr. had always eschewed titles, even preferring *Mr.* to *Reverend*. He was *Father* only to his children and they called him *Daddy*.

If other priests wanted to be called *Father* they had only to let it be known and he would so address them, but he made it clear there was to be no reciprocity. He had been given the honorary degree of doctor of divinity by the University of the South in 1972, an unusual honor for a mere parish priest. Another of the many ironies that seemed to swirl around him; the degree was given because of his strong leadership in the civil rights struggle—his name suggested by Tom Ward, a Mississippi layman. But no one who knew him well called him *Dr. Gray.* Now he had a title protocol required him to wear. He was the Right Reverend Duncan Montgomery Gray Jr. and would be addressed as *Bishop.* Even then, to his close friends he would still be *Dunc,* or *Duncan.*

Gray would be installed on May Day, again an apt date. The inauguration of spring; a new beginning. And an international holiday honoring labor organizations, another cause Duncan Gray espoused. Until then he would continue as rector of St. Paul's Church.

At the consecration the sermon was preached by Professor Albert T. Mollegen of Virginia Seminary. No one was surprised that he would be the choice. Professor Mollegen was known for his own bold stand on Southern race relations, based on the New Testament, his academic discipline. In addition, he was a native of Meridian, had been ordained forty-three years earlier at St. Paul's Church, and in his younger years was vicar at Cleveland and Rosedale where both Duncan and his father had served. Some thought having a liberal academic was an impolitic emergence for a new bishop. No matter. They had thought the same thing when Gray's ordination sermon was preached in Grace Church, Canton, twenty-one years earlier.

While Bishop Gray would be coadjutor for one month, that was in name only. Bishop Allin gave him the reins, turned him loose, and began preparations for his own responsibilities as presiding bishop.

There is a necessary addendum here that in reality should be the body of the text. The vast magnitude of Duncan Gray's work cannot be written. It is too personal, would be an offense to him and unfair to those whose lives he touched. A son or daughter, whether of parishioner or not, might be in trouble with the law. He would be there. Husbands and wives in the spasms of alienation. Alcoholics, the mentally ill, the poor and disinherited, the sick, anyone with spiritual or physical needs; all who fell within beatitudinal reach were his parish. His vocation had been, and continued to be, the kingdom now. His blessedness was that he really wasn't aware of it. His wife had been correct about the tumultuous night at the University of Mississippi: he just didn't know any better; didn't know that what he was doing was anything but what inhered naturally in a baptized Christian. Spiritual instinct. A Christian is one who doesn't think; just responds. Acts of mercy beyond legalism, materialism, secularism, or hedonism.

Those things cannot, and should not, be cataloged or discussed. Those served or rescued by him trusted him and to him the trust is sacred and will not be violated. Many of his acts of generosity have been reported to me in numerous interviews. He would not recognize them now as being his own deeds for, again, they were as natural as breathing. So I leave them be.

Bishop Duncan Gray's first official diocesan act was the regularly scheduled parish visitation to the Church of the Nativity, Greenwood. The rector was Michael Engle, the new bishop's classmate at Sewanee and with whom he had been ordained priest in 1953. Greenwood was where Gray's Grandfather McCrady had been priest 1911–1916 and where Gray's father served 1939–1943, young Duncan's most formative teenage years. The day of the visitation, May 5, was also his father's birthday. He would have been seventy-six, Duncan remembered.

At the eleven o'clock service of Morning Prayer, Bishop Gray confirmed twelve people and received one. It was *deja vu* as he moved down the line of kneeling new communicants, placing his hands on their heads and saying words he had heard his father say so many times:

> Defend, O Lord, this thy Child with thy heavenly grace; that he may continue thine for ever; and daily increase in thy Holy Spirit more and more, until he come unto thy everlasting kingdom. Amen.

While prelates of some denominations have chauffeured limousines to transport them from one station to another, the new Bishop Gray drove his own car of not too recent vintage, his wife and daughter Catherine with him.

The next visitation that day was Starkville, all the way across the state. They had to be there by five o'clock. There would be Evening Prayer, confirmation of six, the receiving of one, and groundbreaking for a new parish house. Then they would return to Meridian.

On his first outing as the Ordinary, Duncan Gray drove over three hundred miles, conducted four services, preached twice, and brought twenty new communicants into the Diocese of Mississippi. Being a bishop was not going to be easy.

His practice of not taking a day off each week would continue. More of necessity now than of preference. There would not be time for a day off. Just to visit each parish and mission church in the diocese at least once each year was demanding. Other early changes would add to that. For example, he began a scheduled visitation with each priest in the diocese on or near the anniversary of their birth. That was in addition to the parish visit. Those were private times, with no agenda and no limits as to what could be discussed.

Gray's commitment to end racial inequality in his beloved Mississippi and elsewhere did not end with the vote declaring him the seventh bishop of the Diocese of Mississippi. That resolve would go on. Early in his tenure he made a point of giving special attention to those congregations that had been most hostile to him personally and most fiery in their opposition to desegregation. The wounds were deep and he saw healing as his first priority. Times were changing and he wanted his church to lead the way. His commitment to changing racial patterns continued and his influence was enhanced by the office. He continued on the board of directors of the Mississippi Council on Human Relations, an agency that kept alive the progress that had been made in racial harmony.

In 1964 the Community Relations Service was established to encourage compliance with the Civil Rights Act President Johnson had managed to get through the Congress. Under the direction of former Governor LeRoy Collins of Florida, state advisory committees were set up. Finding whites to serve in states like Mississippi was difficult. Duncan Gray agreed to serve while still in Oxford. While he was bishop he also served on the State Advisory Committee to the U.S. Civil Rights Commission. A memorable experience from that assignment was getting to be friends with Sam Kinsolving, who then lived in Pascagoula and worked with American Indians who were employed by Ingalls Shipbuilding. Mr. Kinsolving was the grandson of Cochise, the famous Apache chief. His other grandfather had been the Episcopal bishop of the Rio Grande.

In 1975 the only authorized Mississippi history textbook was one written by Dr. John Bettersworth, a professor at Mississippi State and a prominent Episcopalian. Most high school history textbooks in the deep South at the time were blatant nineteenth-century interpretations of history that trashed reconstruction and often romanticized slavery and the Civil War. The Lawyers' Committee for civil rights under law filed a lawsuit to require the State Textbook Board to authorize a more recent text, *Mississippi—Conflict and Change*. Through his daughter Catherine, the bishop was a plaintiff in the suit. At times Gray would find himself testifying in federal court then going immediately to an Episcopal gathering where Dr. Bettersworth was present.

The merger of certain black and white congregations was an important agenda item for Bishop Gray. St. Bernard's, the black congregation in Okolona, was merged with all-white Grace Church in 1982. When a white woman objected, under the guise that the historical integrity of Grace Church should be preserved, she was allowed to have a service for herself once a month. Few doubted that her real objection was kneeling at the altar with black Christians. The merger went forward. In Jackson, St. Mark's, formerly all black, was merged with St. Christopher's, virtually all white.

In 1983 the Diocese of Panama became the companion diocese with Mississippi. Black bishops, clergy, musicians, and various staff appearing at diocesan and local parish functions did much to create a more integrated church in Mississippi.

Gray accepted the first black postulant for Holy Orders from the Diocese of Mississippi since the 1920s. Little that he did was not somehow related to his resolve that the Diocese of Mississippi become an integrated church in a racially united and harmonious place. He realized that the Episcopal Church in Mississippi was numerically small. But by precept and example it could be a leavening in the lump; a beacon in the continuing dark.

I interviewed a number of retired bishops who served in the House of Bishops with Duncan Gray. I was amazed that our discussions seldom got beyond the routine business of the denomination. All recalled him as the energetic and adept chairman of the Committee on Canons of the House of Bishops. Many recalled that he was chairman of the Standing Commission on Constitution and Canons, an office of the General Convention. It was, in a sense, a strange assignment for the presiding bishop to make. Gray had little interest in canons per se previous to that. Yet in that capacity he supervised the revision, updating, and publication of White and Dykman's *Annotated Constitution and Canons,* a project that took nearly six years. To some, that much energy expended on a legalistic matter seemed out of keeping with his years as a social activist. Not at all. From the beginning he wanted things done "decently and in order." That character trait, in part, accounted for his social activism. All things should be in order, conduct and relationships included.

Others recalled that Duncan had also been vice-president of the board of archives of the Episcopal Church and chairman of the Committee on Rules for the House of Bishops. All those things were time consuming but did not compare to the furors that seemed ever to surround him as a parish priest. Only a few of his fellow bishops remembered him as a troubler of the status quo. That did not fit the Duncan Gray I had followed. Maybe, I reasoned, he felt that one could only be radical at the local level for that is where problems exist and are solved or not solved. A battle that is not local is no battle at all.

I recalled that some of those from beyond the basement states of the South with whom I spoke had been among the protesters who occasionally came down during the turbulent sixties to demonstrate against white Southern racism. They had been welcomed by Gray, though I suspect that he must have smiled at the contradiction of their sometimes beholding the mote in the Southern eye while ignoring the beam in their own. Perhaps he recalled Clifford Durr, a white Alabama Episcopalian, attorney and principled integrationist who had what some in those days called the "Durr Law of Righteous Indignation." "The degree of righteous indignation," he said, "is in direct proportion to the distance from the problem." That law seemed to be reversed with Gray. His preachments seemed always to be locally centered and directed.

None of that is to say that Gray got negative reviews from his colleagues in the House of Bishops. All remembered him as a gentleman, a worthy member of their fraternity. Yet seemingly the passing of time often results in revisionist history. Two men connected Bishop Gray with conservative causes to which I knew he was not a party. There was a heresy charge against a fellow bishop. One bishop was certain Gray had supported the charge, the other thought so but cautioned me to check further. I did.

There is no evidence to suggest that Gray ever engaged in homophobic or blatantly sexist rhetoric. There were situations, however, in which his actions were not always clear. In 1974 when eleven women deacons were ordained priests there were charges filed against the three retired bishops who ordained them. Gray, who had been in office two months, did not support the charges. He did, however, in 1989 sign a statement issued by the presiding bishop and his Council of Advice, called together to respond to Right Reverend Bishop John Spong's ordination of a non-celibate homosexual man in the Diocese of Newark. In a statement sent from the presiding bishop's office to all bishops, Presiding Bishop Browning and his council members disassociated themselves from Spong's action, restated and affirmed the church's traditional teaching, and supported orderly process within the church. In the fall of 1990 their statement was presented as a resolution in the House of Bishops and Bishop Gray voted for the resolution. At that time the presiding bishop and some members of his Council of Advice reversed themselves. The motion passed by a small majority. Some saw the supporters of the resolution as voting against homosexuals, maintaining that there were no canons, only General Convention resolutions, forbidding the ordination of non-celibate gays and lesbians to the priesthood. Gray agreed that there was not a specific canon but felt that the convention resolutions were directives for Church procedure.

In the fall of 1987 other charges were made against Spong that involved Gray directly. The charges came from within and without the Diocese of Newark. One charge had to do with a matter of doctrine, others with a dispute between Spong and a local parish over disposal of an insurance payment resulting from a church fire. Presiding Bishop Browning appointed Gray to chair a committee to investigate the charges and determine if they merited a board of inquiry to decide whether or not a trial was indicated. Gray's committee dismissed the doctrinal charges on grounds that canon law prescribed that heresy charges could only be made by "ten bishops exercising jurisdiction in this church." The presentment before Gray's committee had been made by clergy and lay persons. The insurance matter was considered a civil matter and beyond the jurisdiction of the committee. It was immediately dismissed.

A remaining charge accused Spong of improperly using his canonical powers to force a resolution of the civil dispute regarding the insurance payment in favor of his position. The committee determined that this charge, if proved, possibly constituted a canonical offense. A board of inquiry was appointed and after a lengthy inquiry ruled that no trial be held. Bishop Gray was criticized by the accused who saw him as too timid and by some accusers who saw him as afraid to vigorously defend the faith. One Northern urban bishop said to me, "Your man might have been a radical down South but he didn't join our little cadre of hawks in the House of Bishops."

While the authentic radicalism of the new Right Reverend Duncan M. Gray Jr. might not have been recognized in the national body, his pioneering in unplowed acres and unsolved problems in his native diocese where, after all, his mission remained, would continue. He knew, for example, that the matter of race had not been solved. There had been programs by the church and the national government aimed at inoculating against further racial violence such as the sixties had seen. He was grateful for the advances that had been made. But he knew the truce the nation was seeing was an uneasy one; a smooth scar covering a seething caldron of infection sure to erupt on another day.

JEREMIAH GAGE, THEN A FOURTH SERGEANT, HURRIED BY Thomas McKie and the sergeant, spoke to the two men, moved on. Gage had graduated in literature at the University of Mississippi but had returned to the university to study law before the formation of the Greys. For maturity and intellect he would have been a more suitable captain of the Greys, but the pompous, hot-tempered Lowry seemed to the fervent students a more likely leader in battle. McKie, hunkered down and working on his letter, knew an order would soon come to charge the Union line. He neither dreaded nor welcomed it. The vast shadow of his yearning for home distanced him from fear. He didn't care. The ancient affliction was consuming him, an indescribable ache, tugging, emptying him of all but wretchedness.

For several minutes he thought of nothing but his dog back in Lafayette County, Mississippi. He wanted to call him like he used to do. "Here Rattler. Here Rattler," he remembered. Rattler was a smaller than usual feist, a mixed breed, white with black neck and shoulders. Tommie thought of the many times when, after he returned from school, he would load his musket, call Rattler and together they would roam the deep woods and nearby swamps where she never failed to tree a squirrel before the sun went down. Not even the smell of a squirrel frying in an iron skillet half filled with hog lard excited Tommie now. Such was his despondency. Several months earlier, while they were in their winter quarters in North Carolina, he had called Rattler in his sleep. The other soldiers laughed at him next morning, made up a story that six mangy stray dogs had answered and spent the rest of the night in the tent where McKie was sleeping.

Not more than ten feet from where the lad was sitting, Joseph McKie, Tommie's cousin, and Jeremiah Gage were standing. Most of the other soldiers in the Mississippi Eleventh were milling around the area, all looking across the area where the Donaldsville (Louisiana) Artillery was getting a final briefing from Lieutenant Colonel John Garnett.

"Here they come," someone shouted. It was General Robert E. Lee, accompanied by General Pettigrew and General Joseph Davis. General Pettigrew, having replaced the wounded Henry Heth the day before, had never commanded a division before. General Lee wanted to ride the line one more time before the charge to give Pettigrew encouragement but also to inspire the troops. As they rode along the entire Fourth Brigade— three regiments from Mississippi and one from North Carolina—began to chant and cheer. Lee's aids, not wanting his whereabouts so well-known by the gunners looking down on them from Cemetery Ridge, rode in front of the generals trying to hush the noise. Robert E. Lee, the engineer, sitting stately in the saddle, risking his own life and the lives of University of Mississippi boys so that white people could continue to own black people, a cause in which he had no personal stake and in which he did not even believe.

Almost at the same time General Lee was sending his troops across the field of Gettysburg a conversation was taking place little more than a mile away. Colonel Joshua Lawrence Chamberlain was as devout in his religious belief and as well educated in religion as Witherspoon, Corby, or Duncan Gray. Chamberlain was a Maine college professor who had saved the day for the Federals on the second day of battle when he ordered his Twentieth Maine to fix bayonets in defense of Little Round Top. Now he and his younger brother Thomas were talking about the real cause of the carnage they were witnessing. "If it weren't for the slaves, there'd never have been no war, now would there?" Tom said to his scholarly brother.

"No," Lawrence Chamberlain said. "Without slavery there would be no war. We would be back in Maine." Whether that conversation took place with precisely those words is not known. What is known is that the younger brother's question and the elder brother's answer are a summation of a great deal of America's history. Most definitely the history of the Reverend F. A. P. Barnard's Oxford of 1861 and the Reverend Duncan Montgomery Gray's Oxford one hundred years later.

When the generals moved away, Private Andrew Baker and Joseph McKie strolled over to where Tommie continued his writing. "Why didn't you stand up with the rest of us when the great General came by?" Baker asked.

"I'll stand up when it's time" McKie said. "I've never missed a battle yet. And I won't miss this one." He folded the sheet of paper and handed it to his cousin. "See that Mother gets this."

When Gray became bishop in 1974 the national Church was grappling with two issues: the ordination of women and the revision of the 1928 *Book of Common Prayer*. He would join those efforts. But he would not neglect the continuing spread of the cancerous polarization between the races that was still the nation's number one problem. He saw it as the number one sin of the Church as well. Early in his tenure as bishop he put major emphasis on visiting those parishes that had been most recalcitrant on matters of racial progress. He knew that America's racism would still be haunting the church and the nation long after the other matters had faded from memory.

Long before he became bishop he had supported the ordination of women. At one General Convention, while still a parish priest, he was the only deputy from Mississippi to vote yes on the motion. He believed those matters should be settled quickly and amicably so the Church might move on to more important things on which to expend its energies. That did not happen and he found himself caught in the crossfire.

On the revision of the *Book of Common Prayer* his personal opinion was that there was nothing ultimately sacred about the manner in which words were arranged to express a particular petition to God. He loved the language of the 1928 revision of the *Book of Common Prayer* because he had grown up with it. But his logical mind of an engineer reminded him that 1928 had also been a revision that was also a revision, and the controversy could be traced back to the great English reformer Thomas Cranmer who had derived his revision from the Roman Breviary and Missal books. Gray knew of the quarrels of Edward VI, Queen Mary's suppression of the book in 1552 and its restoration by Elizabeth I in 1559 and the Act of Uniformity that has endured in Anglican life to the present. But to Bishop Gray that was a matter of history. Let it be. Better for the Church, he thought, to concern itself with applying the gospel to the social ills of its own day. Again his radicalism of liturgy was, he believed, the proper approach to those problems. His sacramental theology was not something in a vacuum, unrelated to the problems of humanity. Rather the suffering of humanity, whether race, poverty, or classism, is directly related to the Passion of Christ. Participation by means of the symbols—water, bread, and wine—did not free him from the pain. It thrust him into the streets with the pain. In baptism that is the grafting; in the Eucharist the suffering of Christ is brought near at hand. It is not some hocus-pocus that frees us from participation in the sacrifice. It *involves* us in the sacrifice. If those radical understandings of baptism and the Eucharist had been tampered with in the revision of the *Book of Common Prayer*, Gray would have led the line to say them nay. That was not the case. He knew that the greeting "Good morning" could be just as heartfelt as "How are you today?" The difference in the phrasing was not worth an argument. Still there were those in his diocese who saw the wording as of grave consequence and the resulting dissension brought him much grief.

As for the ordination of women, Gray says today, "I must confess that I had really never thought much about it as a young priest. When it became an issue, I thought, 'Well, why not?'" Though neither issue was something he chose to fight about, when he was elected bishop he discovered he had inherited a fight on both points. The two seemed to go hand in hand. The two also seemed to have a speaking relationship with the continuing problem of race. Many who had been most conservative on integration seemed disposed to resist other changes as well. But Gray was a patient man and never arbitrarily imposed his will on others.

Never in his ministry was he one to chase the fads or take a knee-jerk position. Yet if the Church moved in a direction, he wanted to move with it. He did not go out recruiting women priests for the sake of having women priests. He wanted it to happen as a natural flowing of events. The opportunity came in a routine conference with a young man, Jerry McBride, a rising senior at Episcopal Theological School in Cambridge, Massachusetts, to be ordained deacon in Mississippi. As he was about to take leave, McBride added, "By the way, Bishop, as you know, I will be married by the time I am ordained." Bishop Gray's consent and support had come earlier. "Uh, Bishop. Well, I guess I had better remind you of something else. She's a priest." Gray needed no reminding and showed no more concern than when McBride said his fiancee's name was Mary Macsherry but was called *Molly*. "We'll find a place for her," the bishop reassured.

"Don't forget, she's canonically resident in the Diocese of Central New York," McBride went on.

Gray laughed lightly, leaned back and responded, "Jerry, I believe the Diocese of Central New York is in good standing with General Convention. And so are we." It was the opening Gray had waited for. When it came he treated it as the most everyday development. There is no reference to it in his journal. It wasn't that he was trying to be foxy about what to him was an important matter. Rather it was that he was going to set the example of treating the Reverend Molly McBride's coming the same way any other priest transferring into the diocese would be treated. And hope others would be similarly inclined.

That was not to be. Earlier twenty-two parish priests and three monastics issued a statement taking strong issue with the national Church and the General Convention's approval of the ordination of women, and revision of the 1928 *Book of Common Prayer*. They called themselves "Churchmen for Apostolic Faith and Order." In 1971 a national group had been founded calling itself the "Society for the Preservation of the *Book of Common Prayer*." Among the founders were such notable literary figures as Professor Walter Sullivan of Vanderbilt and Andrew Lytle of Sewanee.

In his usual low key and pastoral fashion Bishop Gray gave the dissenting group from his diocese permission to speak to the next Diocesan Council in January 1977. The business sessions were held in a nearby public hall but the host church was St. Peter's, Oxford, where by then Gray had far more support than lingering hostility from his years there. The bishop cordially recognized the Reverend Thomas Waggener who would speak for the dissenting group. The words the priest brought were surely painful to the bishop and his supporters. St. Peter's Church was where Dr. F. A. P. Barnard, president of the University of Mississippi and rector of St. Peter's Church, had stood in 1860 and steadfastly preached against secession and war. And a hundred years later Duncan M. Gray Jr., now bishop, had denounced the evils of segregation and violence. Now he listened courteously as one of his priests attacked the stance the Church had taken on ordaining women:

> To the General Convention and to those delegates here who helped to bring this to pass we say: You have broken faith. You have broken faith with our brothers in Rome, and our brothers in the Eastern Churches. You have broken faith with the Scriptures. You have broken faith with the Holy Fathers, and the Creeds, and the Councils, and the Prayer book, and the Holy Saints above. And you have broken faith with us, your brothers, friends and fellow workers. What dear and precious friendships have been ground up in this hellish mill.

They were harsh words for the gentle shepherd to hear. But like his father before him when similar words were spoken against the document his son, the then vicar had penned—"The Church Considers the Supreme Court Decision"—Gray thanked the speaker. Unlike his father he permitted discussion to follow, not appropriating the chair of authority he occupied to refute words that surely seemed to him unfair and untrue. He would have his say at the appropriate time and in his own way. He could never be deemed a revolutionary in the political sense for he worked through the system; followed the rules.

The bravado of those vehemently opposing the ordination of women had been bolstered by their former bishop, then presiding bishop of the church. At a meeting of the House of Bishops in Port St. Luci, Florida, Presiding Bishop Allin announced that he was "unable to accept women in the role of priests," and that his understanding "prevents my believing that women can be priests any more than they can become fathers or husbands."

Gray declined to comment on his predecessor's position and today, in his character of speaking ill of no one, will say only, "I think Bishop Allin handled his disagreement with grace and dignity."

The controversy was still raging when the Reverend Molly McBride was quietly but forthrightly welcomed by Gray into his domain, with the authority of the waxed seal of consecration as the seventh bishop of the Diocese of Mississippi.

Reading the daily journals of bishops is often a boring manner of research. The nuances are generally not there. There is no mention at all that he learned from Jerry McBride that he was getting married and his bride was a priest of the church. On June 19, 1980, there is an entry that a conference was held with Jerry McBride, who would be ordained two days later. On the day of the ordination it was stated, a seeming afterthought, "Attended reception in late afternoon honoring the wife of the ordinand, the Reverend Molly McBride." It was not an afterthought, however. Introducing the wife as "the Reverend" was on purpose.

Molly McBride is not mentioned again until September 16 when there is a one-line entry for the entire day: "Office. Conference with the Reverend Jerry McBride and the Reverend Molly McBride." I had to interview Mrs. McBride to learn more of what that concerned. The purpose was pastoral. As expected, the presence of a female priest in the diocese had fanned anew the flames of ecclesiastical dissension. Seven priests had written an open letter opposing the assignment of a woman cleric in the diocese. The letter had been disseminated by the state newspapers and the Reverend McBride was smarting under the hostile reception by some of her fellow clergy. In addition, at the first diocesan clergy conference she attended, two priests, while being overly demonstrative to her husband, refused to acknowledge her presence or shake her hand. She was a product of a genteel Eastern family, had for the past three years lived in a seminary community where such discourteous treatment of female priests and postulants was becoming more rare. This was not the good manners of the South she had heard about. "You'll win them over," was the gist of her new bishop's comments.

222

"He was right," reports her husband today. "All but one of the priests signing that letter became close personal friends and active colleagues with Molly. The only one who didn't soon died." The last was reported without commentary.

One bit of advice from the bishop troubled Molly McBride. Gray, noticing that she generally wore no clerical attire, told her that it was customary for his clergy to wear clericals. It was out of character for the bishop. He was not a stickler on such matters. My own feeling is that it was part of his plan of introduction of the change. I believe he was saying, "Get out there and be recognized. Let the word go forth that we have a new priest in town. And the new priest is a woman." The fact that the new priest was a stunningly beautiful woman, with or without clerical neckwear, probably helped to combat the stereotype that still persisted in some quarters.

The Reverend Molly McBride became a canon at St. Andrew's Cathedral where she remains today as one of the most highly respected and beloved clergy in the diocese. On the day she officially transferred from the Diocese of Central New York to the Diocese of Mississippi, the bishop's journal shows no mention of it at all. Except by innuendo. "Good things happening here!" he wrote.

Another storm in the life of Gray was being weathered. It was not a pleasant time for him, nor one without a carrying charge. Despite his patience and enduring pastoral care, a number of priests left the diocese over the ordination of women and revision of the *Prayer Book*. Four renounced their ministry and were deposed.

It would not be the end of the matter, for no usage dies quite so slowly as a religious one. Especially one in which trousers have for so long been akin to stained glass in the purview of the kingdom's cause. It was, however, a beginning. When Annwn Leigh Hawkins, a communicant of St. Andrew's Cathedral, became a postulant the following year the road was not yet smooth. But at least the potholes were a little less forbidding. As associate university chaplain at the University of the South, Annwn Leigh, now Mrs. Myers as well as priest, thinks back over those years and how much easier Bishop Gray made them. "I had been managing the cathedral bookstore and working with the young people of the diocese. The kids were asking theological questions I couldn't answer and I talked to Bishop Gray about going to Virginia Theological Seminary. Just for the education."

She talks of how the bishop asked, ever so subtly and innocently, about ordination. "At that point I really wasn't thinking about that. He made it all sound so natural. So easy." When time came for ordination Gray made no point at all of a female being ordained. He wanted it to be just an ordinary ordination in the diocese. When the priest delivering the ordination sermon began talking about what a challenge this was, how the candidate would face many hurdles, much opposition and prejudice for something she was born with and over which she had no control, Gray impatiently dropped his bulletin three times. He was hearing precisely what he did not want to hear. Finally the preacher, who stood over six feet tall and looked like a giant as he stood in the pulpit, paused, looked at the congregation, then down at Annwn who was barely five feet tall and said, "She will be the shortest priest in the diocese." The bishop relaxed and the congregation burst into warm and appreciative laughter.

Mrs. Myers recalls how the bishop handled the conflict in her first parish. "As a pastor. He didn't intervene. Just came down and was with us, loving us. All of us. And we made it." She remembers his last clergy conference when the bishop was reminiscing about his life in Mississippi. "Suddenly he stopped. Looked at his watch and said, 'Exactly thirty years ago this minute I was standing on the Confederate monument at the University of Mississippi.'" The room grew deathly quiet. "No one said a word after that. We all sat in little clusters crying. Remembering this holy man who never claimed holiness. Giving thanks. I will never forget it."

There came seeking holy orders Ruth Wallace Black. With a Ph.D. degree in French Literature from Harvard University, there could be no question as to her intellectual fitness to be a priest. Dr. Black studied for the diaconate without attending seminary and passed every stage with distinction. She became chaplain at the University of Mississippi Medical Center. Gray's diocese acquired another female priest by way of Europe in the person of Anne Stevenson. Mrs. Stevenson, a Jackson native, was in Brussels where her husband was employed. That robustly ecumenical venture became almost an ecclesiastical comedy of errors. Mrs. Stevenson, a parishioner of St. Andrew's, was studying at the University of Louvain, a Roman Catholic institution in Belgium, preparing for the ministry. Canonically she was under what is called the "Convocation of American Churches in Europe," her bishop being in Paris. As the time for her ordination to the diaconate approached, her Paris bishop, the Right Reverend John Krumm, suggested that she make discreet inquiry as to whether the ordination service might be held in the chapel at the University of Louvain. She did so and was told that it was indeed possible. In mid-April 1983 the Grays took a sabbatical and spent four months in England. At Oxford University the bishop read and studied under the famed Scottish theologian, John Macquarrie. The Grays also lived in the Macquarrie home.

At the end of the term, the Grays spent a month in Europe. It was while they were there that Anne Stevenson was to be ordained. Gray, of course, would attend along with Bishop Krumm. A faculty member, a Roman Catholic priest, would preach and other priests of the Louvain family would participate. Then word came from the cardinal archbishop of Brussels that his priests were not to share in the service. Apparently the ardent prelate neglected to include Mrs. Stevenson's fellow seminarians for they provided the choir. Some faculty members were at the ordination as well.

Following graduation and ordination as deacon, the new Reverend Mrs. Stevenson was given a position at the Anglican Cathedral in Brussels, a congregation of the Church of England. That further complicated the ministerial vocation of the new Mississippi cleric. The Church of England did not ordain women and the issue was even more controversial there than it had been in the American church a few years earlier. However, by some route Mrs. Stevenson did not bother to question, a brief letter arrived from the bishop of Gibraltar, based in London. The bishop sent a license authorizing her to serve in the Belgian congregation. So, some years before women could be ordained in the Church of England, a Jackson, Mississippi, woman was functioning at a Church of England parish in Brussels.

Like a mighty army, moves the Church of God.

Today there are fourteen female priests in the Diocese of Mississippi. Fourteen is not half of eighty-two, but fourteen is more than zero. Perhaps progress will some day destroy all error but in the while inequity abides. It does not behoove me, a male, to implore patience. One thing is certain. When parity comes, it will come largely through the persistent witness of women, and the grace enabling them to forgive an institution that has been slow to recognize their gifts. And it will come through the power of the Holy Spirit who cannot be restrained from calling whomever he pleases to do the work of God on earth. When it does come there will be at least a sizable footnote on the spirit and work of Duncan Montgomery Gray Jr., seventh bishop of Mississippi. The label, church bureaucrat, never fit Gray and I have heard no one use it. "He didn't command respect," Mrs. Myers says. "He just had it. He had it in part because he never shut out the views of others."

In the midst of the most heated and time-consuming discord over the revision of the *Prayer Book* and ordination of women, he was never wedded to the office desk. Hospitals, jails, troubled families, none was neglected under the guise of being too busy.

Nor was his interest and involvement in ecumenical and interfaith ventures abandoned. One organization that claimed considerable time was the southwide Association for Christian Training and Service. With the acronym ACTS it provided consultation and training to address issues of social justice. With Gray as chairman, the organization encouraged judicatories and ecumenical groups to work for minority and economic justice in inner city areas. In his own diocese there was a prison ministry established under his direction but with the leadership of the Reverend Henry Hudson, then rector of Church of the Advent, Sumner. Hudson and the diocese began an Education for Ministry (EFM) program at Parchman, the state penitentiary in Mississippi. EFM is sort of a theological education for laymen and at Parchman the students were both inmates and staff. Gray appointed a priest as full-time chaplain at Parchman and that continues. Gray opposed the death penalty, as he did the taking of life at any stage of life's existence. While in Europe he was troubled that the first execution in Mississippi for many years was about to take place. Hudson, the priest who had ministered to death-row prisoners and championed their survival, was much on his mind. Gray, knowing that he was helpless to stop the execution, called his priest and humbly asked, "What can I do for you?" Hudson replied, "You can get me ten minutes with Governor Winter." Gray, a friend of the governor, immediately called and arranged the meeting. Hudson, now dean of the Cathedral Church in Little Rock, speaks appreciatively and sadly of the meeting. "The governor's wife, also an opponent of the death penalty, was with me. Her husband said he would give us ten minutes. Four hours later we left the governor's office. I had steeled myself not to weep. But as we walked down the corridor the governor's wife and I were pathetically trying to console each other. We did what we could, but Jimmy Lee Gray [the prisoner] was going to die." Before he was executed, the Grays returned from Europe and Gray met with Governor Winter to try to convince him to commute the sentence. Without success.

In an ecumenical venture, primarily with Roman Catholics and United Methodists, a hospice was established in Jackson in what had been a nursing home. Whispering Pines was unique in that it had both AIDS and other patients. The thinking among health care providers had been that AIDS patients had to be isolated from others. Bishop Gray and his colleagues saw that as further humiliation of those suffering with

AIDS. A hospice was for the terminally ill and to them terminally ill meant just that. The program worked and has been an example for other parts of the country.

Another event of intercommunion interest was the Gray's private audience with Pope John Paul II. Roman Catholic Bishop Joseph Brunini of the Diocese of Natchez-Jackson was a close friend and colleague of Gray. When discussing the Gray's upcoming trip to Rome, Brunini and Auxiliary Bishop Houck said they would try to arrange tickets for the Grays to mid-day prayers at the Sistine Chapel. When the Grays arrived at their hotel there was an invitation to attend a Papal Mass at St. Peter's. But their train had been late and the Mass was over. The Episcopal bishop of Mississippi is a humble man and did not want to appear presumptuous. He assumed the invitation might be a mistake. He was, after all, a tourist. The next day there was an urgent message from the Vatican. This time Gray returned the call and was told that the Vatican was anxious to have the Grays come to Castel Gandolfo, the pope's summer residence, where that very day the pope would recite the Angelus. Gray felt that although there would be a large crowd at least he would see the bishop of Rome. When the prayer ended the Grays were ushered into an adjacent room where the pope joined them. There they had a lengthy and cordial visit, talking of human rights around the world and, Gray says, "Whatever I could think of in my astonishment." Ruthie remembered that it was the birthday of Duncan Montgomery Gray IV and the pope said a prayer for the Gray's little grandson. She was so touched by the courtly and nonpatronizing manners of the pope she neglected to express her strong views on the ordination of women and other issues on her agenda.

Bishop Gray was impressed that his Roman Catholic colleagues from Mississippi had such influence with the Vatican. Two weeks later he read that Bishop Bernard Law of the Catholic Diocese of Springfield-Cape Girardeau, formerly a Jackson priest and also Gray's friend, had just been elevated to the rank of archbishop of Boston. Not long after that Law became a Cardinal. Gray then knew what the connection was that enabled an Episcopal bishop of Mississippi to get a private audience with the *bishop* of Rome. He still teased his friends in Mississippi about their weight in Vatican circles.

Following the invasion of Panama under President Bush in late 1989, the National Council of Churches sent a fact-finding delegation to Panama. Gray was asked by Presiding Bishop Browning to represent the Episcopal Church. He was an appropriate choice in that Panama was the companion Diocese of Mississippi and the bishop of Panama, the Right

Reverend James Ottley, was a close friend. After the capture of General Noriega the delegation found mixed feelings among the Panamanians. Those who looked with favor on the invasion, however, were expecting considerable reparations for the war damage. Housing for thousands of people, mostly poor, had been destroyed, Gray says, and the whole economic structure was in shambles. To encourage a rebuilding program he had a lengthy conference with Chief of Staff John Sununu but without the results the delegation recommended.

In May 1991 Gray was elected chancellor of the University of the South. While the vice-chancellor is the one who carries out the day-to-day affairs of the Mountain the chancellor, elected by the trustees, is the lodestar. So Duncan Montgomery Gray Jr. had gone full circle. His seminary years there had been a theological storehouse, yet a tempestuous beginning. There he spent his third year in briery contention with the trustees and his blood uncle who was vice-chancellor and president. When at last he headed down the Mountain, back to his beloved but strife-torn Mississippi where he would spend his life, he vowed never to return. He had entered the University of the South when the twentieth century was at midpoint. Now he would be the one to lead it as the century winds down. America, the South, and Sewanee had seen many changes during the century past. From farming with oxen to planting with airplanes and harvesting with computerized machines. From a rural and agricultural society to an urban and industrialized one. The South had changed from a sharecropping system to agribusiness. Politically it had moved from solidly Democrat to almost solidly Republican. Through all the changes, race had been a prominent factor. That question is not yet resolved. Nor has Gray despaired in his trying.

As the century ends the major controversy within the Episcopal Church is not civil rights, the Great Depression, world wars, *Prayer Book* revision, or ordination of women. The century is winding down with the Church in turmoil over human sexuality. Yet again, the ancient challenge of creation. In 1995 seventy-six active and retired bishops signed a presentment of intent against the Right Reverend Walter Righter, retired bishop of Iowa and then assistant bishop of Newark for ordaining as a priest of the church one who is not heterosexual and had not taken a vow of celibacy. A presentment is the first step leading to a church trial.

Since I am a scribe, not even an Episcopalian, I am not privy to the goings-on within the inner sanctum. As an outsider it seems rather a sad way to end the twentieth century of the reign of the child of Bethlehem. I understand from the media that the preliminary proceedings resulted in a trial of Bishop Righter involving lawyers, hearings, testimonies, depositions, and cross examinations, just like the temporal kingdom uses to deal with its accused criminals. The bishop was acquitted. I do not know what the punishment might have been. He is retired already so he could not have been fired. Some years ago the Christian Church stopped burning its ecclesiastical felons at the stake or cutting off their heads. None of my business, I suppose. Fact is, it would be outside the purview of my subject entirely except the charge of heresy is a serious matter. And since this book is about an Episcopalian who became a bishop it does seem appropriate to report that Duncan Montgomery Gray Jr. was not among the signers of the presentment against his fellow bishop. Those who know him best were not surprised. He knows that a charge of heresy, for whatever reason, against one who has moved from the radical vows vouchsafed for him in baptism to the awesome pledge of the Ordinary, stabs a hole in the heart of the accused, leaving him wounded until the day he dies, with only the brute surge of grace to assuage his hurt.

Duncan Gray didn't sign.

His last official act in the diocese before retirement was a parish visitation with what had been St. Bernard's Church, Okolona. In the sixties this was the black congregation that provided him respite from his imposed segregated life when he participated in the Okolona College religious education training school each summer. Okolona College is a sad casualty of progress, the buildings going to ruin, the soul marching on. As the bishop preached there he reminisced about the good things Okolona College had done and the good times of the old Okolona College summer sessions. I wish I had been there. Mrs. Hattie Raspberry Hall, a woman who was reared on the Okolona campus where her parents taught, wrote a remarkable litany giving thanks for the life and work of Gray. The thanksgiving was for a man of grace, one who fought injustices of all kinds, who brought reconciling words of hope to a race-haunted Mississippi. The litany was a moving tribute by a black native Mississippian for a white Mississippian. Her brother, William Raspberry, columnist for the *Washington Post*, wrote a column about the occasions of Okolona reunions and the miracles a tiny institution for black children in this sleepy corner of northeast Mississippi spawned over the years. He told of a student who had no money on Easter weekend when everyone else had gone home. Embarrassed to admit his plight he told his friends he was going to Memphis to visit his cousin, packed his things and disappeared. For the next two nights he slept underneath a tree behind the agriculture building. His only food that Easter weekend was a jar of unhomogenized peanut butter. That Okolona student is now retired from the military after a successful career. At the reunion another former student, son of a washerwoman, proudly introduced his children—a son who teaches at the University of Oklahoma and a daughter who practices international law in West Africa. The retiring bishop would take credit for no such success stories. But the Raspberry family, and many others, are well aware of at least one strong white hand that was on their side, advocating, bolstering the stronger black hands of familial fidelity. And Gray is well aware of the strong black hand belonging to the aging Raspberry matriarch that contributed much to his spiritual health when his own people so often forsook him. Black and white leaning on each other. The way it's supposed to be.

It has been my biased observation over the years that few men have departed the office of bishop as authentically human as when they began. I would have wanted to testify that night in Okolona that Duncan Montgomery Gray Jr. was leaving with his humanity intact. That he had survived as a genuine human being. But the little Okolona congregation already knew that. "He was just the same old Duncan," the ninety-year-old Mrs. James Raspberry told me.

Then in the fall of 1993, Duncan Montgomery Gray Jr. officially retired as seventh bishop of the Diocese of Mississippi.

There was a big party.

Chapter Seven

REJOICING IN THE
POWER OF THE SPIRIT

There is always something else to learn. I wanted to visit with Gray one more time before ending my research. It proved to be fortunate, maybe even providential that I made the visit. The season of Advent seemed an appropriate time.

It is less than two hours from where we live in Mt. Juliet, Tennessee, to the Gray's second home near Sewanee and the University of the South. I drove there and checked into the Sewanee Inn, a comfortable but not lavish facility owned by the university. The large room I was assigned was tastefully decorated with photographs and posters of Sewanee scenes. Above the bed is a large placard boasting of former Sewanee football prowess and glory. I learned later that it had been a gift of U.S. Steel and that copies were available free from the alumni office.

The headline is in banner lettering:

IN 6 DAYS SEWANEE BEAT TEXAS, TEXAS A & M, TULANE, LSU, AND OLE MISS. ON THE 7TH DAY, THEY RESTED.

Underneath the bold lettering was the story:

SCRAWNY, LITTLE SEWANEE. ALL OF 300 STUDENTS. WHO ˙SEEMED TO PICK THE YEAR 1899 TO BELLOW, "WE ARE THE UNIVERSITY OF THE SOUTH."

SEWANEE WON 12 GAMES THAT YEAR. ALL OF THEM. THEY SCORED 322 POINTS TO 10 FOR THE OPPONENTS.

AUBURN, ALONE, DARED TO SCORE ALL 10. AND LIVED TO TELL ABOUT IT.

LIKE A DAREDEVIL MOTORCYCLIST, MAKING PASSING RUNS AT A SUICIDAL LEAP, SEWANEE TOOK GEORGIA, 12-0; GEORGIA TECH, 32-0; TENNESSEE, 46-0; AND SOUTH-WESTERN, 54-0.

THEN THEY FLOORBOARDED IT. WON FIVE GAMES IN SIX DAYS ON A 2,500-MILE BARNSTORMING SCREAMER.

THEY FELL LIKE THIS: 12-0 OVER TEXAS IN AUSTIN, NOV. 9; 10-0 OVER TEXAS A&M IN HOUSTON, NOV. 10; 23-0 OVER TULANE IN NEW ORLEANS, NOV. 11; 34-0 OVER LSU IN BATON ROUGE, NOV. 13; 12-0 OVER OLE MISS IN MEMPHIS ON NOV. 14.

AND INDEED THEY RESTED.

BUT THAT MUST HAVE MADE THEM NERVOUS. THEY WENT BACK TO TENNESSEE AND TOOK IT OUT ON CUMBERLAND, 71-0.

The rest of the story tells of what, in 1899, was known as the Tennessee Coal, Iron and Railroad Company, and how it eventually became U.S. Steel. In 1886 the Tennessee Coal, Iron and Railroad Company had moved to Alabama and put together the type of mining, coking, and iron manufacturing facilities it would take to pour steel in commercial quantities. On the first day of the 20th century their first shipment was sent to a customer in Connecticut.

The story folds back to 1857 when the company was known as the Sewanee Mining Company. That year they gave 10,000 acres of mountaintop land upon which a university would be built. The poster story concludes: "And that would be The University of the South. Still known as 'Sewanee' throughout the Southland."

Underneath the printed message is a photograph of that wonder team of 1899; eleven young men, each one looking more like Little Boy Blue as a bicycle racer than today's college football players, all leaning against each other, appearing so small, all fast asleep.

Later that day, Gray, now chancellor of the University of the South, and retired bishop of Mississippi drove me around the campus and village. Ruthie, sitting in the back seat, was tour guide. We saw scenes long familiar to them. I wanted to see Woodland, the site of their first home on the Mountain. There is no trace of the tarpaper barracks with ice boxes on the stoops and piles of coal in the yards. Instead there are rows of modest but neat and adequate stone duplexes for married students, many with automobiles with license plates from around the nation parked in the drives. The field where Davis Carter and Duncan Gray collided in a softball game looks the same, they told me as we eased by.

We traced the route Gray took the night he walked to his uncle's house for a heart to heart talk on their differences over integration of the School of Theology. The building, Fulford Hall, stands as magnificently as it did that night the young student sipped tea while telling his uncle that he loved him but would go on opposing him on the delicate issue of race. Fulford Hall is now used as admissions and communications offices.

We rounded the same sharp curves the Grays maneuvered that foggy February night Anne was born, with Duncan's head out the left window and Ruthie's out the other in order to see the road to the hospital. We moved slowly, and it seemed to me reverently, by All Saints' Chapel. Duncan pointed across the way to Thompson Union. "That was the coffee house and movie theater when we were here," Duncan said.

In front of Rebel's Rest we stopped so I could read again the historic marker:

HERE BEFORE THE WAR BETWEEN THE STATES STOOD THE FRAME RESIDENCE OF BISHOP LEONIDAS POLK OF LOUISIANA, A PRINCIPAL FOUNDER OF THE UNIVERSITY OF THE SOUTH. HERE WERE BUILT IN APRIL, '66 THE FIRST TWO LOG CABINS OF POST-WAR SEWANEE BY BISHOP CHARLES T. QUINTARD AND MAJOR GEORGE R. FAIRBANKS. IN THE LATER WERE HELD THE MEETING OF THE TRUSTEES IN 1866 AND THE FOUNDING OF THE EQB CLUB IN 1870.

I stopped reading to ask about the EQB Club. *"Ecce quam bonum,"* the bishop replied. "'Behold, how good and how pleasant it is for brethren to dwell together in unity.' From the Psalms. That's the university motto. In Latin, of course, Will."

"Dwell together?" I inquired. "In unity?" The bishop laughed heartily, understanding that at the root of my question were his seminary years on the Mountain. But no one specifically mentions 1953, a turbulent year when things were neither unified nor pleasant on the Mountain. Instead I asked if the politically correct folk haven't had something to say about "brethren" dwelling. He laughs again. "Nobody knows. The marker just says 'EQB.' *Ecce quam bonum.* Behold how good. You didn't know what that meant yourself, Will." Ruthie stood smiling at my veiled sarcasm on political correctness, not commenting. Perhaps thinking, though, for she quickly changed the subject.

"Duncan, tell Will about Abbo's Alley," she said. "Does the name Abbott Martin mean anything to you?" the bishop asked. I replied that there's a street in Nashville named Abbott Martin. "Same person," he said.

"Was he the bootlegger?" I asked. I knew the story of a mountain moonshiner who used to leave jars or jugs of his fixings in a certain stump, the quantity depending on how much money the students had deposited at the nocturnal rendezvous.

They both laughed. "No, no," the bishop says. "That's another story."

Never interrupting each other, they poured out the story of another celebrated man of the Mountain, Abbott Martin. And Abbo's Alley.

For forty years Professor Abbott taught English at the University of the South. A Mississippian, graduate of Ole Miss, he wore his lack of advanced academic credentials as a badge of honor. His terminal degree was the University of Mississippi Master of Arts. He couldn't be bothered with anything further. Everyone knew Martin, the bishop tells me. "Known as Abbo. People were either crazy about him, or they thought he was crazy. Or were crazy about him and still thought he was crazy. And maybe he was crazy. But brilliant."

Many tales of Martin's years at Sewanee rolled forth. With each episode there were gales of laughter. Abbo was the quintessential Southerner. He made no secret of what he loved and what he hated. The bishop drew on Arthur Ben Chitty, the Sewanee historiographer. "Abbo loved the Confederacy, France, British nobility, kings, queens, bishops, rich people, Republicans, Robert E. Lee, segregation, and bourbon whiskey. He hated Methodists, Yankees, and Germans." Methodists for being prohibitionists, Yankees for not being Southern, Germans for being German.

Because Professor Martin represented the old Sewanee, the old South, he figured prominently in the fracas over integration in 1953. Gray especially relished the account of Abbo's notoriety as a drinking man, before he finally quit. When Martin entered Monteagle Diner, the waitresses always met him at his table with set-ups to match the night's bottle. During the height of the racial crisis, when the allegations of excessive drinking by Professors McNair, Grant, and Reddick were being circulated, Martin came into the diner one night and was seated near Bishop Mitchell, then chancellor of Sewanee and known for his intense aversion to imbibing academics. Also at the table were Bishop Juhan and other dignitaries adamantly involved in the ongoing conflict. Gray's laughter filled the area as he mimicked Abbo's response when the waitress put the routine set-ups in front of him. "With a huffy growl he waved her off.

'Humph! Get that off my table! What do I want with all that soda? Get that stuff off my table!'"

During World War II the university had assigned to it a contingent of German prisoners of war. Abbo was an avid gardener and was given the labors of a platoon of the prisoners. While the professor pestered and lectured them in his broken German on the depravity of Goethe, Wagner, Kaisers, and Hitlers, and the civilizing influences of Wordsworth, Coleridge, and Voltaire, the German prisoners terraced and landscaped the long ravine adjacent to Rebel's Rest with wildflowers, shrubs, exotic plants, and bulbs of all sorts. There were paths, footbridges, and smaller rock gardens. "It was a sight to behold," Ruthie said.

We circled back and saw the large stone building, Clement Chen Hall, the vice-chancellor's residence today. That called for another story. Clement Chen, a native of China, graduated from the University of the South in 1953, the year Gray was pressing the university to change its racial policy, a time when Chen would not have gained admission had he been an American of a different color code. He had been a student in an Episcopal preparatory school in China and was on the last plane to leave Shanghai as it fell to the revolutionary forces in 1949. With a modest scholarship he arrived at Sewanee where he did well, continued to a school of architecture and made a great deal of money designing and owning Holiday Inns and other hotels in America and Asia. As a student he had lived in Fulford Hall when Gray's uncle was vice-chancellor. After becoming rich from his entrepreneurial energy he visited Vice-Chancellor Robert Ayres occasionally and was an overnight guest in Fulford Hall. It was on one of those visits he decided the old mansion was not good enough for his prestigious alma mater's chief executive and decided to build a new one. The day his cashier's check arrived, Mr. Chen died in San Francisco. Dr. Ayres had talked with him that morning. Clement Chen Hall, with spacious banquet, reception, and party rooms stands as a memorial to a man who came from afar and prospered.

The School of Theology has moved from St. Luke's Hall to where Sewanee Military Academy was located and as we drove there, Ruthie pointed out the spot from which she and Duncan Gray III would stand on Sunday mornings to watch her young brother, Lloyd Spivey, now a prominent attorney and businessman in Canton, lead the procession of cadets to Morning Prayer.

We stopped at Morgan's Steep, a spot where many a Sewanee freshman's spine has been tingled by hearing the story of a Confederate general riding his horse over the cliff to escape pursuing Union troops; an incident researchers Arthur Ben and Elizabeth Chitty have proved never happened. The legend lives on, they tell me, as legends should. I thought of something a neighbor alleged to be mentally imbalanced once told me. "Anyone who thinks something ain't true just because it didn't happen is whacko." A worthy axiom for a writer to cherish, I remember thinking at the time. It is factual, however, that Professor, later Vice-Chancellor Edward McCrady took his young nephew, Duncan Montgomery Gray Jr., on cave explorations beneath Morgan's Steep, occasions more exciting to young Duncan than the story of a Confederate general riding his horse over the brink and surviving.

We passed Otey Parish, the Episcopal church for the villagers, and back on campus went into old St. Luke's Chapel, now used for music recitals, where Gray's father, Bishop Duncan M. Gray Sr., baptized Anne in early 1952.

If one did not know of Sewanee's cosmopolitan history he might fancy he was visiting a self-conscious effort to replicate the Old South. The setting, buildings, icons, and ghosts serve as testament and celebration of the Lost Cause. Even the name itself. The University of the South.

The Confederates remain. Major George R. Fairbanks, who had been chief quartermaster for the Army of Tennessee hospital department, is revered at Sewanee for building the first home there, teaching history, serving as commissioner of buildings and lands, and being an invaluable advocate throughout his life. Brigadier General Josiah Gorgas, the man who served his old friend Robert E. Lee as chief of ordnance, was responsible for the death-dealing firepower of the tentative nation. He served as second vice-chancellor. Charles Todd Quintard, chaplain in the Army of Northern Virginia, was second bishop of Tennessee, and first vice-chancellor. Brigadier General Francis Asbury Shoup served under Generals Braxton Bragg and Joseph Johnston, and was baptized on the field of battle. He is remembered as a teacher of mathematics and metaphysics, and as a scholar and writer. And, of course, Major General Leonidas Polk, a slaveowner and bishop who was killed by a shell from Sherman's guns at Pine Mountain on June 14, 1864. Less than a month earlier, May 18, Bishop Polk, then General, had baptized his fellow warrior, General Joseph Johnston. One week earlier General Polk, in his priestly role, had baptized General Hood. Then, with a rifled Parrott artillery shell shot all the way through his chest, the bishop general's dead body lay quivering from involuntary muscle spasms. His fellow general knelt beside him, his hand on the bishop's head in baptismal fashion.

More than anyone else Bishop Leonidas Polk was considered chief founder of the University of the South. Now he and the others are all there, hovering, whispering, remembering, and reminding. Like melting snow of early spring. All, save Polk, were born above Mason and Dixon's boundary. New York, Pennsylvania, Connecticut, Indiana. They had come to the South, stayed on, and fought to sever it from the sites of their cradles. They had created this place, with no malice aforethought, to promote and secure what was called a way of life. Yet here I stood, with a man born in and bonded with the most historically Southern place in the nation: Mississippi. A man whose life has been one of rescuing the drowning victims of the Lost Cause; a people those who preceded him by a hundred years had fought to keep enslaved. For their war, after all else is said, was about slavery. A man who harbors the values, that way of life the South has claimed as its own but has so often perverted and neglected: neighborliness, dignity, honor, courage, good manners, common decency, and yes, though out of fashion now, chivalry. This man standing beside me, I thought, has done more by far to truly bless and honor the South than those whose pictures adorn the walls and whose ghosts haunt every cranny and who resorted to carnage in its name.

AT ONE-THIRTY ON THE AFTERNOON OF JULY 3, 1863, THE shells began to fall in the midst of the University Greys, the Eleventh Mississippi, and the entire Army of Northern Virginia. It was an answer to Confederate guns firing from Seminary Ridge. Generally when a cannonade began it would be intermittent; shells falling and bursting here and there, then calm for a while before starting again. This began more like a sudden hailstorm. From Cemetery Ridge, Big and Little Roundtop, seemingly from every direction and no direction. It was a shelling such as the most seasoned of the warriors had never experienced. On Cemetery Ridge a gunner read aloud a sign, smiled, shook his head, went on firing: ANYONE DISCHARGING FIREARMS ON CEMETERY PROPERTY WILL BE PROSECUTED.

"Get down! Get down!" Baker yelled, dashing from one small grouping of men to another. Joseph McKie threw himself down beside his cousin. Tommie shrugged casually, barely changing from his sitting position.

In all there were 176 Confederate guns. The daylight grew heavy with thunder from both sides. The combined smell of rotting dead horses and men, human waste from impromptu latrines, along with the swirling gun smoke became the harsh incense of Thanatos. Soldiers hugged the ground as trees were splintered by the fiendish fruit from the mouths of sixteen pound Napoleans and Parrott guns. Artillery horses tied in the area squealed in panic when one was hit, lunging to free themselves, running in aimless terror about the open field when they succeeded. Smoke from the guns on Seminary Ridge, the Round Tops, and Cemetery Ridge met in mid-field, the bursts from opposing sides coming together like young lovers in a long-delayed rendezvous; embracing, flitting, crazed, lost in revelry. As the wild clouds darkened the area the continuous eruptions from the throbbing and thrusting cannon barrels were as the lust of Lucifer's imps, impregnating generations to come with deprivation and enmity.

Suddenly Thomas McKie screamed. Actually it was more the sound of whine and delirium than scream. His cousin Joseph nudged closer to him, as close as he could get, and threw his right arm protectively over Tommie's back, pulling him in a tight embrace. The other soldiers couldn't hear the screams above the cannonade. Joseph knew his cousin's panic was unrelated to the shells exploding and falling all around them. Tommie had never shown fear in the face of battle. Joseph had seen the whence of Tommie's hysteria even before Tommie saw it. It was a spider, the only thing Thomas Fondren McKie had ever feared. His mother had told Joseph about it the day they left Springdale.

"He can't help it. It's just something that's in him," she said. "Don't let anyone make fun of him," she had pleaded. "I suppose I was frightened by a spider when I was carrying him," she explained. "Or something. I never understood it. He was like that when he was a tiny baby." For a long time she didn't speak again. Her brow was furrowed and confusion stood out in her eyes. It was as if she was trying to figure it out for the first time. Before she spoke again she took her nephew by the upper arm, her fingernails leaving marks. Then, "Please promise to look after my baby if he sees a spider. I worry about him." Joseph promised that he would. This was the first time it had happened. Joseph had been watching the spider since the shelling began. Normally he would have killed the spider, destroyed the web and said nothing to Tommie about it. This time he didn't risk standing up in the thick of the falling shells. He kept thinking a fragment would hit the spider's web or come close enough to scare it away before Tommie saw it. It was a black and yellow spider and Joseph thought it was quite pretty, though he had no idea as to whether or not it was poison. He knew only that he was not afraid of spiders and his cousin was. It was waiting in the center of the orb it had woven during the night. There was a torn segment on the anchored edge of the web and now the two boys could see the pulsating of the spider's spinnerets as she forced out the liquid silk and rushed out to repair the damage. The dazzling silk flowing from the same invisible pocket as would come the deadly poison if such should be. Joseph marveled that she had survived the bustle of the day at all. And wished she hadn't.

"It can't hurt you," Joseph kept repeating. His words did no good. The words did no good for little Tommie knew, somehow knew, in the deep and primordial recesses of his being, that it not only could hurt but was hurting at that very moment. Did not know but intuited, the way a robin intuits, and thus *knew*, in the deepest sense, that the spider web was like the universe. With a God at the center that can rend asunder or heal, kill or give life, raise up kingdoms from barren rocks or bring princes to nothing. In his innocent, genetic Calvinism knew that this war he had badgered his mother to let him fight was as the spider web. When the most remote filament of the web is touched the spider springs to action, ready to mend or ready to kill. Gettysburg was the web of the universe now. Touched from all sides. There were other screams all around them as soldiers were hit by exploding shells or falling rocks and limbs. Tommie was oblivious of everything except the tiny, eight-legged animal trying to keep its own home intact four feet away.

Joseph felt a strong urge to give his cousin a piece of the tobacco he had bought that morning from a soldier in the burying detail. Tommie had begged him many times for a chew of tobacco. Said he knew it would taste good and settle his nerves. But that was something else Tommie's mother had made Joseph promise. "Tommie is just a little boy," she told him. "I know he has slipped around and used tobacco but please promise me you won't let him do it. I know he'll be tempted by the bigger boys." Again, Joseph had promised his aunt. She wanted her son to be innocent and upright while he was away. Now Joseph was torn between not being true to his word and trying to calm his hysterical cousin and comrade. He was spared the decision when a twelve-pounder shell failed to explode and plowed directly through the stronger-than-iron silk web, leaving not a trace. Tommie continued to whimper but Joseph knew the charge would begin soon and that the fury of battle would quell Tommie's fear completely.

Although the McKie cousins did not know it while they were lying in the company of a spider, their friend Jeremiah Gage had been hit and mortally wounded. Jim Dailey was on litter duty and had taken Gage to the field hospital where he was under the watchful care of Dr. Joseph Holt, a physician from Wilkinson County, Mississippi. The manner of Jeremiah Sanders Gage's dying would be carefully chronicled in future years by some who knew him and some who heard his dramatic story. His dying letter to his mother, sealed with his blood, his release of Mary Ready Wendell, the girlfriend he had courted while he was a student at the University of Mississippi, and instruction for his burial would become some of the most moving drama and romance of the Lost Cause.

Mary lived half a block from St. Peter's Church where Dr. Barnard was rector at the beginning of the war and where Duncan Gray would be rector a hundred years later. The house still stands. One can still stand in the hallway at the foot of the stairs where Jere Gage waited for the beautiful lady to descend. Gage and Mary were estranged by the time of Gettysburg, and Jeremiah was trying hard to find a replacement so that he might be discharged from the Greys and return to Mary. That, however, takes nothing away from the valiant manner of his demise. A human is a human.

When the hundreds of guns of Confederate artillery and a similar number from the Union forces fell silent, the historic and disastrous charge began. The University Greys had been back in the woods of Seminary Ridge during the bombardment. It was 3:30 when General Pickett and General Pettigrew moved their troops forward. It would be over soon. Half an hour and it would all be over. In linear formation they stood, side by side. Each man took up about two-and-a-half feet of space. The line of Pettigrew's men was about three-quarters of a mile. Pickett's men extended about the same distance, with a quarter of a mile separating the two divisions. They were to converge at a rock wall about a mile in front. There was a second row behind the first line. Again the men were standing side by side. A few feet behind the second row were the file closers. They followed to enforce the discipline; see that no one ran in the wrong direction. In a sense it was compelled courage. Better to be shot or bayonetted by the enemy than a friendly file closer.

The line moved forward as if on a parade ground. The enemy was about a mile away. To get to them the Confederates had to cross the open field. There were but thirty of the University Greys now.

Thomas McKie had not completely forgotten the spider but he moved ahead with the others. The vast shadow of his yearning for home continued to distance him from fear of warfare. Strangely, his hysteria concerning the spider was somehow related to his thoughts of home things. His cousin Joseph again considered giving him a piece of the tobacco as they lined up but again decided against it. He had made a promise.

There were the sounds of fife and drums but it was perfunctory. The smoke was clearing since the cannons stopped and they could see across the open field. Time did not exist. They were there no longer for freedom, slavery, rights. None of that. Each soldier was there for the one next to him and the one behind him. There was no other cause. No one was tired, hungry, sleepy, sick now. No one was anything but a weapon of war. Controlled. As unthinking as the weapons they carried.

Back at Sewanee Inn for the night, a friendly employee, the same woman I had seen that morning, skilled at learning one's mission on the Mountain without appearing meddlesome, began a protracted monologue when I told her I was there to visit Bishop Gray.

"Wonderful man. Just marvelous. Lives over on Rattlesnake Springs Road. You want to call? Here. Use my phone. Wonderful man. Oh, you say you have seen him already? Guess you turned off Sherwood Road. After you drove through the campus and the village, and got back on 64. Then left on Sherwood and left again on Rattlesnake Springs. That's the way to get there. Three or four miles is all it is. Keep to the left and you'll find him. Just keep to the left." I started to tell her that some people believe Duncan Gray can always be found to the left but thought better of it.

"Yes, ma'am," I said instead.

I supposed she was still inquiring with her direction giving, waiting as she pushed her forelocks back, still trying to figure out exactly what I was about. She was a woman in what we call midlife, though I have never understood why we say that, how we calculate when one's life is half over. Winter-lean, she had a countenance that intrigued me, that somehow suggested she knew something I wanted to hear. I fumbled in my jacket pocket and snapped on a little tape recorder without asking, a violation of my own rule, as her words poured out like flocks of birds come to feed.

"You know, we're so fortunate to have them here. I just love to hear him read Latin. I go to all the commencements just so I can hear him read all that in Latin. I reckon he's reading it. O, I love to hear that man do Latin. And I'm not even an Episcopalian. Are you an Episcopalian?" "No, ma'am," I said.

Her words seemed to blossom in midair, then hang there without sagging as they sank in with me. So far she hadn't told me anything important but I tarried, still feeling that she would. "Will you be staying for Lessons and Carols? That's this week-end. Tickets are scarce but I'm sure Bishop Gray can get you one. He's the chancellor, you know. That's why he's the one to read all that Latin I suppose."

I told her I wouldn't be able to stay for Lessons and Carols, though I knew I would enjoy it. Lessons and Carols is a traditional service at Sewanee, in origin from King's College, Cambridge. The nine readings range from the Garden of Eden to the prologue of St. John's Gospel where the Word made flesh is described, the readings interspersed with sacred music of the ages. For many years it has been a major event on the Mountain and attracts people from afar. The woman continued. "He's so funny. Wonderful sense of humor. Sometimes I even laugh when he's reading all that Latin. You know, he's short. And a lot of short people are—how should I put it?"

"Grumpy?" I volunteered.

She laughed for the first time. "Yeah. Grumpy. I don't know what makes short people that way." She looked me up and down, seeming to notice that I am about the same height as the chancellor. "Of course, lots of short people are just as agreeable as the next one," she added. "Not all short people are grumpy. Certainly Bishop Gray isn't grumpy. Wonderful man. So friendly. Makes everybody feel at home. And so funny. We're so blessed to have him here. I'm not even an Episcopalian so I ought to know. Of course, we don't have them here year round. They have a home in Mississippi, you know. Jackson, Mississippi." She was speaking faster now, her words more like martins in flight than the soft flow of mountain talk.

I moved to leave as she went on. She looked around as if about to tell me a secret. "You know how to account for all that? You say you're writing a book about him? Well, I'll tell you how to explain all that." She glanced around again, then whispered. "His wife. That explains it all. His wife. Wonderful person. Have you met his wife?" I told her I had. "Then you know what I'm talking about. It's his wife. That explains the whole thing. Wonderful woman. Both of them. Just wonderful."

Deciding that maybe I had been wrong in my first assessment of the woman at the inn, I felt first call for an evening toddy and was starting to ask if the Inn had an ice machine. She quickly interrupted. "He's not only funny. He's smart. One of the smartest men I ever met. And I've met a lot of smart ones. Working here where everybody's smart, you might say. And good. You know how to describe Bishop Gray? He's just a real good man."

She turned back to working on the papers on her desk. Like she had nothing else to say. As I started to thank her and ask about the ice machine she thought of something else. "You know why we mountain people love Bishop Gray so much?"

"No, ma'am, but I would like to," I answered, feeling a strange anticipation.

"It's because he's so ordinary." She paused, as if to see if I would take issue with what she had just said. At first I thought she was making an Anglican pun, for "the Ordinary" is their synonym for bishop. I was growing impatient and was thinking of saying, "Very well, I shall play your silly game. I never thought of Duncan Gray as especially bishopric." I was stopped in mid-thought as she added. "And he's not up to anything." She said that hastily, then seemed content to leave it with that, her surge of words stopping like a convoy arriving at its destination at terrific speed. *He's not up to anything.* I had come here in search of words of acclamation, an index of momentous deeds and accomplishments. Instead I had heard that my subject was just so ordinary. Up to nothing. Somehow, in that moment, I knew that was what I had waited to hear. But how very strange. A bishop of the Episcopal Church not up to anything? A seeming oxymoron. How would one ever get to be bishop if he were not up to something?

Back in the room I considered what the woman had told me. Over two years, many documents, and thousands of miles trying to find out just who Duncan Montgomery Gray Jr. was, what had shaped him, and precisely what made him tick, I had found it at the starting place. From a neighbor who is on the mountain but not of the Mountain. Here was a woman not caught up in all the benefits and hazards of academe, with a job that probably does not pay her what she's worth, a person of another religious declension, standing aside and seeing a bishop as an ordinary man not up to anything. And declaring him good.

What else is there to say? He's just a good man. As I replayed the tape I thought of a character from the Four Gospels. The man who took Jesus from the cross. I checked the Bible on the table as I sipped the toddy. All

I could find about that man was that he was a good man of Arimathaea. The Scripture doesn't tell us anything else about him. It says simply that he was a good man. Who stepped in and offered his services when the world had done all it could do to the Son of Man-Son of God. Maybe to say someone is a good man is enough to say of any mortal. It seemed then an apt description and summary of one I said at the beginning of this project was my hero.

DUNCAN MONTGOMERY GRAY JR.: A GOOD MAN.

The woman had added something else. "He's not up to anything." I remembered that as I drove down the mountain the next day. I thought of all the happenings of the years. All those who have come to this mountain. From those who nudged the Indians off the peaks, to missionaries, Sewanee Mining Company and the Tennessee Coal, Iron and Railroad Company. From General Leonidas Polk to the Appalachian Volunteers of the Great Society; all have been up to something. Often with good intentions; nevertheless, up to something.

I considered some of those Gray has influenced over the years who are now priests. Protégés in a sense. The Reverend Tom Ward, now Sewanee's chaplain. Sam Lloyd, nephew of Mrs. Gray, who left Sewanee for Boston's historic Trinity Church, where Phillips Brooks held sway in the mid-nineteenth century. David Elliott of Vicksburg. And Duncan Montgomery Gray III of St. Peter's Church, Oxford. I hope it can be said of them that they are not up to anything.

For two years I had been tracking a man, an ordinary man as the woman put it, who has never held political office, received the Nobel Peace Prize, coached a Super Bowl team, led an army, starred on television, accrued great wealth. None of the things that make for fame and glory in our day and time. Content to be a clay pot, an earthen vessel, the treasure within radiating the Light of the World, affecting change, making things better wherever he went. One of whom a mountain woman could tell me all I needed to know in the first place. She had told me that Duncan Montgomery Gray Jr. was just an ordinary man, a good man who was not up to anything. I recalled a letter from the Gray's Delta-born son Lloyd, journalist and editor. He wrote, "Two years ago when Duncan III and I were talking in preparation for an article we did in the diocesan newspaper at Daddy's retirement, we agreed that the most remarkable thing about our childhood was that it was so ordinary."

The word "ordinary" has taken on new meaning for me. Remarkably ordinary, the son had said. I had never thought of anything ordinary being remarkable. The two seemed contradictory. Ordinary: Plain.

Average. Common. Inferior. Mediocre. Normal. Everyday. Quotidian. Those are some of the synonyms for the word ordinary. Not one is edifying. Not one describes Duncan Gray. It made me question the manner in which the nation's history has been written. Wars are its generals; not the thousands who stormed the beaches or held firm against incredible odds. Gettysburg is Lee, Longstreet, Pettigrew, Pickett; not Raines, Ballard, Heslep and Brewer—Greys from the ranks whose intrepidity was never measured. The Pacific fleet is Admiral Nimitz; not mothers with gold stars in their windows. Periods of Church history are its popes. American history is measured by its presidents; industry by its barons. Even the word "ordinary" as used for church prelates is of humble origin. One of the earliest English usages was for priests appointed to attend convicted criminals at Newgate.

In the beginning I had wanted to write a book about Duncan Gray because from what I knew of him already he was one of my heroes and I believed he was a great man. But *great* seemed a rash adjective with which to measure a fellow transient. So I abandoned that notion. I just wanted to learn the truth about him. Now a mountain woman had given me a succinct recital of greatness. Or so it seemed to me.

I had a question or two to ask myself. What exactly is the principal mark of a good man? Even a great man? That morning, after checking the biblical references about one good man, the one who took Jesus from the cross, I had scanned the collects, prayers, and appointed readings from the Epistles and the Gospels in the *Book of Common Prayer*, the 1928 revision I had used throughout. I was struck by the number of times I found the words "joy" and "joyous." They were the same words many who have known Gray well had used to describe him. "He is the most joyous person I have ever met," his wife had told me on one occasion when we were discussing a troublesome period of his life and I was not understanding. A good man, I concluded, will be a man of unceasing joy. Joy in the biblical and *Prayer Book* understanding. Not joy as happy-go-lucky for he is capable of deep sadness. Over the years, through trials and tribulations, good times and bad, victories and defeats: joyous. Springing from assuredness that God has intervened in human history. Advent. Easter. Pentecost. Joy not dependent upon highs and lows of feeling or changing conditions of affluence or misfortune.

A person close to Gray had said, "Duncan is what the Episcopal Church would be if everyone in it believed (lived by) the words they repeat every Sunday." The radicalism of liturgy had made an ordinary man good. Joyous. And a truly joyous person is never up to anything.

For the moment the thought of his not being up to anything lingered. It seemed somehow incongruous with the way so many have viewed Duncan Gray over the years: liberal, radical, social activist, crusader, disturber of the status quo; a priest of doing. Then, looking back and reflecting on what I had learned of him, I realized the woman at the inn was right. He really hasn't been up to anything. Why should he be? For him there is nothing left to do. Simply something to be. Not trying to do anything at all. Just trying to live, and lead others to live, knowing what has already been done, knowing that celebration of liturgy brings the past to present. Free in obedience. Be what you already are: reconciled to God and all creation. That was his understanding of the teachings of the apostle Paul.

I went back to what Ruthie had told me when I asked where her husband got the courage to face the mob at the University of Mississippi when the first Negro citizen was admitted as a student. "He simply saw this as part of his priestly duty. The same as celebrating the Eucharist that morning," she said. "He thought, 'That's what a priest does.'" That's what someone who knows him better than anyone told me. He didn't know any better, she had said. Passing the paten and chalice, quelling a riot, going up against the political establishment, the White Citizens' Council, the KKK; all the same; all in keeping with the New Creation. Liturgical instinct. Some might call it Eucharistic madness.

Too many of us are up to something, I thought. Several months ago our closest and dearest neighbors suffered a great tragedy. Their sixteen-year-old grandson, who lived with them, was murdered by his mother who then killed herself. All we were able to do was be with the grandparents in their intolerable grief, trying, as best we could, to bear a little of their pain. A few days after his death, it was Christmas Day. They were coming over to share our Christmas table. We would not feast for it was not an occasion for feasting. The food would be ordinary, in the sense Duncan Gray has been ordinary. And it would be eucharistic. We would talk of young Matt, so early gone. Of yesterdays they enjoyed and tomorrows they would never know. Maybe it will help a little, this brief passing of time together. To spite her estranged husband, a mother murdered her child. Up to something.

Until they arrived I sat in my cabin, trying to write what I learned from a wise and perceptive innkeeper. Beside my desk sat an aging Dalmatian, abandoned on these acres years ago because he was born with one eye blue, the other brown, signifying total deafness the veterinarian told us. Not fit for training nor breeding we supposed his callous master

thought. As if servility and breeding are the only purpose for earth's creatures. Twice he has been attacked, once almost fatally, by a rottweiler up
to something. Canine mayhem. Once he was hit by a passing truck he
intended only to salute in peace with yelps he cannot hear. Again he
almost died. His enemies were up to something. But not he.

Those mismatched eyes focused sharply on mine, trying, it seems, to
tell me something. I reflected on some words Martin Buber wrote many
years ago, words I have found useful on other occasions. "An animal's
eyes have the power to speak a great language," he wrote.
"Independently, without needing cooperation of sounds and gestures,
most forcible when they rely wholly on their glance, their eyes express
the mystery in its natural prison, the anxiety of becoming." Who has not
marveled at those fixed eyes, trying, sometimes desperately, to express
understanding. In this instance, condolence.

The continuing eye contact with Doops, the deaf Dalmatian, mingling
with the anguish for my neighbors, took me again to what the woman on
the Mountain told me. Not up to anything. Mischief is being up to something. A woman is up to torturing her husband so she murders their son
and leaves her world in shambles. A Mississippi man is up to nothing at
all and leaves his world a little better than what he found.

What were the University Greys up to? Gage, McKie, Montgomery,
and the rest? Were they not as liturgically driven as Duncan Gray? Flags
and banners. Drums and fifes. Songs and prayers. Sermons and the
General's command: "Charge!" In faithfulness they had responded. In
obedience they stood against infeasible odds. *Stranger, go tell the
Lakedaimonians that we are lying here in obedience to their command.*

When I read those lines from Simonides on the Confederate monument at the University of Mississippi, on the very spot where Duncan
Gray had stood in his vain effort to stay the wrath and projectiles
hurled—presumably in promotion of the Greys' memories—I was at first
offended. How dare they address those classical lines to so ignoble a
cause as a war in defense of slavery? Yet. Valor? Who can say them nay?
Upright, conscientious, honorable, honest, scrupulous? Those are virtues
we ascribe to them today. Maybe we attribute those things to them
because that is what we yearn to be ourselves. Or, if they were all those
things, their individual morality somehow tempers the immorality and
assuages our own guilt for their common cause. In any event, they were
ordinary men as the innkeeper had described Duncan Gray as being.
They lay in graves, lying in obedience to commands as surely as the
Lakedaimonians, some of their graves to be forever unmarked, scattered

from Gettysburg to Marshall County, Mississippi, or in prisons far from the then ravaged halls of Oxford from which they had marched so certain of victory and early return four years earlier. *"Our cause is of the Lord."* They still believed, and theological adjustments would be forthcoming.

What were they up to? And how then shall we distinguish between the University Greys and Duncan Gray of the university? Is valor of the victors alone? The righteous only? What do we say of honor, conscientiousness, honesty, scruples among those whose cause was not only lost but wrong? To make the distinction, we must go back a lot of years with Gray. Back to the time in 1953 when he stood in the office of his friend and teacher Robert McNair, with Dr. Allen Reddick and his pal Davis Carter, agonizing over the vice-chancellor and trustees' intransigence in the admission of the sons of former slaves to a school that taught of Jesus. Dr. McNair handed Gray the Bible and told him to read:

> We wrestle not against flesh and blood, but against principalities, against powers, against the rulers of the darkness of this world. . . .

I have tried on these pages to stay clear of a flood of theological jargon. If there is to be a treatise called "The Systematic Theology of the Right Reverend Duncan Montgomery Gray Jr.," certainly I am not the one to write it. In the first place, I am not a theologian. In addition, it seems to me the life one lives *is* his theology and needs no exegesis. But if the distinction is to be made between the bravery, honor, and scruples of the University Greys and those marks in the life of Duncan Gray, then his understanding of the biblical allusions to principalities and powers must be considered. Principalities in the Bible refer to the utter fallen condition of creation. Not just original sin of human beings but a fallen state of everything. It is not some romantic allegory. It is reality. So even virtues like honor, scruples, uprightness are relative terms, subject to fallenness, and require an antecedent and object. Honor to what or whom? Uprightness in what context? All of these virtues can be corrupted, perverted, and become idolatry. For everyone, Duncan Gray would insist.

Principalities can best be understood in modern language as institutions. Or ideologies. The State is a principality. The ideology of a "justified state," ordained of God, the notion of Manifest Destiny that led to the slaughter of the Indians and gave America license to commit the most outrageous acts—all are principalities. Powers and principalities with a being of their own. All are blasphemy for they usurp the authority of the one true God. All isms are principalities. An Episcopal layman,

248

lawyer, and theologian named William Stringfellow went further when he wrote in "An Ethic for Christians and Other Aliens in a Strange Land":

> The very names and titles in biblical usage for the principalities and powers is some indication of the scope and significance of the subject for human beings. And if some of these seem quaint, transposed into contemporary language they lose their quaintness and the principalities become recognizable and all too familiar: they include all institutions, all ideologies, all images, all movements, all causes, all corporations, all bureaucracies, all traditions, all methods and routines, all conglomerates, all races, all nations, all idols. Thus, the Pentagon or the Ford Motor Company or Harvard University or the Hudson Institute or Consolidated Edison or the Diners Club or the Olympics or the Methodist Church or the Teamsters Union are all principalities. So are capitalism, Maoism, humanism, Mormonism, astrology, the Puritan work ethic, science and scientism, white supremacy patriotism, plus many, many more—sports, sex, any profession or discipline, technology, money, the family— beyond any prospect of full enumeration. The principalities and powers are legion.

If that seems a bleak picture of the human condition consider the account of the wild man Jesus encountered in St. Mark's Gospel. He was a man totally senseless, disheveled, and violently mad. When Jesus asked the man his name the man replied, "My name is Legion, for we are many."

What Stringfellow was describing was a society that makes no sense when compared to the kingdom of God that Christians pray will come to earth. He was enumerating some—but only some—of the false gods we serve and worship. The powers and principalities that grip us are legion, innumerable. And individuals, such as those members of the University Greys, as well as all of us, are caught up in, with, and by these powers. This was why Professor Robert McNair pointed to that particular passage that day on the Mountain. To say to his students that their fight was not with Bishops Juhan and Mitchell, not with Vice-Chancellor McCrady, but against the powers and principalities that were real and were seeking to wreck the kingdom God in Christ had established. The ism against which they wrestled on that occasion was racism, an idol with a life and power of its own.

None of this is to excuse Captain Lowry, Lieutenant McCaleb, Private Thomas McKie, or the whole of the University Greys. Nor is it to say they were less honorable, heroic, conscientious, courageous than Duncan

249

Montgomery Gray Jr. Rather it is to put both the University Greys and Gray of the university under the white heat of the First Commandment: "Thou shalt have no other gods before me." It is only to pose the question, who has more nearly followed the commandment of the God who said to Moses from a burning bush, I AM WHO I AM?

There are many gods, many powers and principalities to be served and worshiped. Gray saw the fallen state of Sewanee as institution in 1953. Yet he came back to it. But still wary of its fallenness, even—he would say, especially—with himself at the helm.

Duncan Gray is a biblical scholar, and as student, priest, bishop, and chancellor he has held the Bible as the rule and guide of his life. Yet on these pages I have not sought to place him within the various spheres of biblical criticism. From what I have learned I assume that if forced to place himself in some camp he would choose the one called *biblical realism*, generally understood as the view of those who see the tragedy of human history as occasioned by the existence of original sin, and he would see the call of the people of God (the Church) to be responsible acts to limit sin and advance human good, based on the teachings of Jesus and the Prophets.

I began to feel I was discovering the real Duncan Gray when I examined his tough and substantive understanding of grace vis-á-vis principalities and powers. One of the few doctrinal questions I asked him had to do with that. I had gleaned something of the answer from my readings of his sermons preached on occasions of crisis and controversy but felt it best to let him answer for himself. "What do you mean when you say 'grace'?", I asked him.

He said:

> I think of "grace" as God's special gift to us of his love and acceptance, his mercy and forgiveness, all without reference to our own merit or deserving. . . . "Grace" is the power of God at work in our lives, but it is a power that comes largely in and through these gifts. To be loved unconditionally, to be forgiven for all of my sins, and to be totally accepted is power; the power to be better than you ever thought you could be. . . . It is power and it is joy. And it is this "grace" that is ours by faith and trust in Jesus and His presence with us.

I began to understand Duncan Gray better after that. Grace and joy, I concluded, are inseparable. Also, the *doing* follows the *being*.

Chapter Eight

AND THE
BLESSING . . . REMAIN
WITH YOU ALWAYS

T he story of Duncan Montgomery Gray Jr. has not ended. He blossoms on the Mountain he vowed in the spring of 1953 never to see again. In 1977 the Grays had never lived in anything except church-owned houses. Realizing that some day they would not have that privilege, Ruthie suggested they build a house near Sewanee that could serve as summer vacation residence, for trustees' meetings, seminary guests, and be rented out during other times to graduate students or short-term faculty. Finally it would be a place of retirement. She met considerable resistance from her husband. Partly because she was always a persuasive partner in the union and partly because she had a modest inheritance of her own, she prevailed. With budget limitations and displeasure with professional offerings, Ruthie decided to design and contract the building herself. With a builder friend giving her standard dimensions for such things as bathtubs, doors, windows, and appliances she went about the task of doing something she had never done before. She drew the blueprint. Her primary concerns were a good view, a large fireplace, and lots of storage space. She chose cedar siding for the entire house and Sewanee sandstone for the massive fireplace and chimney.

A New Jersey lumber company that owned much of the land of Lost Cove, that area that dawdles down the mountainside with implications of endless time, was cutting the giant cherry, walnut, and chestnut oaks as her building began. The workmen needed an egress across the Gray driveway. Ruthie cheerfully agreed. Perhaps in return they gave her some of the rough-hewn cherry lumber to fashion into furniture. Not as payment for the egress. That was free. And the very heart of one of the biggest walnut trees, the dimensions six inches thick and ten feet long for a mantle. That too. And just enough of the imperfect chestnut oak boards for a fence around the property. Yes, that too. When the cutting was done, there were plenty of boards for Nelson Wright and his carpenters to put up a fence for her. Appreciated lagniappe.

The cherry was fashioned into a dining table and some large chests. The carefully dressed and polished walnut accentuates the mountain stone that forms the huge fireplace and most of an inside wall. Wide pine planks salvaged from an antebellum home next door to Grace Church, Canton, brought a touch of Mississippi to the mountain haven, forming most of the floors. Ruthie's first jaunt into the field of architecture resulted in a house best described as elegant, all blending with and complementing what the grand architect of the universe has done with rocks, dirt, trees, and creatures.

Adjacent to their acres is a place belonging to Kyle Rote Jr., a graduate of Sewanee who abandoned his father's game to become an internationally known soccer player. Also nearby is property once owned by William Alexander Percy, the kinsman who raised Walker Percy, the novelist. Walker Percy spent considerable time there—Brinkwood, the estate was called—in the summers and told Gray that the Lost Cove Cave in Percy's novel, *Second Coming*, was actually at Sewanee, though he had taken literary license to move the cave to North Carolina.

Officially Gray presides as chancellor at functions such as commencements and meetings of the board of trustees. That is the same body he challenged in 1953, though not one of that number remains. He takes serious counsel with all who come his way on university concerns, prays, reads, writes, and answers mail in his untroubled study. He also sits with Ruthie counting wild turkeys that come calling, their stylized plumage registering the drift of the wind. White-tail deer wander by, close enough to be in harm's way, secure in their priestly refuge, all amid the genial sounds of creation on a mountaintop smelling of goodwill, with even the smoothest scars of past hurts forever gone. He loves this place. With the same tenacious energy he used to fight its ancient wrongs at twenty-six, he appropriates and embraces it now at three score years and ten.

In Jackson, Mississippi, between stays on the Mountain, he proceeds with his priestly chores when called upon, sees old friends, plans ahead for grandfathering, works for peace and justice, comforts and disturbs with his presence. No piece of his world has been put away. Never idle, he seems as heedless of the sands of time as when he made his first communion at the age of eleven. Reminiscing is in response to prodding and is always pleasant. Never judgmental. He shows no signs of disenchantment with his fellow human beings, no matter the sorriness he sees in us. I suspect it is because he was never enchanted with us in the first place, seeing us always for the frail things we are. Yet precious in God's sight and his own. Perhaps that accounts for something I have been told time and time again by those who have known and worked with Gray most closely. Canon Fred Bush told me something I found hard to believe about any human being. But I knew that Canon Bush is not given to superlatives and flattery. I also knew that during the years Gray was bishop, Fred Bush had probably spent more time with him than any person outside of family. Though they did not always agree, the canon knew the Ordinary. He said, "I have never, ever heard Duncan Gray say an unkind word about another human being." "Not ever?" "Never." "What about General Edwin Walker?" "Not one unkind word." "What about all the people who deserted him and St. Peter's Church, Oxford?" "Not one unkind syllable." "Have you ever seen him angry?" "Many times. At injustice, tyranny, poverty, inequality." "But not a harsh word against the perpetrators?" "Not one."

Strange.

Seeds planted in the past continue to grow and bear fruit. At a recent Cursillo gathering for racial reconciliation at Gray Center, the Episcopal encampment north of Jackson named for his father, something happened that could not have occurred when Gray was blazing a trail of justice, peace, and reconciliation, yet was the flowing of water from a well he dug through granite. *Cursillo,* a Spanish word meaning "short course," began in the Roman Catholic Church in Spain right after World War II and is now worldwide. It seeks to provide spiritual renewal and to discover and train leaders within the Church. The Right Reverend Alfred C. "Chip" Marble, a disciple of Gray since childhood and now bishop of the Diocese of Mississippi saw the idea as being an opportunity to promote racial reconciliation. He saw old wounds festering anew in the state and he believed what can change people in terms of racism and prejudice is the personal experience, getting to know people across racial lines, the one-on-one sharing of deepest feelings. Thirty-four people gathered for the three-day session. Twenty-two of them were white, twelve were black. They were roommates, tablemates, and prayer partners. Nothing was off-limits. Any pain, any bruising slur or physical wound could be shared. The sessions were designed for healing, not denial.

Among the participants was Duncan M. Gray III, rector of St. Peter's Church, Oxford, in the lineage of his father and, many think, marked already to be third generation of the Ordinary, though he harbors no such ambition. In an opening homily he spoke of many courageous people in the racial struggles of the past. He claimed no special courage for his father. Instead he said, "What was key for me was not so much his courage; there were a lot of courageous folks in those days. What set him apart was his refusal to hate. He would say, 'If you hate, they've won.'" His modesty regarding his father was fitting, as was his not saying in such a setting that most of the courageous ones were black. It was also proper that he said his father refused to hate. Humility regarding his father is not the only place that trait appears in the life of Duncan Gray III. Prior to the gathering, he had just removed his name from consideration for one of the most prestigious ecclesiastical positions his denomination has to offer, remaining instead at the relatively small St. Peter's.

A white woman, now too old and frail to stand, told of participating in the formation and early days of the Mississippi Council on Human Relations, the organization Gray served as president. A middle-aged white woman talked of their daughter marrying a man of another race who was not a Christian, and of how they dealt with the situation. What they did was evangelize him and then, in the words of the apostle Paul, "worldly standards ceased to count" in their estimate of him.

Black members of the group shared the pains of humiliation, indignity, and economic inequity wrought of a system of segregation and discrimination. Also actively participating in the Cursillo was George Street, a man who had fought unrelentingly to keep James Meredith out of the University of Mississippi at the same time the father of Street's present rector (Duncan III) was risking his life to assure the black student's safe entry. George Street was an attorney, director of development and chief spokesman for the university during the crisis and riots when Duncan Gray Jr. made his bold stand. Now George Street was an old man. As he spoke to the Cursillo he had an illness that would soon claim his life. He was confirmed in the Episcopal Church by Gray not long before his retirement. Street's testimony to this interracial group was both confessional and declarative. He told of his stiff resistance to the admission of Meredith to the university, acknowledging that Ole Miss had his ultimate allegiance at the time. "It was my idol." Then he told of being asked by Duncan Gray III a few months before the Cursillo to stand at St. Peter's front door and welcome members of their companion black congregation.

"So here is the irony," he told the group. "In 1962 I'm standing there [on campus] to keep black people out, and in 1996 I'm standing at the Episcopal Church to welcome them in. It's quite a switch, don't you think?" At the close of the weekend, pleased at what he learned late but in time, and standing erect like the brave soldier he was, with no maudlin inflection on the fact that more than longevity was overtaking him, he told the gathering, "I am winding down now. I don't have any hatred in me. I don't have anything to get off my chest." Three months later George Street died. A free man.

From Sewanee to the Mississippi Delta to Oxford to Meridian to Jackson, then back to the Mountain, those were words Duncan Gray Jr. had worked and longed to hear. Bread cast upon the waters.

Gray's words about grace spoke also of his own and my relationship to those considered enemies. From his youth he had known that the Scriptures counseled him to love his enemies. But nowhere did the Scriptures say he didn't have enemies. After my last visit on the Mountain it occurred to me that I had spent much time with Gray and with his friends. Little time with his enemies.

Gray's old friend Kenneth Dean invited me to spend a few days in Mississippi with him during Christmas week. Dean had been executive director of the Mississippi Council on Human Relations when Gray was that agency's president. We were to relive some of the events of the civil rights movement in which we and Gray were involved. One of our days was to be spent with Samuel Holloway Bowers Jr. Bowers, according to government documents, was the imperial wizard of the White Knights of the Ku Klux Klan during the bloody sixties. That organization was considered the most angry and violent of the many Klan organizations that sprang up during that era. Bowers was said by the FBI to have masterminded nine murders and three hundred bombings, burnings, and beatings. Gray was thought by some to have been on the "hit list" of the White Knights for a number four—murder. The list included the Meridian chief of police, an FBI agent, several black activists, and some prominent Jewish citizens. I was not able to document that Duncan Gray was actually on the list but it was widely known that he fit the mold of those the Klan considered dangerous enough to be eliminated. The thought of spending an entire day with Sam Bowers, a man reputed to be one of Duncan Gray's enemies, was both frightening and energizing.

Bowers served more than six years in federal prison for his conspiratorial role in the murders of James Chaney, Andrew Goodman, and Michael Schwerner, the three civil rights workers whose killings led to the most extensive FBI engagement of the civil rights era. Since the Meridian entrapment when Ken Dean had tried in vain, with the support of Gray, to stop the shoot-out where Kathy Ainsworth was killed and Thomas Tarrants was critically wounded, Dean had become friends with the major players on both sides of the drama. The manner in which he succeeded in gaining the respect and confidence of black and white activists and the FBI agents, along with that same respect and confidence of notorious Klan men and women who knew exactly where he stood on the issue and knew well his personal involvement in the civil rights struggle, is a remarkable story itself. I welcomed the opportunity of being in the presence of both the imperial wizard and Mississippi's best known white civil rights activists. Here would be one of Gray's closest civil rights friends and confidants, side by side with a man I assumed would hold Gray in utter contempt. Each had been a weighty antagonist of the other.

Before the scheduled day with Bowers, we spent an evening with Danny Hawkins, the man whose place Kathy Ainsworth took the night of the entrapment and fatal shooting in Meridian, a woman whose life Dean and Gray had attempted to save, although Dean had thought at the time it would be Hawkins on the ill-fated mission. He was described by the FBI as the "hit man" of Klan activities. His father, Joe Denver Hawkins, was said to be a chief night rider for the White Knights of the KKK until he was killed in 1974 in what was reported by the police as a robbery, although the circumstances were mysterious and continue to be suspicious. I had not seen Hawkins since I assisted Dean at Hawkins's father's funeral twenty-one years earlier. Hawkins was never convicted of any of the Klan bombings but spent thirty months in prison during the mid-70s for giving untrue information regarding a gun purchase. During the evening, when I mentioned Gray, Hawkins talked in detail of his activities the night of the Ole Miss riots. He grew emotional only when describing the huge bonfires he and his father saw along the route to Oxford, and when he spoke of the army troops that moved onto the campus after midnight. Somehow the U.S. Marshals who did battle with the mob earlier did not bother him. They were doing their duty, he thought. He saw the soldiers as going to war against their own people and thus traitors.

Before going to Danny Hawkins's home, we stopped by WLBT television station, a station that once had its license lifted in a lengthy court battle over racial discrimination and had become a fully integrated facility, owned and operated by black men and women. Ken Dean had served as president of the television station during the interim while commercial ownership was being established. The black manager, black newscasters, as well as black and white technicians and staff men and women were genuinely glad to renew the friendship with Dean. When we reached Hawkins's home, he was watching the black anchor giving the news, apparently without offense at the pigmentation of the broadcaster.

The next day we had breakfast with a man who was an FBI agent in Jackson during the height of the violence directed at blacks and Jews. We then visited with a Jackson attorney who was attempting to gain freedom for Byron de la Beckwith, the man convicted of the murder of NAACP director Medgar Evers, a poet now found in anthologies; prophet and bard reviewed through the scope of a deer rifle and cut down. We visited the farm of a woman who has known Duncan and Ruth Spivey Gray since childhood. She accompanied us to a long lunch in a Chinese restaurant (that seemed somehow out of keeping with what I had known as a small rural town) and we talked of the Grays. The woman's deceased husband had been sheriff of a county through which the Meredith March from Memphis to Jackson passed in 1966. That march had been organized after James Meredith had been shot near Memphis during what he intended to be a solitary walk to demonstrate to Mississippi Negroes that it was safe to walk a public highway. A march against fear, he called it. After he was wounded soon after his march began, the leading civil rights organizations banded together to complete the march.

The town we were visiting was where the Meredith marchers had been gassed when they attempted to camp overnight on a schoolyard, and it was here that Stokeley Carmichael, then head of the Student Nonviolent Coordinating Committee made his famous Black Power speech. The sheriff, though not remembered among the civil rights workers as being at all partial to their cause, had heard that dynamite had been strung along the route the marchers were supposed to pass. Ken Dean had heard the story that the sheriff worked into the night dismantling the string of dynamite bombs that would have exploded if tripped over, doubtless causing many injuries and loss of life. After lunch we went to a small abandoned barn and examined a box still filled with dozens of sticks of dynamite, blasting caps, and fuses, weather-soaked but still intact. "The real Movement was a lot of different people playing a lot of different roles," the sheriff's widow said. When no one answered she added, referring to her late husband, "He tried to be fair."

The day with Sam Bowers was spent in Sullivan's Hollow, a legendary region of Smith County seen today more as a metaphor for the racial darkness of that period when the KKK sought to be a law unto itself than as a geographical entity. Still one knows when he enters the ancient domain and when he is leaving it. Settled by the Sullivan patriarch in the early nineteenth century, it was populist from the outset. Stories still abound of interlopers being dragged from cars and forced to pull a plow, sick cows dragged onto the railroad to be hit by a train, followed by lawsuits against the hated railroad, killings at high school basketball games, and family feuds that lasted for decades.

Bowers, now in his early seventies, remains agile, alert, and articulate. He grew up in an educated, well-to-do family in New Orleans and Mississippi. His father's father was a prominent lawyer who served four terms in the U.S. Congress and spent a lot of time with young Sam reading and talking of history, politics, religion, and patriotism. His other grandparents were wealthy planters. Sam talks philosophy, politics, and theology with honed rhetoric and appears on the surface to be at peace with himself and the world.

Traversing the countryside, back and forth across unnamed Smith County bridges and side roads, we talked of many things in Sullivan's Hollow's past. And of many other things. We saw the original Sullivan house, several abandoned pioneer cabins with underpinnings of cypress that have outlasted the drop sidings, latticed windows, and shingle roofs, yards marked by condom wrappers, beer cans, empty wine bottles, and other suggestions that modernity has not neglected the issue of Mr. Tom Sullivan.

Smith County claims to be the watermelon capital of the world. The county seat is famous for its annual tobacco-spitting contest. Many of the roadside farms had massive broiler houses and parked vehicles with TYSON printed on the sides. "That's modern day sharecropping," Sam Bowers explained. "The farmers have a little piece of land, Don Tyson of Arkansas furnishes the baby chickens and the feed, the farmers furnish the labor and get a little of the profit." When we didn't comment Bowers added, "You know, Espy was a good secretary of agriculture." He was referring to Mike Espy, a black Mississippian who was President Clinton's first secretary of agriculture and who resigned over some offense involving the Tyson chicken conglomerate.

When the subject of some still pending court action regarding a Klansman came up, Bowers would parry that we were there on a mission of fellowship and he did not wish to discuss it. Once when Dean seemed to press him on a Jackson attorney's attempt to free de la Beckwith, Bowers, a navy man during World War II, patiently explained that

"Landlubbers dig their own foxholes. On a ship everyone, from the captain to the lowliest seaman, have the same assignment: to keep water out of the hull of the ship. When the ship goes down, everyone goes down." He didn't pursue his metaphor. It wasn't necessary.

Only once did he alter his rule of not commenting on the past. Toward mid-afternoon he directed Dean to turn on what appeared to be a wagon road. "Right here," he announced, as we pulled alongside a small, well-kept cemetery. There were not more than fifteen graves, all marked with delicately tasteful headstones. In silence Bowers led us to the newest grave. Several sprays of artificial flowers and greenery stood in place on their three-pronged stands. He took a solemn stance at the foot of the grave. We stood beside him. I reverently removed my hat as he began what I thought was going to be a prayer. But it was not a prayer. Instead, calling the man by name, and addressing him directly, he said, "I am not here presuming anything, but if your spirit still lingers nearby I just want you to know that I love you, I still miss you and . . ." His voice trailed off and he began to weep softly.

"Amen," I said, in as pontifical a tone as I could muster, as if to indicate it was an appropriate ending to his brief requiem. Dean said Amen.

Bowers walked in front of us back to the car, dabbing his eyes as he went along. "He was a trusted friend. A staunch Tri Kappa," I heard him say, not talking to us. I had never before in all my life heard the KKK referred to as Tri Kappa. The ugliness of past deeds has given KKK an unwrought standing in the language. Tri Kappa had a soft literary ring about it. It was as if the speaker was equating KKK with the most familiar collegiate fraternities. And probably he was.

"This is where we've been on our way to all day," Bowers said as we stopped at the very end of the seldom traveled narrow road a few miles from the cemetery. An elderly man sat alone in a pickup truck as we appeared. As if by appointment. Roaming the area were sixteen dogs of indeterminate lineage. Bowers walked through the passel of dogs, with an air that indicated he knew the dogs might harm others but not him, spoke a few moments with the man, then came back to where we had parked and said we had permission to stay in the area as long as we wished. "Gentlemen, we are now in the very bowels of Sullivan's Hollow," he announced as we got out of the car and moved along. Then, in the manner of a triumphant safari scout, he added, "That's the Cohay Creek." A stream of crystal clear water rushed furiously toward its rendezvous with the Leaf River to the south. A white sand bar edged into the water; a beckoning it seemed. Moving back and away from the

259

rippling water was a clearing consisting of several acres, forming a neat park area, earth-clean and groomed. Except for the whispers of wind and willows there were no sounds. Not even birds could be heard, as if they, too, were barred from these cryptic grounds, lest they call out sullied secrets of the years. The area appeared well-suited for outdoor gatherings but the arbitrary remoteness of it made it clear that it was not for public use. One could envision scantily clad Choctaw mooring their canoes, then standing on these very banks bartering peltry with Spanish traders for knives, guns, and ornaments. Or he could imagine nocturnal, clandestine gatherings where inviolable oaths were sworn and dark rituals uneased the night. The very air exuded secrecy. We asked no questions.

There was a wide area in the bend of the creek, with overhanging vines, reminding me of the spot where I had been baptized in the Amite River when I was seven years old some hundred miles away and sixty-five years ago. Huge beech trees, live oaks, cypress, sweet gum, and tall pines that seemed virginal cast a heavy winter shade to the far side. It was four days after Christmas and red berries of holly, flanked by sun-starved but green magnolia saplings, were friendly reminders of the season. As beechmasts, cypress cones, dry leaves, and acorns crunched beneath our feet, we walked along the bank, Dean describing the dissimilarity of this and the Jordan River where Jesus was baptized. Bowers talked of the Christmas program at his church in which he had read the Luke account of Jesus' birth and of how he had talked the preacher into changing the litany to read, "He is the Christ" instead of "Some say he is the Christ." A small bandstand faced the clearing. Mr. Bowers described a reunion of the man's family whose grave we had just visited and told of how he had performed a little dance as the band played patriotic songs. The winter solstice had just passed and the sun was going down with little warning.

JOSEPH DID NOT REMEMBER THE DAY ON THE ROAD FROM Springdale when he asked Thomas to come with him. He remembered only a letter in his pocket. And a little piece of plug tobacco. He thought perhaps he would share the tobacco when this battle was over. At least he would consider it. When is a promise no longer inviolate? He didn't know.

260

Most of the Greys knew Jeremiah Gage was not marching along with them now. They did not know he had been given a tablespoon of concentrated opium, mixed with vinegar and whiskey and called *black strap*, much stronger than laudanum, to soften the journey he was making. A cannon ball had blown away his bladder, a great deal of his intestines and a third of his pelvis. He had shared a toast with those near him and, seeing the first hazy moment of what the clinicians call death, he, with a violent, yet somehow tranquil shudder, moved on. As the remnant of his once beloved University Greys moved across the field to extinction, Jere Gage, lying on his back on a pile of straw, his pain-wracked features rested and serene, was asleep. His last sleep. One who might have been a great jurist, governor, educator, or literary figure was gone.

At first the lines of troops marched like wound-up toy soldiers. Periodically one tumbled to the ground and the others kept going. It was getting worse by the second now. The lines were gone. At a heavy post and rail fence the Federal guns were taking direct aim with exploding shells, grape, canister. Canister, a large group of small balls enclosed in what looks like a lard bucket, was especially damaging. The miles of gray that started out as swarms of bees flying into the wind was now more like the inside of a giant tornado. Bodies and parts of bodies whirling, falling, in no pattern. It was the Eighth Ohio firing from the left flank. More destructive than firing from the front. From the front, only one man was hit. Maybe there was a man directly behind him and he went down also. But there were no more in the line of fire. If fired down the line from the flank, a whole row may go down. And row after row did go down.

The basic mandate was victory, with no regard for losses. The wall was in sight but seemed farther and farther away. The Greys were scattered, their earlier buoyant spirit of optimism gone. They had no way of knowing that the South's fortune that seemed ascendant early in the war was receding on the slopes of a theological seminary town, never to return. When they crossed the Emmittsburg road they were facing Federal guns directly. They were close enough to fire their muskets now and within small arms range of the Bluecoats. The stone wall that ran north and south, forming an angle near the center of the Confederate line and right in front of where the Greys and the Eleventh Mississippi would cross was within reach. General confusion. No one appeared in charge.

"Close it up! Close it up!" a voice kept calling from somewhere in the rear. With no resonance of authority. It was not one of the assigned file closers. When the neat lines were broken, turned into absolute chaos, the file closers were useless.

"For God's sake, John, give the command to charge," yelled Private Andrew Baker to Captain John Moore who was supposed to be commanding Company A on that day.

"No," Moore yelled back above the screams of hurting and pandemonium. "I can't take the responsibility for this." He knew they were losing, that the lines were hopelessly destroyed and there would be no regrouping.

"Then I will," Baker yelled above the tumult. "Charrrge!" he bellowed. Only a few of his comrades were still standing to try to follow. Thomas McKie was one of them. Twenty feet to the left of Bryan's barn and a few feet from the wall Baker fell, wounded but still alive. Soon he would be captured. DeGraffenreid was wounded after crossing the wall. The few survivors scampered over the wall in the shouting, turbulent, animalistic confusion, each man his own army. One by one the Greys went down, the others pressing on, without design or reason. Grey and Blue were snarling, slashing, screaming, irrational creatures. Lashing out at whatever came close.

"Virginians! Virginians!" It was the dispirited General Pickett, behind and far to the right of Pettigrew's troops, screaming for the fealty of a regiment he knew no longer existed. Still in desperation he continued to yell. "Virginians! Virginians! Follow me! Follow me!" How he had coveted this fight. Now it was lost and he knew it. The generally coiffured locks that accentuated his perfumed and handsome face hung in tangles. Like a mountain lion hemmed in a crater with no escape. Then he seemed to disappear. Those who will try to chronicle the day will be vague as to his whereabouts. The charge will carry his name forever and forever the questions will remain.

Back in the trees of Seminary Ridge, behind the silent Confederate artillery a few body servants were bunched together. What were these black men thinking? For what did they wait? For what did they hope?

Thomas McKie stopped to reload his musket. As he knelt on one knee he felt a burning, tearing in the lower abdomen. He fell, rolled over, was still conscious, hugging the musket. The pain was not severe. He reached down and felt something soft and slippery. Like a wad of pond mud or the lamprey eels he used to catch in the creeks of Lafayette County. It was a section of lower bowels dangling through the threadbare trousers that were held on with a rawhide sash. He dropped the gut as he might a snake. His Cousin Joseph saw him fall, saw him lying there like a broken toy, tried to get to him. He remembered the tobacco Tommie so often begged him for and wished he had given it to him. What would it have hurt? Still, there was the promise. At that moment Joseph, too, fell, shot by a cap and ball Colt at close range. He was captured immediately and never saw his cousin again. Both had reached what came to be called "the high-water mark of the Confederacy," forty-seven yards beyond the place reached by the Virginians.

The war the University Greys fought did not end at Gettysburg on July 3, 1863. But the notion of a separate nation did. Likewise, the war over *Brown* v. *Board* did not end at Oxford in 1962 when the first nonwhite student was enrolled, but never again would a state's leaders convince its citizenry that it could defeat the nation with violence and massive resistance. Tommie McKie and Duncan Gray both witnessed the high-water mark of resistance to Federal force.

Tommie McKie lived through the night but would die the next morning, July 4, 1863, lying in the rain where he fell. His body would never be recovered.

The casualty rate for the University Greys during that half-hour battle was one hundred percent. Of Company A, Eleventh Mississippi Infantry Regiment, only Jim Dailey who brought Jeremiah Gage to the makeshift hospital behind Seminary Ridge began the sad retreat back to Virginia with General Lee. On the fourth of July in a torrential rain.

The Mississippians left to rot in the soil of Gettysburg did not know of the ignominious defeat their people in Mississippi were experiencing at the moment of their death. Nor would they have understood the irony of the day; the ghosts of Dancing Rabbit Creek. As the sad wagon train carrying the wounded of Gettysburg began the long trek back to the Potomac and Southern soil. General John C. Pemberton was surrendering Vicksburg to General Ulysses S. Grant. Just thirty-three years earlier a jubilant throng of white settlers stood on the very spot where the Southern abdication was taking place. They were cheering the departure of the Choctaws, robbed of their land in the nefarious Treaty of Dancing Rabbit Creek, sure now of great wealth in a new kingdom that would last forever. It was a short forever. Their Cotton Kingdom was now ended as 29,000 Southern soldiers laid down their arms and gave up in Vicksburg while more than 20,000 were casualties in Gettysburg. In 1830, when the steamboat *Brandywine* weighed anchor and began the journey taking the Choctaws into exile, there was jubilation in Vicksburg. And abundance of food and drink. Now, in 1863, after a year's siege, some who had feasted in baroque mansions following Doak's Stand and Dancing Rabbit Creek survived on the flesh of mules and rats in riverbank caves.

How are the mighty fallen in the midst of the battle.

From Harpers Ferry to Manassas to Seven Pines, Gaines Mill, the cornfield at Antietam, and finally Gettysburg, the University Greys lie. Company A of the Eleventh Mississippi Infantry Regiment would continue on the Confederate rosters as a company of the Eleventh. But the University Greys that stacked their books and boarded the train more than two years earlier were no more.

Stranger, go tell the Lakedaimonians that we are lying in obedience to their commands.

And over the years Grey would turn to Gray.

In the deep, foreboding swamps of Cohay Creek I was searching for Duncan Gray, a man I was sure had never been there. Beside me was Bowers, a man alleged to have been responsible for multiple murders, bombings, and mayhem. On the other side of me was Dean, a man who had risked his own life trying to save the lives of black citizens, as well as the lives of Klansmen about to be killed in what he saw as a reprehensible and extra-legal entrapment arranged and paid for by private citizens and carried out by agents charged with enforcing the laws of Caesar. It was the greatest test my tentative understanding of unconditional grace as overshadowing, overcoming, conquering humanity's inherent sinfulness I had ever known. The scandal of the Gospel I had heard preachers and theologians talk about in generalities all my life assumed an even more outrageous posture. Is grace abounding here in this darkening arcane forest? Truly unconditional grace? Something as crazy as Golda Meir chasing Hitler around the pinnacles of heaven, and after a thousand years he stops and lets her pin a Star of David on his chest? Who said that? I couldn't remember but it was an awesome simile to ponder there in those cowing woods. Grace, not just as homiletical rhetoric. Not some quaint, metaphysical, abstract speculation purloined from ancient scribes. Concrete-hard reality. My mind dredged the cesspools of human behavior I had witnessed over the years, coming up with numerous exceptions I would have made were I the dispenser of grace and forgiveness. To contemplate Gray's St. Luke Society and Bowers's Tri Kappa standing on equal footing before the Deity was more of a scandal than I could deal with at the moment. What will the preachers do without the threat of hell? I pondered. How will they build their spires and steeples? Who will bring the gold if their congregates need have no dread of God?

I felt a strange oneness with the two men with me. And an even more unfamiliar concord with those I knew had convened on this ground to plan missions of atrocity.

Is this the thing Gray has talked about and lived by all these years? When he answered my question about grace, though it touched me at the time, and especially when I applied it to the University Greys, it still had a somewhat catechistic ring; not what I was face-to-face with in the Cohay swamp. "Grace . . . that special gift to us of his love and acceptance. His mercy and forgiveness, all without reference to our own merit or deserving . . . loved unconditionally, to be forgiven for everything . . . to be totally accepted." That is what Gray had told me. To be forgiven for everything? Scandalously scary! In the abstract of seminary halls and lofty pulpits it is tame enough. But when one considers that it may be here, on the banks of Cohay Creek, well, that's a different matter. Right now? Here and everywhere? For Gray, the University Greys, and for me? For the fallen Tri Kappa lying in the cold ground of Sullivan's Hollow, and the imperial wizard who had danced at his friend's party and wept at his graveside? Surely tears and joy are both the ritual of the reality and realization of grace. What, then, of the mob that attacked Gray and pulled him from the Confederate monument on the Ole Miss campus the night the first black student came? The triumph of grace here is not that Gray has forgiven his trespassers. The marvel is that, while deploring their actions, he never condemned them.

I felt an intuitive hankering to sing the song, and began humming it ever so faintly as we moved along. ". . . Through many dangers, toils and snares. . . ." I suppose I had never really appropriated the infuriating profundity of John Newton's lyrical treatise. I had been fearful all day. Now the lines of a hard-living slave-ship captain's song nudged me down the illogical path of Gospel folly, and for the first time all day I felt untroubled in the presence of the Imperial Wizard of the White Knights of the Ku Klux Klan. "'Twas grace that taught my heart to fear, and grace my fears relieved."

Amazing.

Finally, as the day was ending, deep in a Mississippi wilderness, as remote a place as I had ever seen and the purpose of which I could never approve, was the subject of my research mentioned. "Sam, Will here is writing a book about Reverend Duncan Gray," Ken Dean said. "What did you think about Duncan Gray? I mean, back then?"

There was a long silence while the tape recorder Bowers had given us permission to use continued to roll. The quiet prevailed as we made our way out of the deep recesses of Sullivan's Hollow. Bowers's silence troubled me. Is it silence as being golden or silence as the ultimate insult? I remembered again those of the Lost Cause. I remembered Nathan Bedford Forrest. What now of him in the light of what Gray had told me? In the beginning I had seen those with whom I differed on race relations as misguided mortals. The University Greys were, at most, to be pitied. I tried to get to know them. At the outset I spent many hours with them at the University of Mississippi as they drilled and frolicked, posed for pictures in their new grey garments, cleaned their weapons, said their sanguine good-byes. I had trembled with them on Seminary Ridge as Federal batteries rained their carnage upon them and watched them fall like tenpins as they rushed the bloody angle of Gettysburg in one last, desperate flirtation with destiny. I had stood in the rain at their graves on lonely hillsides in Marshall and Lafayette counties. Still, convinced that they were fighting for an evil cause, the perpetuation of slavery, I could not love those boys. Now as in the silence I thought of Gray's words about grace I began to see them through new eyes. The Imperial Wizard of the White Knights of the Ku Klux Klan. A civil rights radical. The University Greys. And me. Is it true that we are all the recipients of a special gift, the gift of love and acceptance, mercy and forgiveness? Everyone? For everything? Unconditionally? If it is so I need not feel pangs of guilt for admiring, loving, even celebrating these boys of the Confederacy; the Lost Cause. I can even exult in their honor, their courage, steadfastness, uprightness, loyalty. I had started out to write of Greys and Gray in stark contrast, to play on the irony of such variance when only one letter made their names different. It was my intent, I suppose as I look back, to pass judgment and feature approbation. The admiration of Gray has not dimmed. But now I can be at ease with the Greys. Moreover, I can spend a winter's day in Sullivan's Hollow with the Imperial Wizard of the White Knights of the Ku Klux Klan although I, too, had once been in the crosshairs of the Klan's scope. What began as my gift to Duncan Montgomery Gray Jr., the story of his life, was becoming his gift to me; a new understanding. At least a beginning.

I looked back at where Sam Bowers sat on the back seat of the rented Oldsmobile. I wanted to break through this disturbing quiet. Or maybe I shouldn't. Maybe the Imperial Wizard of the White Knights of the Ku

Klux Klan knows now of grace as surely as Duncan Gray. Here I was, asking a man alleged to have been a leader of anti-black terrorists a question about a priest who had spent most of his adult life wrestling with America's dilemma. Race.

Bowers said nothing. But surely there must be something left to say. Something neither the Imperial Wizard, the bishop, nor I have said. Is there not something left to say when all movements have been lived out, all martyrs forgotten, all social activists resigned, all research and interviews ended? Or is the silence the hidden God, the paladin of all history? With folk such as Duncan Montgomery Gray Jr. celebrating the mystery?

I turned and addressed the Imperial Wizard directly. "Mr. Bowers, I am writing a book about Bishop Duncan Gray, a man with whom you have had major differences over the years." As we pulled onto the main road heading west, back into what the world calls civilization and progress, there was still the impenetrable silence. Nothing more.

Index

269

270

271